AN INVITATION TO JAPANESE CIVILIZATION

Robert S. Ellwood, Jr.
University of Southern California

Wadsworth, Inc., Belmont, California

ISBN 0-87872-237-8

For Audrey Ann
Sister and artist

An Invitation to Japanese Civilization by Robert S. Ellwood, Jr.,
was copyedited by Amy Ullrich and prepared for composition
by Pamela Byers. Cover and interior design were provided by
Cindy Daniels.

Wadsworth, Inc.

Library of Congress Cataloging in Publication Data
Ellwood, Robert S 1933–
  An invitation to Japanese civilization.
  Bibliography: p.
  Includes index.
  1. Japan—Civilization. I. Title
DS821.E513   952   79-15381
ISBN 0-87872-237-8

Printed in the United States of America
  2 3 4 5 6 7 8 9

Contents

Foreword

Civilization in Asia is a series intended to make available to college students and teachers the current state of scholarly thinking in various Asian subjects. The proliferation of specialized monographs of high quality during recent years makes it possible to write well-informed general summaries in many fields, and makes it essential to bridge the ever-widening gap between specialist knowledge and undergraduate education.

To write texts of the sort described is a task that requires the best scholarly awareness of the current state of the art, the ability to compress and summarize without distorting the subject, and a style of writing that is lucid and literate. Fortunately, the sound rationale for this series has attracted some of the best-qualified scholars in the field as its authors. These are all persons who have distinguished themselves by published research that gives them high reputations in the profession. That they have willingly devoted their learning and talents to provide sound, basic texts is a sign of their recognition of an urgent need.

Perhaps the most overriding concern shared by all who are involved in *Civilization in Asia* is that American education should continue, and increase, its efforts to bring all of humankind within the purview of our students, who must function intelligently and humanely in what is now undeniably one world.

Laurence G. Thompson
Series Editor

Preface

How does one capture the essence of a great civilization in a single short book? Not, certainly, by telling all about it, or even as much about it as would be told in a long book.

Instead, all one can hope to do in a book like this is to provide a few bearings for a journey that, I hope, many readers will continue after the last page of this invitation to Japanese civilization is turned. An introductory work like this can be compared to a single glimpse through the gates of a Zen garden, or the previews of a Kurosawa film. It can only hint, I would like to think intriguingly, at the fascination of one of the world's richest, most complex, and often most paradoxical cultures. If the introduction leads many readers to go on to the long books—or to visit the garden and see the entire film—it will have served its purpose.

A few practical matters. Since the purpose of the present writing is to acquaint readers with as much as possible of the usages, major and minor, of Japanese life, names are written in the Japanese manner, surname first, given name second. The long mark is used where pronunciation requires on the vowels *o* and *u*, except in a few proper names like Shinto, Toyko, and Kyoto and in Japanese words like No and koan, now found in English dictionaries, where common usage in English writing does not employ them. The beginner will not go far wrong in pronouncing the vowel sounds of Japanese written in *romaji* (Western letters) like Spanish, but stretching out the long vowels. *G* is always hard. Syllables with *y* like *gyo*, *hyo*, and *myo* are strictly one syllable, not "my-o." Diphthongs like *hei* ("hay") and *ai* ("I") are also one syllable. *A* is always "ah"; *e* is English "a"; *i* is English "e"; *o* is "oh"; and *u* is pronounced as in "too," just as in Spanish. With these few guidelines in mind, pronounce Japanese fearlessly—pronunciation is by far the simplest thing about it.

Let us now turn our thoughts to the Land of the Rising Sun itself. Until little more than a century ago, Japan and America were barely aware of each other, save through rumor and legend. In this century, both in tragic conflict and as increasingly important trading partners, these two very diverse nations have become inseparably linked to each other's destinies. Since the Second World War, each has experienced a virtual explosion of knowledge about the other. We can now participate in that knowledge.

R.S.E.

Time Chart

Period	Religion and Philosophy	Literature	Art	General History
Jōmon 8000–200 B.C.	Preliterate religion—animism, fertility cults, perhaps comparable to Melanesian and Polynesian religion	Unknown	Pottery, *dogū* figures—half animal, half human with slit eyes	Prehistoric
Yayoi 200 B.C.–A.D. 250	Agricultural rites, shamanism	Prototypes of *Kojiki*, *Nihonshoki* myths	Ritual swords, mirrors, bells	Pimiko?
Kofun 250–552	Same as Yayoi—ritual burials, sacred kingship	Mythology develops	Immense tombs, *haniwa*, grave goods	Unification under Yamato house about 350, Korean immigration
Asuka and Hakuhō 552–710	Introduction of Buddhism and Confucianism	Beginning of written literature	Buddhist art flourishes, Hōryūji built	Consolidation of state under Shōtoku and other reforms
Nara 710–794	Buddhist high point	*Kojiki* and histories, *Manyōshū*, *Kaifusō*	Magnificent Buddhist sculpture, Nara Great Buddha	First permanent capital, Dōkyō scandal
Heian 794–1185	Shingon, Tendai, later Pure Land most influential	*Monogatari*, *Nikki*, the *Kokinshū*	Buddhist and Shinto sculpture, *Yamato-e emaki*	Fujiwara dominance, *Insei* after 1072, rise of *buke*

Period	Religion/Thought	Literature	Art	History
Kamakura, Kemmu, and Nambokuchō 1185–1392	New Buddhisms—Pure Land groups, Nichiren, Zen	*Gunki*, especially the *Heike Monogatari*, the *Shinkokinshū*, Yoshida Kenkō	End of great sculpture; portraits, *emaki*.	Warlord domination, the Kemmu restoration and two courts, rise of Ashikaga
Muromachi or Ashikaga 1392–1568	Zen dominant	No plays, *Renga*	Zen-related painting, gardens, etc.	Weak Ashikaga rule, civil disruption, Ōnin war 1467–1477
Momoyama 1568–1600	Christian influence	No	Castles, screens	Unification under Nobunaga and Hideyoshi, European contact
Tokugawa 1600–1868	Official Confucian ideology, Buddhism static	Ukiyo-e stories, kabuki, haiku	Kanō screens and landscapes, Ogata, Ukiyo-e	Isolation, relative stability
Meiji 1868–1912	Separation of Shinto and Buddhism, Confucian ideology of loyalty, Christian missions	Influential Western translations, rise of novel in Western form	Western styles	Japan becomes modern world power
Taishō and Early Shōwa 1912–1945	Rise of extremist imperial ideologies and State Shinto	Stories and novels of Akutagawa, Kafū, Tanizaki, modern poetry	Partial revival of traditional forms, cinema	Nationalism, repressions, Pacific War and defeat
Late Shōwa 1945–	Rise of new religions, secularization	Novels of Mishima and Kawabata	World-famous cinema	Occupation, recovery, democracy, rise of unprecedented affluence

Mt. Fuji, a mountain of many moods, is represented in countless paint-ings and photographs and is known worldwide as a symbol of Japan. Here, it is seen rising above the serene countryside. (Courtesy Japan Air Lines.)

Part One
Islands of Wind and Sun:
An Invitation to Japan

The *Kojiki* (*Record of Ancient Things*) is the oldest Japanese book. Compiled from oral traditions in A.D. 712, this collection of myths and legendary history was intended to tell the story of the Japanese islands and gods and to establish the divine origin of its ruling imperial line.

One key story set back in the "Divine Age" at the beginning of time tells of the beautiful goddess Amaterasu, often identified with the sun, and the male god Susa-no-o, whose violent moods seem borrowed in part from the tempestuous storms and typhoons that frequently shatter the calm of the island nation. Though both are the offspring of the primal parent Izanagi, Amaterasu and Susa-no-o have a rocky relationship. Sometimes they cooperate in producing multitudes of new gods; sometimes they quarrel. On one famous occasion Susa-no-o, in a strange combination of exuberance and temper, destroyed the fields and desecrated the sacred harvest celebrations of his sister. Amaterasu hid in a cave, and the impetuous god was expelled from heaven.

The story of Japan is like the story of Amaterasu and Susa-no-o, for in its geography, climate, history, and culture sunny calm and wild storm contrast to a striking degree.

In our opening chapter we set the stage by exploring some of the contrasts that comprise the complex civilization of Japan. We also begin direct contact with the past of Japanese civilization by glancing briefly at three crucial times and places in its development.

In the second chapter we look at some of the values of Japanese culture and their sources, from age-old Shinto and shamanism to the hierarchicalism that emerges in modern education and business.

1

Popular culture and its values, in Japan as everywhere, are the powerful backdrop of "high" culture. We shall see the same themes and tensions that animate village or corporate life appear again as the stuff of drama, cinema, and even poetry.

In the final chapter of this introductory section, the long history of Japan is surveyed, and we focus on its major periods and events. This survey provides a chronological framework for the discussion of specific aspects of Japanese culture; it provides an acquaintance with the basic cultural motifs of each period that is necessary to understand the relation of historical events to cultural accomplishments.

Introducing Japan and the Japanese Heritage

1

Japan has been called a nation of contradictions. Certainly it is a land of paradoxes and polarities. Only by looking at both sides of its manifold pairs of opposites can one begin to understand these islands on the eastern frontier of the world's largest and most populous continent.

A LAND OF PARADOXES

Geography and Climate

Japan is set in the Pacific Ocean opposite North China, Korea (which extends out toward the island nation to provide the closest access to the mainland), and Soviet Asia. To the south, the Ryūkyū Islands, now Japanese, provide a link with Taiwan and southeast Asia. To the north, the Japanese island of Hokkaidō and the Russian Sakhalin Island offer close approaches to frigid Siberia. All these points of contact have been important in Japanese cultural history. Prehistoric Japanese culture contained southern motifs, brought by people with Indonesian affinities. For example, despite the much cooler Japanese climate, the early traditional Japanese house and building is very similar to traditional Indonesian architecture and seems better designed for the tropics than for the temperate zone. Northern motifs from Siberia and Inner Asia also reached Japan, and horseback riding, a prerogative of warriors, was most likely introduced from the north.

Japan's climate, moderated on the Pacific side by the Japan Current, is temperate and generally mild. Summers tend to be hot and humid, with considerable rain, and winters—except in the storied but lightly populated "snow country" of the north and west—are usually clement. Spring and autumn days amidst the fabled cherry blossoms or falling colored leaves of Japan can be exquisite enough to beguile one into thinking the mythic isles of

3

paradise have at last been discovered. Moreover, most of Japan is possessed of marvelous natural beauty, even though modern industrial pollution has left its ravages. Japan's splendid mountains, deep mossy forests, whitewater streams, and rocky seashores are countless. Its agricultural areas, with their irregular bright green rice paddies or knobby tea plants in deeper green, interspersed with thatch or tiled houses and Shinto shrines, are equally appealing.

But to this scene stand contradictions symbolic of all the contradictions of Japan. The calm beauty of Japan is not infrequently disrupted violently by typhoons and earthquakes. Typhoons, which fell trees and walls and leave torrential rains, regularly batter the islands in late summer. Major earthquakes are less common, but tremors occur often—in some places every few days—as though reminding the inhabitants of this beautiful land of the precariousness of existence.

A distinguished Japanese philosopher, Watsuji Tetsurō, has written a book entitled *Fūdo* (*Climate*), which argues that a people's religion and temper can be understood as a response to climate. Certainly much can be said for viewing the Japanese in that light. Like their weather, the Japanese can exhibit extremes of gentleness and violence, of profound appreciation of beauty and of rapacity. The same man can be—and many have been—at once a warrior and an aesthete.

Japan and the World

Yet another set of contradictions lies in Japan's relations with the rest of the world. The sunrise land lies on the edge of Asia, yet it is separated from the mainland by often stormy seas. No invading army has ever conquered Japan from the mainland. Much has been imported over the centuries, but always by way of missions or trade; Japan has had time to assimilate and change newly arrived cultural gifts to its own style. In modern times the volume and speed of the cultural importation is greatly increased, but the process is not really much different.

Borrowing and assimilating foreign cultures has always been full of ambiguities for the Japanese. They usually want to import, as would anyone, what seems good; yet they have also usually been very conscious of the uniqueness of their own culture and have desired to protect its fundamental integrity. This contradiction has sometimes led to violent swings of attitude toward the outside world. Sometimes Japan has appeared eagerly and uncritically willing to import and assimilate—even to idolize—anything foreign. At other times it has lashed back with xenophobic passion, trying either to isolate itself from other cultures or to impose Japanese culture on them.

Perhaps related to this ambiguity is another paradox of Japanese history: its tendency to be late in getting started, and then to show an incredible ability to catch up. Japan did not enter the mainstream of world history as a proper nation or advanced culture until around the sixth and seventh centuries A.D. The foundations of the Chinese culture from which Japan initially borrowed had been laid well over a thousand years before. But once the borrowing process started, it led to the pervasive introduction of art, letters, religion, and statecraft from the continent, and Japan with amazing alacrity assimilated and adapted the imports to produce art and literature that was distinctive to its own culture, yet no less magnificent in quality than the foreign models. The same process occurred in the nineteenth and twentieth centuries with a rapidity that was the wonder of the world; Japan suddenly awoke from two-and-a-half centuries of isolation to compete as an economic and political world power.

The Japanese Language

Finally, we might note that the Japanese language itself reflects the paradoxes of the culture. Its complex writing system includes both *kanji* (Chinese characters representing words or concepts that indicate the Chinese origin of Japanese writing) and two forms of *kana* (syllabic "letters" used for the conjugated verb endings Chinese does not possess and for simpler words—particles, conjunctions, and the like). Often the choice of *kanji* or *kana* depends on the whim or style of the writer.

Of the two kinds of *kana*, *hiragana* is usually used for true Japanese words and endings, and *katakana*, somewhat comparable to italics in English, is employed for modern loanwords. Many loanwords, predominantly from English, are used for all sorts of modern and foreign things, from bread to elevators. The names of foreign places and persons (except Chinese and Korean) are also usually written in *katakana*—for example, in newspaper stories. *Katakana* words and names occur frequently on many a modern page, and they also stand out; even though frequently and fluently used, they never indicate words that are fully assimilated into "real" Japanese.

Even "real" Japanese has two strands, roughly comparable to the Germanic and Greco-Latin strands in English. The first strand may be called "original" Japanese. It is descended from the language in use prior to the Chinese influx and the introduction of writing that began in the early centuries A.D. It controls the basic grammatical structure and is used for particles, prepositions, and for innumerable common household words—much the same sort of words that is of Anglo-Saxon derivation in English. These words are now usually written in *hiragana* or in *kanji* that are pronounced in the indigenous Japanese way.

A second type of word, roughly the same sort likely to be of Latin or Greek derivation in English (like "immediate" or "telephone"), is taken from Chinese. These words are of a slightly more elegant, literary, or technical flair than the "original" Japanese; like the English examples given, many are in very common use. These words, most often written in *kanji*, are pronounced in a medieval Japanese adaptation of certain Chinese dialects that has little to do with standard modern Chinese.

THREE POINTS OF REFERENCE IN JAPANESE CULTURE

We have just looked at certain bedrock conditions of the Japanese experience—geography, climate, relations with the world, and language. We have seen that these conditions are replete with potential paradoxes and tensions, but out of them has come a complex and striking culture. This culture is deeply attuned to the beauties of nature, as one might expect of people who dwell in such lovely islands. The rich racial and linguistic background of the Japanese has, moreover, given them a subtly nuanced language with which to express both feelings about nature and the intricacies of human emotion. At the same time, the contradiction of violence amidst calm beauty that tinctures the nature of Japan runs through its history and culture as well. Other significant conflicts are as basic to human experience as wind and sun to nature: social obligation versus inner feeling; family commitment versus the call of the heart.

We can now begin to establish bearings in Japanese cultural history by looking at three points of reference: a scene from Japan's greatest literary classic, *The Tale of Genji*, which exemplifies the Heian period; the culture of the medieval *shogun* (dictator ruling in the name of the emperor) Ashikaga Yoshimasa, which exemplifies the pervasive cultural influence of Zen Buddhism; and the culture of the early modern "townsman" class that supported the famous *Kabuki* (popular drama) and puppet theaters of the Tokugawa period. These three great "moments" are important in themselves; at the same time, each offers an easy entrée into the values and atmosphere of traditional Japanese culture and to a preliminary understanding of some of its shapers and background influences, such as courtly manners and Zen.

Farewell to a Heian Princess

In the third of its nearly four centuries, the culturally brilliant Heian epoch was in its silver rather than golden age. The first burst of expansive confidence was past, troubles had increased, and a melancholic sense of the transitoriness of all things was in the air. Poets sang of the slow irretrievable departure of all that is beautiful, and monks and moralists preached of the corruption eroding the rectitude of better days. Out of such a mood can come profound portraits of the human condition; the third Heian century gave us some of the greatest works of all of Japanese letters.

Among them is the *Genji Monogatari* (*The Tale of Genji*), accounted the greatest classic of Japanese literature. This long novel tells of the life and loves of Genji, a young prince of supreme beauty and sensitivity. His universe was the imperial court at Heian, modern Kyoto, where the fortunate ones "above the clouds" passed lives at once given to pleasure and aestheticism, infinitely constrained by meticulous considerations of etiquette, social rank, and taboo. The book affords an incomparable vision of people unbelievably appreciative of exquisite refinements of psychological and sensory experience. It gives us a priceless window into the customs and routine, the aesthetics, and even the inmost attitudes and mood-spectra of a memorable era now vanished forever.

It was long ago. The broad-avenued ancient capital of Heian (Peace and Tranquillity) was, as it is today, the heart of classical Japanese culture. The century was, by Western reckoning, the eleventh A.D. In Europe the flame of culture burnt low. At the time, Europe had scarcely heard of Japan, even as the Japanese had heard of Europe, if at all, only as a place beyond China and even India on the farthest rim of legend. The eleventh century was the third century of the period historians of Japan now call the Heian era.

In one scene from *The Tale of Genji*, a young princess, "a charming, delicate girl of fourteen, dressed by her mother with very great care," was attending the sovereign in an audience hall of the palace. She had been appointed priestess at the Grand Shrine of Ise, a lovely but rustic temple set many miles from the capital amid deep woods, not far from where the eternal waves of the Pacific roll. This house of worship, dedicated to Amaterasu, the greatest ancestral deity of the imperial line, was the most exalted in the empire. In the Heian epoch, only persons of the blood could visit the Ise shrine. By ancient custom, a virginal imperial princess always served the shrine. She would be appointed at an early age, and prepared for the awesome responsibility by long periods of purification and rites of lustration that were undertaken chiefly at a shrine just outside Kyoto called the Nonomiya (Shrine in the Fields). Then she would depart from home in a great procession, to remain at Ise until the death of her father or mother, when she was permitted to return to the glittering capital and marry.

The great progress of the fourteen-year-old princess was about to depart. A number of gala-carts were pulled up before the palace, waiting. The mother of the priestess, the Lady Rokujō, had herself resided at the Nonomiya and had been a paramour of Prince Genji; in a memorable earlier scene, the subject of the play *Nonomiya* (which we shall examine later in this book), Genji had violated custom by visiting her there. As the departure was about to get underway, however, Genji found himself half in love with the pretty young servitor of the great goddesses herself, and he sent her poems half-revealing his heart in the proper Heian manner. She dismissed him with verses sprightly and coy enough to infatuate him further.

Within the palace the priestess, accompanied by palace ladies, received the *kusa-wakare* (comb of departure) from her ruler. Tears bespotted the eyes of the emperor, himself a sentimental young man. That evening she left through the Osaka gate whose name was taken to mean "Hill of Meeting." The next day, a morning of heavy mists, Genji spent alone sunk in reverie. He whispered to himself the verse:

> I see her on her way. Do not, O mists,
> This autumn close off the Gate of the Hill of Meeting.[1]

The splendor, the mood of wistful love, the poem with its yearning tone and its play on words, are all typical of *The Tale of Genji* and of Heian life and literature in general. In this vignette we note, above all, the fundamental tension between the inner life, in which feeling and taste are supremely important, and the outer life of society, in which even the highest must conform to obligations built into the social structure. Even the emperor, even imperial princes and princesses, are subject to structural law; all their tears and poetry will not avail against the custom that sends a vivacious young maiden to a life of icy purity at lonely Ise, far from the gay capital.

The Shogun of the Elegant Life

On the outskirts of Kyoto, in the district called Higashiyama (Eastern Mountain), is the serene Ginkakuji (Temple of the Silver Pavilion). In the Muromachi or Ashikaga period (1392–1568), this site was a fountainhead of what has been called Higashiyama culture. Higashiyama culture is a distinctive set of interrelated arts that expresses superbly an attitude that has shaped much of Japanese civilization.

At this time the country was ruled in the name of the emperor by a series of shoguns (dictators) of the Ashikaga house. An early figure of this line was the famous Ashikaga Yoshimitsu (1358–1408) who came to the throne at the age of nine. In his youth he became far more interested in Zen Buddhism and Zen-related art than in government. Although he impoverished his people and was accordingly keenly hated, his patronage enabled the development of many Zen arts: the No drama, landscape painting, and architecture. This shogun retired in 1394 to take Buddhist orders and built for himself as a place for Zen meditation the famous Kinkakuji (Temple of the Golden Pavilion), which is reflected like a golden flower in its lake on the western outskirts of Kyoto.

Yoshimitsu's grandson, Ashikaga Yoshimasa (1435–1490), the builder of the Silver Pavilion, was even more intoxicated by Zen and its arts. The apparently hereditary disinterest of these shoguns in practical affairs of state reached a high point with Yoshimasa. The resultant vacuum at the center was like a trumpet summons to local warlords and ancient enemies to rise against each other in a senseless rampage of violence that culminated in the vicious Ōnin War of 1467–1477. Even though the carnage was immense, and nearly everything old and lovely in the capital was put to the torch, the war accomplished nothing.

But Yoshimasa was little touched by the destruction, even though the succession crisis engendered by his wish to retire had initated the conflict. He was finally able, amid the ruins all about him, to build the Silver Pavilion in 1482 and to retire to the appreciation of Zen aesthetics and meditation within it. Called the *furyū shōgun* (shogun of the elegant life), he lived only for the love of refined beauty.

The Furyū Aesthetic Among the arts advanced by Yoshimasa and the cultivated Zen priests he retained were painting, poetry, gardening, *chanoyu* (the tea ceremony), and *ikebana* (flower arrangement). Yoshimasa loved to sit in a tea room in the Silver Pavilion. The straw-matted room was only nine feet square, austerely ornamented with the tasteful simplicity that emphasizes the beauty of the few accoutrements in view. On one side might have hung a painted scroll, and under it would have rested a pleasing arrangement of flowers. Looking up, the tea-sipping shogun would have gazed over an irregular pond banked by mossy, rocky terrain scattered with evergreens and rhododendrons. Beyond it, his eyes would have risen to the low eastern hills, covered with the varied greens and restrained tree-flowers of a moist but temperate land.

One priest in Yoshimasa's company, Sōami (d. 1525), was particularly skilled in gardens and flowers. He wrote a book on ikebana. Another flower-arranging priest of Yoshimasa's court, Ikenobō, later became incumbent of the Rokkakudō temple in Kyoto, where he established a school in the art that is even today the largest in the country.

What is the essence of Japanese floral art? Perhaps the first thing that strikes an observer is a lack of contrived symmetry or rigorous balance of color and form. The Japanese garden boasts a seemingly "tossed" naturalism that is the opposite of the straight rows and geometric shapes of the Western formal garden, and ikebana art creates a subtly pleasing effect without forcing a sense of arrangement. Ikebana is, rather, an infinitely painstaking reconstruction of a naturalness that is "just right." The arrangements have a studied irregularity, simplicity, and use of the natural structures of the materials.

All this is at the heart of *fūryū*, the true elegance mastered by Yoshimasa, the tranquillity-loving ruler around whom war swirled beyond his control. But *fūryū* itself is subject to the unsurpassed elegance of nature.

A *fūryū* object may seem at first glance to be of imperfect shape and unprepossessing appearance. Sometimes a flaw will have been deliberately left in it. The object may seem frail, old, and delicate—a twisted and dwarfed tree, calligraphy with curt freehand strokes, a bowl whose laquer is old and cracked, an ikebana of a harmony transcending simple regularity.

How do such objects give one a sense of peace, of aesthetic satisfaction, even of entering through them the Great Way of nature itself? The answer is said to be that their very frailty induces no pride or passion, but feelings of tenderness.

A regular and perfect object impels envy of the master who made it, covetous desire to possess the perfection, fear lest it be marred, or pride if it is one's own creation. The careful imperfection of true *fūryū* art leads one away from distasteful psychic interaction with the powerful personality—the Michelangelo or Rembrandt—behind the masterpiece, or from one's baser capacities for jealousy or acquisitiveness. Instead one is drawn to the art itself; a tenderness, almost a pity, for the deformed thing leads one into a peace and beauty that is nonetheless there. In the very absence of feelings of ego and desire dwells peace. The fragile ikebana in the alcove of Yoshimasa's tea room suggested this peace, which was fulfilled by the incredible richness of the view of water, rocks, trees, and mountains. Yoshimasa was inspired by the humble, unbalanced flower

Buddhist monks leave very early on a winter morning for takuhatsu, *or solicitation of donations from the faithful in exchange for the chanting of a sutra. This practice, followed in some temples, expresses egoless humility on the part of the monks and the exercise of charity on the laity's part. (Courtesy Japan Air Lines.)*

arrangement at his side to see these natural beauties as they are, shorn of all films of fear or desire in the eye of the beholder.

Zen Buddhism   Behind *fūryū* aestheticism is Zen Buddhism. Zen, like all Buddhism, teaches that our ordinary sense of ego, of being a separate individual self, is a misleading illusion that creates in us feelings of "me against the world." Egosim, fortified by webs of fear and desire, leads to no peace.

Instead of the ego, our true nature is the universe, whatever it may be called—the Void, the Buddha-nature, Reality. This true nature is realized only by actualizing one's identity with all things and with the wondrous emptiness at their cores. Zen emphasizes that a true nature underlies the complexity that appears on the surface of things, and the true nature is perceived by seeing beneath what is created or perceived by ego, fear, and desire.

In Zen practice, true nature is realized for the individual in *zazen* (Zen meditation). In the stillness of meditation, one becomes who—or what—one is. One can discard the myriad memories, forms, fears, and fancies that make up the separate personality and get down to true nature. Zen art endeavors to do the same thing: to show the true nature of a tree or bird or mountain through a few strokes that reveal its essence and nothing else. The result is natural and not artificial, irregular and not contrived—yet pleasing and harmonious. To the Zen eye, any part of nature is deeply harmonious with all the rest of nature and with the enlightened being. The *fūryū* arts are an introduction to this Zen vision.[2]

The Cultural World of the Tokugawa Townsmen

In the late seventeenth and early eighteenth centuries, the era of Louis XIV in Europe, another shogunal house, the Tokugawa, held the reins of power. Unlike the cultivated but weak and callous Ashikaga, the Tokugawa were able to give the nation two-and-a-half centuries of relative peace and prosperity—though at the cost of hidebound and xenophobic policies. The Tokugawa established their seat in Edo, modern Tokyo; during their era Edo and other major commercial cities like Osaka and Kyoto developed a very distinctive cultural flavor.

The dominant class was nominally the *samurai*, the proud but sometimes improvident caste of knightly warriors. Only they were allowed to wear swords, and their lives were supposed to be governed by the code of *Bushidō* (the Way of the Warrior), which inculcated unflinching fearlessness and loyalty to one's feudal superior. Rather than suffer disgrace to himself or his lord, the samurai was obligated to commit ritual *seppuku* (*hara-kiri*, suicide).[3]

Some 6 percent of the Tokugawa period (1600–1868) population was of samurai class; another 80 percent were peasant farmers in the countryside. Theoretically, as primary producers of food, they were second in honor only to the samurai. In practice theirs was a hard life, though perhaps not quite as hard as during the preceding centuries of incessant warfare, when burning and looting armies left little but plague and famine behind, and the tax collector took of that little to pay the armies.

In the cities, above all Edo and Osaka, other classes were becoming stronger, and with them developed another lifestyle and another cultural world. Shopkeepers and artisans represented no more than 15 percent of the population, but their influence on cultural life was disproportionately great, like that of Heian courtiers and medieval Zen monks.

The world of the new townsmen was quite different from the world of those earlier cultural vanguards, and on the face of it far more worldly. Theirs were cities of shops, apprentices, money, entertainment, loves licit and illicit, gay pilgrimages to Ise, and secular realistic art that portrayed sensitively the faces and moods of a lively era.

Something of the Edo spirit can still be captured in certain sections of modern Tokyo. Side streets around the Ginza and Roppongi still boast tiny eating places, which have paper lanterns and purple curtains, and which sell such traditional delicacies as sushi, eel, and noodles. These teeming narrow streets still house bustling places of amusement for all tastes and the shops of a hundred crafts. A moment's reverie, and one can see in the laughing, pink-cheeked shopboys the storied apprentices to Edo, and in the hurrying expense-account crowd the prosperous merchants of the shogunal city, who carried plenty to spend on art and entertainment, since the laws of the Tokugawa state severely limited what sort of clothes they could wear or houses they could live in.

Kabuki and Bunraku Nowhere does old Edo come back to life more vividly than at the Kabuki-za, a great modern theater near the Ginza devoted to the form of drama called *Kabuki* that flourished in that era. Like much Western opera, Kabuki depends for stories on stock melodramas of love and battle and makes great use of costume and stage effects. It is not actually sung in the Western sense, although actors present lines in remarkable modulations of voice, accompanied by various traditional instruments that convey immense emotional range. Together with the equally impressive gestures, Kabuki exudes an almost unbearably potent sense of controlled strength, like a coiled spring. It requires consummate mastery of the actor's craft. When the principal, perhaps playing a samurai warrior seeking revenge, enters the stage, he moves up a long runway called the *hanamichi* (flowery path). His every heavy step is a powerful menacing thump, followed by a dramatic pose—arms out, the face a mask of frozen rage and determination. Finally he breaks into a piercing cry that moves the house to waves of applause.

The heyday of Tokugawa culture is traditionally said to be the Genroku period, strictly 1688-1703, but often expanded to cover roughly 1680-1730, when the greatest writers and actors of the age flourished and the characteristic Edo exuberance had not yet begun to decline.

In this expanded time period, the Genroku era was also the heyday of a form of Japanese theater even more remarkable than Kabuki, the *ningyō jōruri* or *Bunraku* (doll or puppet theater). Japan's greatest dramatist of the era, Chikamatsu Monzaemon (1653-1725), first wrote for Kabuki. After the retirement from the Kyoto stage of the most eminent performer of the day, Sakata Tōjirō (1647-1709), Chikamatsu moved to Osaka, home of *jōruri*,

Bunraku, the unique Japanese puppet theater, developed during the Tokugawa period and was a vehicle for the dramas of Chika-matsu. Here a Bunraku doll performs under the control of its black-robed puppeteer. (Courtesy Japan Air Lines.)

and turned his exceptional gifts to puppet theater as the medium of his more mature writing. Some of his puppet plays were later adapted for Kabuki. *Jōruri*, although it is still alive and sometimes revived, declined to a minor place after the middle of the eighteenth century.

Westerners tend to think of puppetry only as a novelty or a children's entertainment for which the *Punch and Judy* sort of farce is adequate. We must make some mental adjustment to conceive of it as a vehicle for the dramas of Chikamatsu, whose poetic subtlety and tragic power has been compared to Shakespeare's.

To understand Chikamatsu's theater, we must first acquire a new image of puppets. These were not silly-looking hand puppets or marionettes on the ends of strings, but three- or four-feet-tall dolls, carved and colorfully dressed by master craftsmen whose life-pride was the perfection of their handiwork. The puppets were moved about the stage by as many as three professional puppeteers, robed in black to render them a nondescript background to their brilliant charges. The observer had to imagine away these crouched attendants and see only the bright *ningyō* (dolls). Puppet artists could give their inanimate vehicles gestures so polished that even Kabuki stars would study and imitate them. As the dolls performed on stage, a reciter would chant the lines and connecting narration to the accompaniment of the lute-like stringed instrument called the *samisen.*

This *ningyō jōruri*, this puppet theater, had a peculiar effect. The realism of the stunning portrayal of emotional feeling by an unsurpassed skill in movement of the arms, legs, and head was combined with the timeless, archetypal effect of the puppets' unchanging painted faces and the bardic chanted narrative. Together, these two features would pull the audience deeply into a sensitive yet storyland mood that no other medium has quite achieved. Bunraku avoids on one hand the cult of the great virtuoso performer that afflicts both Kabuki and Western opera, and, on the other hand, the harsh realism of *shingeki shibai* ("modern" drama of the Western sort).

Chikamatsu wrote both the popular *jidaimono* (historical plays full of battle and bombast) and also domestic tragedies. The latter were the first mature plays anywhere in the world in which ordinary common people, rather than the aristocratic paragons with the tragic flaw of Aristotelian theory, attain the dignity of poignant feelings and deaths that is exalted by circumstances of genuine tragedy. The traders and craftsmen of Tokugawa rightly saw themselves ennobled in these plays and loved them.

The Love Suicides at Amijima For example, the protagonist of Chikamatsu's *jōruri The Love Suicides at Amijima* is Jihei, an Osaka paper merchant who owns a thirty-six-foot shop. (Business establishments were measured by the length of their footage on the street.) Jihei hardly represents a classic hero. He is a whining, weak, emotional man who has an understandably furious father-in-law and an outspoken, though loyal and compassionate, wife.

The little paper-seller is in love to the depths of his humdrum heart with Koharu, a prostitute in the gay quarter, on whom he spends inordinate amounts of time and money while the business and his wife and two small children languish. Jihei is heedless when he thinks he can get by with something and snivelling when caught. There is little to admire in him. Koharu, from the lowest stratum of society, seems just another practitioner of her trade, exploited, yet no better and no worse than a thousand others.

Despite their manifold weaknesses, the love between Jihei and Koharu is real. Somehow Chikamatsu, with the magic of his drama and poetry, is able to make us believe in its reality, so that the foolish but recklessly sincere lovers gain our own love, if not our approval. When Jihei and Koharu finally commit suicide rather than give up their vows to each other—even as the ostensibly worthier samurai would do, rather than betray his liege or honor—we cannot but feel that, for all their folly and irresponsibility toward others, they have achieved a certain grandeur.

In his final words Jihei prays that he and his paramour may be reborn in the Buddha's paradise on the same lotus. The narrator, to the twanging strings of the *samisen*, intimates that the pure single-heartedness of their love may have won the pair Buddhahood, for he ends by saying: "People say that they who were caught in the net of Buddha's vow immediately gained salvation and deliverance, and all who hear the tale of the Love Suicides at Amijima are moved to tears." And Chikamatsu managed to catch in the net of his own marvelous words a moving tragedy of lowly yet deeply human lives, which even Shakespeare, for all his catholicity, would have relegated to his interludes of comic buffoonery about the passions of townsmen and servants.[4]

The Values
of Japanese Culture

In every advanced human society, "high culture" and "popular culture" can be set off against each other. High culture is the culture of the elite, those well educated in the traditions of the society and influential in shaping them. It is usually a culture of books, refinement, and philosophical reflection; in premodern times it may be the literate and courtly culture. Popular culture is the way in which ordinary people, whether in towns or rural villages, express their values; it may be a culture of storytellers, festivals, popular songs, and folk art. In Japan both high culture and popular culture can certainly be discerned, yet to a remarkable extent the two are in close interaction. Fundamental values and themes are shared by both, and motifs move rapidly between the two; in fact, it often seems that the distinction is artificial. Yet the distinction does help us to see what is truly universal in Japan and where the ultimate roots are.

HIGH CULTURE

Obligation and Human Feeling

Donald Keene has rightly pointed out that the basic conflict in the plays of Chikamatsu is between *giri* (obligation resultant from the social order) and *ninjō* (human feeling).[1] This conflict is not different from that felt by the Heian emperor and courtiers when the young princess was sent to the sacerdotal palace in remote Ise, or from that of Ashikaga Yoshimasa between his role as shogun and his personal life as lover of Zen arts. Indeed, the conflict between *giri* and *ninjō* can be regarded as a fundamental dynamic of Japanese culture. Many more examples could be adduced. The *Manyōshū*, the earliest great collection of Japanese poetry, is full of "poems of departure" in which a nobleman weeps as he is ordered to service in some remote province and must leave his love behind.

The Japanese tradition is clear that *giri* must take precedence; this tradition is deeply influenced by Confucianism and by an earlier cultural pattern of paramount loyalty to the clan. The obligations of *giri* are really part of a cosmic machinery that will destroy the honor and even the person of those who flout it. Torturous conflicts can arise between opposing *giri* obligations, and no shame is attached to feeling deep sadness when *giri* forces a hard choice that goes against personal feelings and loved ones. These conflicts are the stuff of song and story.

Few Japanese have been unfamiliar with this conflict. The fictional Prince Genji could sympathize with the princess-priestess; he was himself both pampered and enslaved by his privileged station. In the same way the aesthetic shogun Yoshimasa was trapped between an inner need for the experience of beauty that the perquisites of office enabled him to fulfill and the onus of a great national task laid upon him, for which he was not made and which he could not begin to do well.

Zen In fact, the whole idea of the Zen tradition Yoshimasa loved is to bring the tension between obligations to a climax. Then the tension becomes a dynamic to remove attachment to either obligation or feeling; peace can be found in living egolessly fulfilling obligation, or in living as a feckless "Zen lunatic" who forgets obligation and just follows human feeling and beauty. It is not easy, however, to untangle the knotted coils of the human psyche so that the cords all flow one way or the other. Zen assumes that one's true nature, at one with the infinite and therefore free, is not the superficial nature of moods and feelings that we think we liberate when we really indulge ourselves. The training of *zazen* requires a highly controlled posture for meditation, but lets the mind release all thoughts and fancies whatsoever. Zen predicates that discipline, not giving in to whims, produces the true freedom of pure service or love.

Tension between inwardness and social role would have been drawn even more tightly—until perhaps it also finally snapped and was resolved—in skilled people like Kabuki actors and the operators of *ningyō jōruri*. They had prepared for their roles, to which they had come by heredity or adoption, from early childhood, and their power depended on exquisite control.

Resolution of Conflict

The Japanese, then, are deeply aware of a hereditary social order and hereditary obligations. Yet they also profoundly value paths for resolving or transcending the conflicts created by the obligations, or even for symbolically or actually breaking out of the order of society and obligation for a time, if permanent release is impossible.

Travel and Pilgrimage   Travel and pilgrimage have long been important to the restless Japanese spirit. Travel narratives are common, and it was not only the Heian princess who went to Ise. The princess's journey to Ise was like a pilgrimage. In the Tokugawa period mass pilgrimage to Ise was a common way of temporarily breaking with the rigidly hierarchical order. In Japan an eagerness for movement flourishes incessantly—defined, ritualized, yet definite movement out of structure and back again.

Nature   This theme can be recognized not only in the great importance of pilgrimage in religion and the travel genre in literature, but also in the vitality of nature as a literary and artistic theme. Nature is pictured in Japan as that which is invitingly outside of structure as people know it, though under karma and the gods. People think of nature as mystical, vague, elusive, and yet infinitely fascinating, the realm of ultimate freedom and equality. Nature is one extreme of a persistent Japanese sense of polarity between structure and freedom, obligation and feeling, the place of humans and the liberty of nature.

The ancient Japanese feeling for nature as the reservoir of the pure and the sacred led to the isolation of the priestess and the shrine in a fresh, clean spot, uncontaminated by other human habitation; it also lies at the roots of the Higashiyama arts of the tea ceremony, ikebana, and the Zen garden. This sense of the natural is quite different from Western romanticism, in which natural beauty leads to exaltation through greater and greater enhancement of feeling. Rather, nature as sheer "otherness," in which human patterns derived from egocentricity are broken, brings contemplative tranquillity as it drains away pride and emotion. This egoless calm, which Yoshimasa presumably felt as he sat in his tea room viewing garden and mountains, calls to mind the reverence of the earlier Japanese for the sacred mountains and outdoor sanctuaries (*shiki*) where *kami* (gods) were believed to come down to break the ordinary order with their supernatural power.

FOLK CULTURE

The high culture of Japan, with its feelings about society, the heart, and nature, is not fully understandable without reference to the folk and popular culture out of which much of the high culture has arisen. Interaction between art and basic Japanese attitudes is to be sought not only in these great themes; one must turn to folk culture for full understanding of certain prevailing motifs.

Shinto

Shinto as a religion is far more than a popular phenomenon; it has an intellectual and institutional tradition as strongly connected with the court and other centers of elite power as with the common folk. But certain basic motifs of Shinto need to be mentioned at the beginning of any discussion of popular culture, for they are deeply symbolic of its profoundest values.

Purity We have already observed that the ancient Shinto idea of sacred space in a pure place is fundamental to the Japanese garden. Nothing is more basic to Shinto than the sense of a great divide between purity and pollution. A pure spot, like the precincts of a shrine or the heart of a sincere person, is bright, fresh, clean, simple, and in harmony with nature. It is uncontaminated by blood, sickness, or death and is set apart from the realms of pollution. From its vantage point, the impurities are invisible. The purity-pollution concept to this day affects deeply rooted Japanese attitudes on numerous matters, including some very secular-seeming problems.

Localism Another Shinto-related value is localism. The *kami* (deities) of Shinto shrines are generally thought of not as universal God, but as the finite spirits of particular localities (a village or mountain) and its people. Localism encourages a deep sense of region, community, and family as the primary divinely sanctioned foci of loyalty. Localism views the universe as a whole as a pluralism of diffuse divinity broken into many diverse local expressions, rather than as a focused monotheism.

Pilgrimage In contrast to localism, pilgrimage is a quest for the sacred in faraway places of great purity and numinous quality; it also has deep Shinto roots. From time immemorial, wizardlike ascetics and ordinary pilgrims have sought especially close ties to *kami* atop mountains or under waterfalls. They have combined a general Japanese love of travel with a feel for its spiritually refreshing quality. Pilgrimage had its greatest development in the Tokugawa period, when millions combined piety with temporary leave of the constricted social climate by making for Ise, the most popular shrine, or for a holy mountain like Ontake. Like Chaucer's Canterbury-goers, these pilgrim bands were merry and uninhibited; the popular side of Shinto religion in Japan has rarely been overly solemn, and has often given vent to that side of religion expressed in festival and dance. At the same time, the pilgrimage aspect of Shinto doubtless offers an ultimate model for all travel literature and poems written

The lively spirit of the Shinto matsuri *is well represented by the Kenka ("Scuffle") Matsuri of the Matsubara Hachiman Shrine in Himeji City. On October 14-15 of each year,* kami *spirits are carried in seven gorgeous* mikoshi *(palanquins)—each weighing nearly a ton. The sight of the* mikoshi, *which are carried on the shoulders of young men, jostling with each other is an unforgettable spectacle. (Courtesy Consulate General of Japan, N.Y.)*

along the way, which both suggest that movement enhances the spirit.

Festivals The festive face of Shinto is seen in the *matsuri*, the great festivals of Shinto shrines. Virtually every shrine has an annual *ujigami* festival (festival of the patronal deity of the place) and perhaps other important holidays as well. These festivals usually take place in the spring or fall, since they are basically agricultural rites of planting or harvest; some shrines have colorful midsummer rites to ward off insects and disease, and New Year's ceremonies as well. They remind us of the great importance of seasonal awareness in Japanese literature and life.

The *matsuri* has four ritual steps: purification, when the priest purifies the congregation by a gesture like waving an evergreen branch over them; presentation of the offerings; prayer or petition, when the priest chants the *norito* (prayer); and participation, when worshippers may be given a sip of rice wine as a sort of communion, and the mood of the festival changes from slow solemnity to a vivid, almost frenetic carnival atmosphere. Sacred dance and sports may be performed; the deity is carried in a palanquin through the streets at a half-run; eating, drinking, and games are the activities of the day.

The *matsuri*, with its many local traditions, at once affirms the importance of ritual, celebration, performance, and occasions of release in Japanese life. As with Greek drama in the West, the roots of the classic Japanese theater, especially No, are probably to be found in the sacred dances and popular celebrations of the Shinto *matsuri*. The revelatory importance of the theater, the employment of nonordinary tempos—slower or faster than normal—the use of masks, and strained oracular voice of Japanese drama all remind one of the *matsuri*.

Shamanism

One of the most fundamental ancient Shinto motifs of all, which has had considerable cultural influence even though it is no longer an important aspect of Shinto proper, is shamanism. Characteristically a shaman is one who, after selection by deities, initiation, and preparatory ascetic practice, is able to go into ecstatic trance. In trance, deities or spirits of the departed communicate through the possessed one, or the shaman is able to travel mystically to the world of the gods or departed souls. In trance, shamans serve as healers and diviners. Japanese shamans have been predominantly female.

The institution of the Ise princess-priestess, for example, has roots in ancient shamanism. Long before the Heian period, a female relative—sister, wife, or niece—of a clan chieftain or emperor would usually serve as shaman. She would go into trance, be possessed by a deity, and give advice on matters of state. Frequently, in order to maintain the absolute purity her vocation required, the shaman lived apart from the court, across a purifying stream or on the slopes of a sacred mountain. The Ise priestess, while not in historical times primarily a shaman, undoubtedly is in the heritage of that prehistoric institution. Comparable independent shamans still practice in some remoter districts of rural Japan.[2]

The model shamanism has offered of the powerful, spiritually possessed individual has had a far-reaching effect in Japan, despite the fact that actual shamans are now few in number. The influence of shamanism can be seen in the peculiar potency of the charismatic individual in Japanese religion down to the important "New Religions" of the nineteenth and twentieth centuries. One can also trace its influence in the theater and in dance. Shamanism, with the legitimation it has given to the power of charisma and unusual states of consciousness, has long offered the Japanese a countervailing force to the power of *giri* as determinant of human destiny in family and community obligation, even though in practice the two often uphold each other.

Popular Culture and the Arts

The subject matter and mood of Chikamatsu's *The Love Suicides at Amijima* are Edo; however, because the story is about very ordinary people, the backdrop of popular belief breaks through in incidental, yet cumulatively pervasive, ways. We read that Jihei and Koharu consummated their pact in "the tenth month, the month when no gods will unite them." The tenth month was the *kannazuki* (the "month without *kami* or gods"), when, according to popular teaching, all the deities of Japan gather at Izumo for a conference, leaving the rest of the nation bereft of their blessings. Again, Koharu reflects popular concepts of Pure Land Buddhism when she says just before the final deed, "If I can save living creatures at will when once I mount a lotus calyx in Paradise and become a Buddha, I want to protect women of my profession, so that never again will there be love suicides."

Much more could be said about the fascinating world of popular Shinto, folklore, and the like. We could talk about the strange widespread belief in foxes with powers of enchantment; about widespread popular Buddhist celebrations like Ōbon, the late summer season when the departed are commemorated and believed to return; about the great importance of the New Year's holiday. But we must proceed to discuss another aspect of popular life, the structures of family and loyalty.

FAMILY LIFE AND ETHICAL VALUES

Family and Community   The fundamental unit in Japanese society is the *ie* (house or household in the sense of family or kin). Patterns of relationship within the family are manifested by customs. Within a traditional household or *ie* the eldest son and his wife live with the son's aging parents and carry on the family farm, business, or estate, while younger sons set up branch houses. A more inclusive unit, in some places, is the *dōzoku* (extended family), composed of several *ie* of the same surname presided over by the senior line and its head. The senior line of this extended family constitutes the *honke* ("main family") that has primacy of honor and a certain authority over the branches. Branch families visit the *honke* at New Year's, the main holiday for affirming traditional relationships, and assist it in such ceremonial ways as helping to clean its cemetery at Ōbon. The *honke* may keep ancestral tablets of the *ie* or *dōzoku* at its Buddhist temple and may maintain a *dōzoku* Shinto shrine apart from the village or community shrine.

The typical traditional Japanese rural community, and even

This mealtime scene suggests the life of the Japanese family today. Note the combination of Western and traditional dress and customs; the family sits on the floor and uses hashi *(chopsticks), but some of the furnishings are Western. (Courtesy Consulate General of Japan, N.Y.)*

certain old and traditional neighborhoods of cities, is made up of one or more *dōzoku* comprised of *ie* whose interrelationships and intermarriages are carefully arranged. Community leadership, and sometimes ceremonial functions in the Shinto shrine, may rotate among the heads of the households, or perhaps among young men of certain ages.[3]

In addition, we should mention the class of outcastes (*eta* or *bunrakujin*) who live in villages outside the "regular" communities and perform, among other lowly occupations, tasks such as butchering that are impure in Buddhist eyes. They have often suffered harsh discrimination in Japan's otherwise cohesive society.

The Work Group An important point about Japanese society, which has not always been fully appreciated by outside observers, is that the first loyalty of Japanese, especially working males, is and always has been not to the family as such, but to the work or activity group.[4] The family is secondary to the work group, though there is usually no conflict. At New Year's, calls by subordinates upon superiors are more frequent than calls between collateral kin—married brothers, sisters, cousins—though the *honke* call remains important.

The work group may be the modern office or corporation. Japanese firms are more paternalistic and more strictly governed by seniority than their American counterparts. A person customarily enters employment for life, and kinship terms are extended to the occupational context. In a real sense, the work group replaces the medieval *daimyō* (feudal lord) and his retainers, the spiritual master and his disciples, or even the ancient *uji* (clan) headed by an *uji no kami* (chieftain).

Very often the extended family is an *uchi* (familial economic unit), a farm or mercantile house, so that the two loyalties are convergent. But this is not necessarily the case. Despite the influence of Confucianism, family loyalty beyond the point of mere courtesy is actually weak in Japan, except when reinforced by economic cohesion. Relations between adult siblings, or between adult children and their parents, unless they live or work together, are probably less intimate and more perfunctory than in America.

For this reason, Japanese Confucian thinkers have long tended to rationalize the extension of the central Confucian virtue of loyalty to parents to other objects of absolute devotion: the feudal lord and, more recently, the emperor and the state.

Today, family loyalty is still easily and quite explicitly transferred. Corporations like to speak of themselves as families, and they frequently have patriarchal elder statesmen in paternal roles. Formerly, feudal lords explicitly adopted promising successors as sons to maintain a fiction of familial continuity, and abbots made families of their novices. In Japanese universities, graduate students generally make themselves followers of an *oyabun* (a professor who is like a parent). The student, even if he becomes a junior professor, assiduously serves his *oyabun* in both scholarly and personal ways and certainly does not criticize the senior's work before anyone else. One can change *oyabun*, but that is a serious matter. The same pattern obtains in business, government, even the underworld.[5]

Nonetheless, the *oya* or *oyabun* (the head of a family or family-like organization such as a business) is far from being an individualistic autocrat. For another basic principle of Japanese society is that group actions and decisions are always preferred. Everyone, high or low, avoids personal responsibility and seeks instead to formulate group responsibility through consensus. The consequences of failure, for a person who assumes direct responsibility, are devastating to the Japanese psyche and social standing.

Rather, the Japanese tradition is one of close cooperation and joint responsibility within a family, business, or other unit.

Basic decisions in families were traditionally made in long family conferences that went on until consensus was reached. Today business decisions are often preceded by the circulation of memos (*ringisho*), to which each ranking employee who approves it affixes his seal. The functions of a family or business head, who has reached his position of honor largely by seniority, are (like that of the emperor in the state) to a great extent ceremonial and social. The real decision-making power is broadly based, though it works not by formal vote so much as by a complex, intuitively understood process of discussion and negotiation until a consensus appears to be reached; the entire unit takes responsibility together for what it is going to do.

One view is that close cooperation and shared responsibility goes back to the requirements of the rice-cultivating village. Rice-growing demands much hard intensive work that must be done together, from transplanting to maintaining irrigation ditches for the benefit of all, and if anyone fails his or her part all suffer. Certainly these social attitudes have roots in the feudal system and the clan system that preceded it.

Personal Relationships   Japanese society, shaped by this family model and driven by the dynamics of *giri* obligation, is nonetheless a society of vertical relationships insofar as language and deference are concerned. In any encounter, Japanese immediately see themselves as superior or subordinate; this understanding of position will shape the tone and govern the language of conversation, for Japanese has many verbal and grammatical modulations appropriate to different types of relationship. For this reason, the marvelous range and subtlety of the Japanese language come into their own in interpersonal conversation. Conversely, Japanese often find addressing a group, in which persons of several different types of relationship to the speaker may be present, an awkward task, and public rhetoric is not a particularly well developed art in Japan.

The Japanese tend to assume that really important decisions are made through interpersonal relations structured, as all are, by the family model and patterns of obligation. In a society of vertical relationships, the Japanese have trouble accepting anyone as a true equal, except in relationships going back very far, as of schoolmates of the same age who may remain equal friends for a lifetime.

Since loyalty is to a relationship and its structure rather than to abstract principles, Japanese ethical values tend to be situational rather than absolutistic. Rather than absolute ethical laws, the relational and human nature of each situation calling for ethical decision has its own rights and wrongs that must be perceived.

Traditional ethical writings, harking back to Confucian thought and the Shinto concept of purity, speak of *makoto* (sincerity) as the key virtue in such a moral order. The truly sincere mind—simple, pure, fresh, bright, wishing to do right, and without a trace of duplicity—will intuitively perceive what is right in each situation as it comes.

Periods in Japanese History

Japan's long history can be divided into several periods, each marked by significant political and cultural transitions. Perhaps the periodization is too convenient, for it tends to give undue emphasis to unities within each period and discontinuities between them. However, these nearly universally accepted units do serve to break history down into manageable units in the case of Japan. In this chapter, then, we shall introduce the conventional periodization and briefly describe the political and cultural scene in each period.

PREHISTORY: JAPAN BEFORE WRITTEN DOCUMENTS

Jōmon Period Although remains of Stone Age cultures going back thousands of years have been found in Japanese soil, the earliest culture likely to have much continuity with historical Japan is that called the Jōmon. The word literally means "rope pattern," and it refers to a characteristic rope-like design often used to decorate Jōmon pottery. The earliest Jōmon relics are dated to about 8000 B.C., and the period extends until about 200 B.C. It is noted not only for its pottery, but also for *dogū*, striking half-animal, half-human earthen figures, perhaps magical in intent. The Jōmon people practiced hunting, fishing, and in some instances simple agriculture; archaeologists have suggested that their culture may have been not too dissimilar from that of recent Polynesians and Melanesians.

Yayoi Period The next cultural period, the Yayoi, is dated from around 200 B.C. to A.D. 250. Wet rice agriculture, evidently introduced by immigrants from Southeast Asia during this period, gradually extended northward from southern Kyushu. Metal was introduced to Japan, probably from Korea. The earliest metal objects were of ritual rather than practical use: swords, spears, mirrors, and bells, which probably served as sacred objects in shrines and as grave goods buried with important persons.

The accounts of travelers from China give a vivid picture of life in Japan in this era. They tell us that people ate raw vegetables from bamboo or wooden trays, were long-lived, clapped their hands for worship rather than kneel, were fond of liquor, and were generally honest. The chronicles inform us that Japan formerly was ruled by a man, but more recently (apparently in the third century A.D.), after a period of turmoil, a woman named Pimiko (Sun-princess?) took power. She was a shaman who lived in seclusion with a thousand female attendants and a single male, who mediated between her and the outside world; this sorceress-queen remained unmarried and "bewitched the populace."

Involved and fascinating attempts have been made to reconcile these accounts with archaeological evidence and the mythological narratives. We cannot follow them here, but we can note that the Chinese records give a most intriguing picture of early Japan.

Kofun Period The Kofun (Great Tomb) era is A.D. 250-552. This period might be called "protohistoric," for archaeology and legend give us a general view of events, even if precision is lacking. The archaeology of the Kofun period is rich, for, as the name suggests, great rulers built immense earthen tombs, often in a keyhole shape and surrounded by a moat. On the flanks of these edifices were placed clay figures, charmingly and skillfully executed; they represent retainers intended to follow the great man to the Other World and in their diverse garb and work give a valuable picture of many aspects of Kofun society. Within, the deceased was surrounded by sacred mirrors, swords, and jewels (still the regalia of the Japanese emperor), and sometimes by remarkable paintings and accoutrements.

After a time of troubles, Japan is believed to have been unified under the Yamato house, progenitors of the present imperial line, about A.D. 350-450. Their seat was in the Yamato basin, the area around Kyoto and Nara. In an expansive burst following unification, Japan may have occupied southern Korea in the late fourth century, but the last foothold there was lost in 562.

The Kofun era, the last in which the Japanese were a vigorous but barbaric and unlettered people on the outskirts of more civilized areas, came to an end with the introduction of Buddhism. With that great faith came many other cultural gifts: writing, Chinese political and philosophical thought, new forms of fine arts, and new technologies.

The traditional date for the introduction of Buddhism corresponds to 538 or 552. The acceptance of Buddhism, and the increasingly voluminous inflow of the other benefits of the mainland's advanced culture, was certainly more gradual than such an exact date would indicate; however, the dates suggest when Buddhism became politically significant. The chief early source of mainland culture was Korea; its transmission was no doubt largely a byproduct of the Japanese occupation and came with Korean craftsmen and teachers who immigrated to Japan in the sixth century in considerable numbers.

THE ASUKA PERIOD (552-645) AND THE HAKUHŌ PERIOD (645-710)

The Asuka and Hakuhō periods were times of gradual and often painful assimilation of the new culture and religion. From the perspective of the time, adjustment doubtless seemed slow and difficult; looking back, we are amazed by the islands' change in little more than a century and a half from a country of illiterate outlanders to the site of a brilliant civilization worthy of comparison with any in the world, as were our grandparents by Japan's modern transformation.

The era began with trouble over the new Buddhist faith. The Buddhist cause was taken up by the politically powerful Soga family but was understandably opposed by the Mononobe and Nakatomi clans, who had traditional Shinto priestly roles. The rivalry degenerated into civil war, in which the Soga prevailed for a time. In 592 the prime minister, Soga no Umako, consolidated the Soga's seizure of power by arranging the murder of the reigning emperor; he placed his own niece on the throne as the Empress Suiko. An imperial prince, Shōtoku (573-621), was made regent.

Prince Shōtoku However underhanded the means that brought him to power, the rule of the brilliant Prince Shōtoku was beneficial and became the turning point in the emergence of Japanese culture and nationhood. A devout Buddhist like the empress, Shōtoku founded the first major national temple, the celebrated Hōryūji, in 607. Although most of the remaining structures are later than Shōtoku's time, this great temple near Nara remains a trove of priceless early Buddhist art. The prince endeavored with some success to use Buddhism and its culture as a national unifying force transcending the individual *uji* (clans). The so-called Seventeen Article Constitution (traditionally dated 604) is also attributed to him, though the authorship has been disputed. The document was not really a constitution in the modern sense, but a setting-forth of very lofty ethical principles for public officials, based on Confucianism but mentioning Buddhism also. It was a first important step in the transformation (at least on paper) of the Japanese government to a rationalized and hierarchical bureaucracy administering fixed laws by established principles on the Chinese model.

The process of transformation was continued in the Hakuhō period, though under different auspices. In 645 the Nakatomi recouped their earlier losses when Nakatomi Kamatari and Prince Naka killed the ruling Soga minister, the arrogant Iruka, and seized power. The Fujiwara, who were to become all-powerful a little later in the Heian era, were a branch of the Nakatomi house; this coup d'état of 645, then, deeply affected the fortunes of Japan for many centuries.

The Taika Reform   The first major result of Nakatomi rule was the Taika Reform of 646, a revamping of government that further rationalized the ministries of state and attempted to complete centralization of the nation in an absolute monarchy. Even private property was abolished in theory; all land was transferred to the crown, which was then to redistribute it equitably. This provision, like others, was to prove unenforceable, but the "Great Reform" set a precedent for extreme centralization that was to have lasting consequences.

Several sovereigns of the last part of the seventh century, especially Tenchi (r. 661–671), Temmu (r. 671–686), and Temmu's widow, the Empress Jitō (r. 686–697), were relatively strong rulers who did much to promote Buddhism and governmental authority. Temmu and Jitō also assured that the court Shinto rites dear to their Nakatomi counselors were updated and given parallel prestige to Buddhism; the Nakatomi family's senior branch became chief court Shinto chaplains and chief priests at Ise around this time, positions they held until 1872.

The Taihō Code   The process of strengthening and reorganizing the state culminated in the promulgation of the Taihō Code, which inaugurated the legal system called Ritsuryō (Laws and Regulations). Ritsuryō was to remain the fundamental law of the state through the Nara and Heian eras and, in theory, until the modern constitutions. Modeled on certain Chinese codes, this constitution promulgated by the Emperor Mommu in 702 defines the organization, rituals, powers, and duties of the court, the provinces and the ministries.

THE NARA PERIOD (710-794)

In 710 the first permanent capital of Japan was established at Nara, a new city modeled on the capital of the culturally splendid T'ang dynasty then ruling in China. Until then, the capital had been a more or less temporary affair that was moved after the demise of each monarch because of Shinto taboos against the pollution of death. When that practice ended, the potential richness of Japanese culture broke through, not just in a temple here or there, but in an entire city of palaces and opulent monasteries.

Much of the artistic legacy of the golden age of Nara can be seen today in that now-quiet town. The traveler to Nara enters, almost as if by time travel, the beauties of another age. He or she can walk through the famous Deer Park, thronged with tame animals and dotted with exquisite temples and pagodas. Trails lined with stone lanterns lead to the vermilion-porticoed Kasuga Shrine, seat of the patronal gods of the great Fujiwara house. Not far away is the Daibutsu, the Great Buddha of Nara, over fifty feet high.

The magnificent Great Buddha of Nara was built by order of the devout Emperor Shōmu (r. 724-749) as the national centerpiece of a system of provincial temples (*kokubunji*), where sutras were to be constantly chanted for the protection of the state. The immense cost in money and labor entailed by the project required that the court and several disgruntled factions in the nation seek reconciliation, so that taxes could be collected and labor brigades levied without hindrance. At least temporarily, the construction of the huge edifice accomplished its purpose of bringing the nation into political and spiritual unity. Upon its dedication, the emperor abdicated to enter the Buddhist priesthood.

The Buddhist paradise of national unity suggested by those events was soon shown to be superficial, however. The very success of Buddhism had led the major temples to acquire great wealth and concomitant political influence, an influence much resented by the old aristocracy. The matter came to a head in scandals involving Shōmu's successor, the Empress Kōken, and an ambitious priest named Dōkyō who came near to ascending the throne as consort and emperor. His actions eventually discredited female rule (there were no important reigning empresses after Kōken), priestly intrigue at court (thereafter usually resisted), and the location of the capital at Nara, where it was susceptible to the influence of powerful temples in the same city. In 784, the court moved out of Nara and in 794 was established in Heian, modern Kyoto.

For all its problems, the Nara period has left a glowing cultural legacy: its rich architecture and its literary bequest of poetry and histories. The chief of these is the mid-Nara assemblage called the *Manyōshū*, a collection of poems often concerned with nature, love, or separation, written in a wistful, yearning mood often expressed with great delicacy. A volume of poetry written in Chinese, the *Kaifusō*, appeared at about the same time, for the Nara century was a time of considerable cultural and religious importing from the mainland.

THE HEIAN PERIOD (794–1185)

The Heian period was the golden age of imperial court society. The emperor reigned nominally, but real power fell into the hands of the Fujiwara house. Its daughters became imperial consorts, and its leading men were chief ministers of state and religion. The most effective Fujiwara ruler finally became a virtual dictator (insofar as he could enforce his rule in the provinces), with titles like *sesshō* (regent for a minor emperor) and *kampaku* (regent or administrator for an emperor of age). The greatest of the Fujiwara rulers, Fujiwara Michinaga (966–1027), saw the domination of his house reach its height as his power and privilege continued unabated even after his formal retirement. During this time no less than eight figurehead monarchs came to the throne, and each abdicated after producing a minor heir. Michinaga himself enjoyed supreme contentment, complete with a private temple designed to reproduce the wonder of the Buddhist paradise; it had jeweled nets on the trees and peacock islands in the pond. "My aspiration," he allegedly said, "is fully satisfied like a full moon in the sky."

Others were less well pleased with Fujiwara domination, including the stronger-minded emperors themselves. A sovereign customarily abdicated after performing his primary nonceremonial function in life, the begetting of male heir to be married in due time to a Fujiwara maiden. This practice insured that the nominal ruler would most often be a minor with a Fujiwara mother as well as a Fujiwara regent, doubly insuring the suzerainty of the Fujiwara house. But beginning with the Emperor Gosanjō (whose mother was not a Fujiwara), who abdicated in 1072, these retired sovereigns, stripped of tiresome ritual duties and possessed of the freedom and energy to act, sought to exercise real political power from behind the scenes. This curious system of *insei* (cloistered rule) gradually weakened the power of the Fujiwara, who were already afflicted by increasing dissatisfaction in the provinces with the moribund and luxurious capital.

That discontent was abetted by the gradual appearance of a new class in the outlying reaches of the empire, the *buke* (samurai or warriors). Although some structures of the old clan system were retained, the leaders of the *buke* were not traditional chieftains, but rather they were predominantly scions of younger branches of aristocratic Heian families (even the imperial one) who were sent out by the rigidly hierarchical court. They accepted *shōens* (tax-free estates) in the provinces, where they gradually gained power bases and private armies. Often, indeed, they had been assigned distasteful military tasks by the effete court, which abhorred bloodshed (capital punishment of the aristocracy was abolished during most of the Heian period); to its ultimate distruction, the court had no substantial military forces directly loyal to it. Having once tasted the decisive power of the sword, those knights, now more used to the field than the Heian drawing-rooms, were not satisfied to be the military lackeys of men they inwardly despised.

Cultural Life　More important in the last analysis than its political history, however, is the Heian period's cultural heritage. As the glorious era of court life, it was the age of *miyabi* (courtly elegance and taste), an elusive quality of life unforgettably portrayed in *The Tale of Genji*. For the *bijin* (the "beautiful people" of the court), the people who were *kumonoue* (above the clouds), life was shaped more by aesthetics, by form, wit, and propriety, than by any other standards.

Although Shinto usages like the sending of the princess to the Saigū at Ise were carefully observed, attitudes were preeminently colored by Buddhism. The major Buddhist sects were Shingon and Tendai, new foundations started by charismatic leaders about the time the capital moved to Heian, which were not tinged with the poor reputation of the Nara temples. Both were, or soon became, heavily ritualistic and esoteric and offered gorgeous spectacles and subtle doctrines for courtiers and commoners to enjoy or mull over as best they could. Later in the period, the Pure Land doctrine gained popularity; this doctrine stated that those who simply call upon the name of Amida Buddha in faith will be brought into his paradise—a splendidly sensuous paradise well represented by Michinaga's temple garden. Most pervasive, though, was a general Buddhistic mood that, on the one hand, saw eternity reflected in the glory of *miyabi* life, but on the other hand was deeply conscious of the transitoriness of all things and the inevitability of destinies governed by karma. Life, even of brilliant exquisites of the court, is like cherry blossoms that bloom for a few days, then fall; in their time they nonetheless suggest something of the mysteries that lie beyond the visible world.

The chief forms of Heian literature were the *monogatari* (novel-

The Heian shrine in Kyoto is a modern reproduction, on a smaller scale, of the Daigokuden (Great Hall of State) of the first Heian Imperial Palace built in 794. It is brilliantly colored in vermilion and green. (Courtesy Japan Air Lines.)

istic tale), of which the *Genji* is the supreme example; the *nikki* (diary), which was often somewhat fictionalized and interspersed with poetry; and verse, a form used—as we have seen in the case of Prince Genji—by courtiers for routine courtesy and communication, the best examples of which were collected in court anthologies.

In all this courtly literature two moods prevail: the *mono no aware* (sensitivity to things) feeling that sees both the transitoriness and the dimension of depth in all objects and events and communicates that sense, as does *Genji*, with moving subtlety if not understatement; and the *okashi* mood, which appreciates in a light, witty, ironic way the passing parade of life. The best example is the *Makura no Sōshi* (*Pillow Book*), a diary and miscellany by the bright and observant court lady, Sei Shōnagon.

For all its flaws, the Heian era has continued to hover like a bright ghost at the back of the Japanese consciousness. The Heian epoch was a time when truly Japanese culture reached supreme quality and when a way of life of peerless refinement was constructed in Japanese terms. In more bloody or frenetic times to come, nearly all Japanese of sensitivity have known nostalgia for the timeless elegance of the Old Court.

The great poet Bashō Matsuo (1644–1694) caught in a few words the eternal meaning of Kyoto, the Old Capital, the home of Heian splendor, a place that has ever been as much an ideal, a dream, as an earthly reality. The last line refers to the *hototogisu* (the Japanese cuckoo), here written with characters meaning "bird of time." Rather like the Western nightingale, the *hototogisu*, which appears not infrequently in Heian poetry, is a bird of rich and

romantic associations, whose call inspires thoughts of pathos, yearning, and unattainable beauty. Bashō wrote:

> I am in the Old Capital
> Yet still I yearn for the Old Capital—
> Ah, the Bird of Time.[1]

THE KAMAKURA OR MINAMOTO PERIOD (1185-1333), THE KEMMU RESTORATION (1333-1336), AND THE NAMBOKUCHŌ ERA (1336-1392)

The eagles of war set in flight when military duties were farmed
out by the Fujiwara government to *buke* came home in the mid-
twelfth century. Owing to differences between the *insei* and reigning
emperors, and between branches of the Fujiwara and other noble
houses, the court was divided into two factions. Each enlisted the
help of a powerful *buke* house. The two aggregations of samurai
warriors, the Taira and the Minamoto, clashed in the Hōgen War of
July 1156, and again in the Heiji War of 1159, when the Minamoto
were decisively defeated.

For some twenty-five years (1159-1185), the Taira, under their
ambitious and autocratic leader Taira Kiyomori, controlled the
country. He married his daughter to the emperor, dismissed ministers
wholesale and replaced them with members of his own family,
and razed temples whose monks he thought opposed him. He strove
to promote trade in the Inland Sea and with China. For all his
pretensions to the elegance of the Fujiwara he was replacing, Kiyomori's regime had an aggressive vigor such as had not been seen
for centuries.

The regime did not, however, last long. The Minamoto had
been recouping their forces upcountry, and in 1180 they rose against
their hated rivals. In 1185 the Gempei War between the Minamoto
and the Taira, whose commander Kiyomori had died in 1181, came
to an end in the great sea battle of Dannoura. The Minamoto, under
their outstanding leader Minamoto Yoritomo, were now the dominant house in the land and their opponents were forever vanquished.

The Bakufu Believing that the Taira had become enervated in their
twenty-odd years in the luxurious capital, Yoritomo determined to
establish his political headquarters in more austere surroundings.
The site selected was Kamakura, on the shores of Tokyo Bay. The
imperial family and a toy court complete with elegant Fujiwara

ministers stayed in Kyoto. While the court remained an arbitrator of refined culture, the emperor's only political function was to appoint the ruling Minamoto shogun (in full, *seii taishōgun*, "barbarian-quelling generalissimo," a title ironically first given by Mommu, founder of the Heian court, to his commander fighting the Ainu in the far north). As such, the shogun was a military dictator entitled to rule the temporal affairs of the nation from his capital in Kamakura. The shogunal regime was called the *bakufu* (tent government).

Yoritomo and his soldiers established firm but effective control, welcome after an era of civil war. Following his death in 1199, real power went to the Hōjō family, from which Yoritomo's wife had come. For a century a situation obtained in which a Hōjō administered the land in the name of a Minamoto who ruled in the name of the emperor.

The Mongols The greatest crises of the Kamakura *bakufu* came in 1274 and 1281, when Mongols from overseas sought to invade Japan in the aftermath of Genghis Khan's world-sweeping conquests. The assaults were repelled with bitter fighting; during each ferocious attempt, the alien fleet was destroyed providentially with the aid of a great gale, a storm called the *kamikaze* (divine wind).

The Kemmu Restoration Although the Minamoto regime survived the Mongols, the battles weakened it. Victory left the state with many debts, not least to disaffected samurai who could not in this case, unlike most victories, be rewarded with spoils in the form of the enemy's land. The Minamoto period ended in 1333, when the Emperor Godaigo (1288–1339), a stronger figure than most, restored direct imperial rule. By conspiring with samurai who felt no loyalty for Kamakura, he succeeded in overthrowing the Minamoto and Hōjō, establishing the period of direct rule called the Kemmu Restoration. The emperor's dream did not last long; in 1336 one of his generals, Ashikaga Takauji, of a branch of the Minamoto house, led a band of warriors in a conspiracy against him and forced the sovereign to flee.

The Nambokuchō Era Takauji set up another member of the imperial house in Godaigo's place, who duly made the victorious warlord shogun. Godaigo, fleeing to Yoshino, set up a rival court, which was called the Southern Court. Although it was a lost cause, the Southern Court with its faithful samurai has ever held the sentimental affection of imperial loyalists. After Godaigo's death, Ashikaga Takauji himself, as a work of merit, established the famous Tenryūji Zen temple to the northwest of Kyoto with its wonderful gardens, and dedicated it to the eternal welfare of the deceased imperial soul. The Kyoto court aligned with the Ashikaga house;

because Kyoto is north of Yoshino, it was called the Northern Court. The rival imperial courts lasted for some sixty years, 1336–1392, when a compromise led to the dissolution of the Yoshino house and the consolidation of all power in Kyoto under the Ashikaga shogun. The period of two courts is called the *Nambokuchō* ("Southern and Northern Courts"); it oddly parallels the contemporaneous great papal schism in Europe, when rival claimants to the throne of Peter held court in Rome and Avignon.

Culture in this tumultuous era was understandably dominated by the values of the newly dominant warrior class. One of the early acts of the Hōjō regency was to issue a new legal code, partly supplementing the old *Ritsuryō* of the Taihō reform, called the *Jōei Shikimoku (Formulary of the Jōei Period)*. This document of 1232 emphasized provisions basic to the warrior way of life: the sanctity of lord-vassal relations, paternal power, and the right of female inheritance. Female inheritance was important in maintaining property intact in dangerous times, but it was also a token of the enlarged role that highborn Kamakura women enjoyed in the world of affairs.

Literature and Religion

The most characteristic form of literature is the *gunki* (account of wars). The preeminent example is the *Heike Monogatari*, which relates the intrigues and battles by which the Minamoto humbled the Taira. It is remarkable for the lingering sense of *mono no aware* it casts over those murderous events; the deeds of heroes are truly heroic, but framing them is a sense of contemplative sadness that knows that victor and vanquished alike will in the end come to dust. However, the samurai ideal of a proud, austere warrior, utterly loyal to lord and honor, indifferent to death, retained its grip on this era and, indeed, on several subsequent eras.

The samurai triumph and the general re-sorting of values of the Kamakura age had far-reaching religious implications too. New Buddhist movements swept the country, garnering finally more than half the souls of the nation and resulting in forms of Buddhism more deeply attuned to samurai, and Japanese, temperament than any before. All represented both a popularization and a simplification of Buddhism. No longer was the ancient faith accessible only to leisured courtiers or monks with the capacity for complicated meditations. The new forms were based upon simple, sure techniques suitable to what many considered a degenerate age, as easy for the peasant in the fields, or the warrior facing death on the field of battle, as for the priest.

Hōnen and Shinran taught Pure Land Buddhism: all that is needful is simple faith in the saving vow of Amida Buddha, expressed through saying the *Nembutsu* (*Namu Amida Butsu*, "Hail, Amida Buddha"). Shinran, the more radical of the two, so believed (like Martin Luther) in the saving power of faith alone that he gave up his monastic robe and married, trusting in Amida rather than in works. The powerful prophet Nichiren taught faith in the mystic power of the Lotus Sutra, the preeminent text of Tendai. He, with a typical Kamakura radicality, saw it not simply as the crown of the sutras, but as the *only* saving text, alone to be venerated. Zen, imported from China early in the Kamakura period, especially attracted the admiration of the new aristocracy, which could appreciate the stern training, stoic indifference, and sublime poise of the Zen adept, as well as the understated elegance of its arts.

One of the most influential and admired literary works of this period is the *Tsurezuregusa* (*Essays in Idleness*) of the cultivated hermit-monk Yoshida Kenkō. Written about 1340, during the nostalgia-laden Nambokuchō era, it yearns on one hand for the lost elegance of the Old Court, and on the other hand sets forth the chastened *fūryū* aesthetic of the future. *Fūryū*, in admiring that which is imperfect, old, cracked, and unbalanced, appealed to warrior and aesthete alike. Old things from the bemourned Heian past could thereby be treasured, and the best a more violent age might afford could have value despite its unavoidable frugality. Michinaga compared himself to the moon when full; Kenkō, in an age far more aware than was Michinaga's of its deep flaws, informs us that only boors admire the moon just when it is shining full on a clear night. The man of true breeding, he relates, admires it more when it is well past its prime, visible only near dawn, and half-obscured by rushing clouds.

THE MUROMACHI OR ASHIKAGA PERIOD (1392-1568)

The next era indeed afforded beauties as singular as the moon, and they were much tormented by roiling clouds. In discussing Ashikaga Yoshimasa and Higashiyama culture, we have already referred to the strange combination of brilliant aesthetic accomplishment and dismal political administration that characterized his shogunal dynasty.

Yoshimitsu The Ashikaga established their *bakufu* in Kyoto. The strongest ruler among them was Takauji's grandson Yoshimitsu, who set up his headquarters in the Muromachi district of the capital, after which the period is sometimes named. He succeeded by 1400 in establishing relative peace; the two courts were reunited, and ob-

The shogun Ashikaga Yoshimitsu built the Kinkakuji (Golden Pavilion) in Kyoto in 1394 as a place for Zen meditation. (Courtesy Consulate General of Japan, N.Y.)

streperous local magnates were subdued. He retired to build the Golden Pavilion in Kitayama; as we have observed, Yoshimitsu was also an enthusiastic patron of the No theater.

Like all the Ashikaga he sought vigorously to promote trade with China. New cultural ideas, therefore, were introduced and flourished in this colorful but troubled period. It is important to note that only at certain periods in Japan's long history has overseas trade—chiefly with China in premodern times—flourished. That trade led to a great influx of new religious, philosophical, political, and aesthetic ideas. At other times policymakers have discouraged overseas trade, and Japan has fallen into what might be called periods of assimilation and compensatory fostering of indigenous culture. In premodern times, the chief promoters of trade and the education of Japanese abroad have been the Asuka, Nara, Taira, early Minamoto, and Ashikaga rulers. Interestingly, however beneficial their trade and cultural policies have been in the long run, these regimes were not well-loved or even highly successful in the eyes of their contemporaries.

Certainly the Ashikaga rulers were neither. A principal motivation for their promotion of the China trade was the profits the ruling house itself realized, which helped to alleviate the monumental debts the Ashikaga cultural and building ventures incurred. Even so, they found it necessary to impose oppressive taxes when and where they were sufficiently in control. This, and an increasing mood of popular independence, led to serious uprisings by farmers and lower samurai in the first half of the fifteenth century. Indirectly, this cynicism and dissatisfaction produced the disastrous Ōnin War of 1467-1477. That war, a pointless and futile struggle between rival warlord factions, ostensibly over the shogunal succession, devastated the capital city.

Yoshimasa The politically inept shogun during the period of this war, as well as before and after, was Yoshimasa of the Silver Pavilion, the promoter of Zen-related arts of the tea ceremony, gardens, floral arrangement, and painting. The Ashikaga period was indeed the golden age of Zen. Zen was then the most influential Buddhist sect, its monks the most educated men of the society, and its artistic style the most emulated. The era's characteristic arts had about them the qualities Kenkō loved: *sabi*, a feeling of being aged or antique; and *wabi*, the "poverty" quality of being simple, rough-hewn, imperfect, asymmetrical.

After Yoshimasa the central government became weaker and weaker; the Ashikaga shoguns were only figureheads in a country essentially divided into the domains of feudal lords. In such a situation, some among the feudal lords could be expected to contend for the highest prize under the throne.

THE MOMOYAMA PERIOD (1568-1600)

The first of the warlords to achieve national power was Oda Nobunaga (1534-1582). He seized Kyoto in 1568 and five years later deposed the last Ashikaga shogun. Nobunaga was a violent man in a violent age, one who did not shrink from destroying the vast and ancient monastery of Mt. Hiei northeast of the capital when its warrior-monks appeared to be conspiring against him. As his power expanded outward from Kyoto, he took great strides toward unifying the country. A man who lived by the sword, he died by the sword when an assassin felled him in 1582.

Nobunaga was succeeded by one of his generals, Toyotomi Hideyoshi (1536-1598), who finally brought the entire country under his sway by 1590. Hideyoshi was no less a soldier than Nobunaga, but he was also a man of many other talents, who set the pattern of a flamboyant age. He fancied himself a connoisseur of art and culture in the grand Ashikaga tradition; indeed he was, though his modest background and meteoric rise showed in a penchant for garishness and conspicuous aesthetic consumption.

Tea paraphernalia, for example, were virtually a craze in the Momoyama era as a means of display. Hideyoshi paid astronomical prices, as earlier did Nobunaga, for tea services of great value, some imported from China. The climax of the fashion was a great outdoor tea party Hideyoshi gave in Kyoto in 1587, attended by thousands, at which he placed his most famous pieces on display. It was presided over by Sen no Rikyū (1521-1591), the greatest of all masters of the tea ceremony, whom Hideyoshi patronized. Ironically, Rikyū's specialty was *wabicha* (poverty tea), a style of the tea rite that emphasized austerity and the appearance of the commonplace in setting, service, and manners.

In the same way, Hideyoshi conspicuously patronized No, even writing plays himself and taking a portable theater with him into the field so that performances might be uninterrupted.

Appropriately, though, in such a warrior age the main vehicle for artistic expression was the castle and its ornaments. While the great castles that Nobunaga and Hideyoshi built have not survived, striking examples from around this period of the white, wooden Japanese castle with its curved roof can be seen in such cities as Osaka, Nagoya, and Gifu. One of the most typical Momoyama arts is the silk screen painting; perhaps because of the dark castle interiors they often embellished, these landscapes and studies of picnics or actors are placed against a brilliant gold background. The familiar secular topics are typical of the period's mood, as is the showy treatment that catered to the taste of swashbuckling samurai and was beginning to reach the new market of townsmen with money and a desire to prove it.

European Influence　Another new factor in the Momoyama period was the arrival of Europeans. Portuguese sailors, shipwrecked on an island off Kyushu in 1543, were the first to set eyes on Japan. Within six years, in 1549, the great Jesuit missionary, St. Francis Xavier, arrived in Kagoshima, Kyushu. He stayed only two-and-a-half years but came to love deeply and respect Japan. His work, and that of the Jesuits and Franciscans who followed him, so prospered in the troubled times that by the end of the century as much as a tenth of the population, largely in Kyushu, was Roman Catholic. These converts included certain feudal lords. Indeed, Nobunaga and, at first, Hideyoshi looked with favor on the Christian missionary activity, both because they saw it as a counterweight to the powerful Buddhist denominations, and because they liked the European trade that accompanied it. (The Europeans brought firearms—for which, needless to say, the warlords found ready use—in the same ships that carried the Gospel.) For a time *namban* (southern barbarian; i.e., Portuguese) culture was in vogue in Hideyoshi's world; pictures survive of his court trying on European dress, and such artifacts as clocks, lenses, and muskets were much in demand. When Hideyoshi, seeking new worlds to conquer (and new games with which to divert his restless samurai) launched his ultimately unsuccessful invasion of Korea in 1592, one of his two leading generals was Buddhist, the other Christian. It is not clear that the faith of either warlord mitigated in any way his customary bloodthirstiness, but this division does suggest the brief but impressive spate of Christian influence in the late sixteenth century.

However, for not entirely clear reasons, toward the end of his life Hideyoshi became suspicious of the European Christian influence. His Tokugawa successors opposed it entirely, forcing Christians to recant or face fearsome persecution and restricting European trade to one Dutch ship a year. One cause of this reversal of Japanese attitude was certainly a fear, all too justified by events in the Philippines, the New World, and elsewhere, that trade and Christianization would lead to colonization.

The Momoyama epoch was a time of expansive dreams, tumultuous change, and worldwide exposure. But, with a suddenness often characteristic of Japanese history, the openness was to be reversed into something almost its opposite.

THE TOKUGAWA PERIOD (1600-1868)

The struggle for succession to Hideyoshi was brief. Tokugawa Ieyasu, one of his generals, defeated the supporters of Hideyoshi's heir at the battle of Sekigahara in 1600. Final victory for the Tokugawa house, however, did not come until 1615, when Hideyoshi's son Hideyori perished with his followers in the seige of Osaka castle, their last redoubt. Ieyasu established his capital at Edo, modern Tokyo, which has ever since been the major administrative and commercial center of Japan, even though the figurehead imperial court still remained in Kyoto.

The Tokugawa rulers strove to end the centuries of confusion and bloodshed Japan had suffered; they wanted to construct a new kind of society, based on both Confucian philosophy and the best ideals of the warrior class to which they, of course, belonged. They envisioned a tightly ordered, heirarchical society, sealed off from the rest of the world. This ideal was far from consistently achieved despite draconian strictures from above; sometimes—especially in the hedonistic townsman culture we have observed in connection with Chikamatsu—society seemed more than anything else a mockery of the official virtues. Yet the ideal shaped the political life of the nation for two-and-a-half centuries; Japan resembled a speci-

The lavishly ornamented Tōshōgū Shrine in Nikkō was built at great expense by the Tokugawa government to enshrine the spirit of its founder, Tokugawa Ieyasu. This photo shows the famous Yōmeimon (Gate of Sunlight) entering into the main hall of the shrine. (Courtesy Consulate General of Japan, N.Y.)

men of feudalism preserved under glass, outwardly static and isolated, though inwardly dynamic enough.

The New Social Order   In the new Tokugawa social order, which produced such unexpected results, one-fourth of the land, the ultimate source of wealth, was owned directly by the Tokugawa, who also ruled most of the major cities. Other land constituted the *han* (fiefdoms) of *daimyō* (feudal lords), who were theoretically independent in their own domains, but who in fact were moved around and deposed at the will of the *bakufu*. The shoguns also kept the daimyo on a short leash by requiring that their families reside in the capital virtually as hostages, and that the lords themselves alternate residence between the court and their domains. The lavish processions the lords affected in moving from one place to another were a vivid Tokugawa institution, but the expense and inconvenience involved served the purposes of the government.

According to the official Confucian-based ideology, society had four classes, each with its own prerogatives and responsibility to maintain itself as a separate caste. First were the samurai, in theory the privileged but sternly self-disciplined ruling class. They alone were allowed to wear swords. In practice, many samurai fell on hard times after the descent of the Tokugawa peace. They had no more wars to fight and were squeezed by the inflationary pressures of a changing economy. Not a few envied the often high-living townsmen they were supposed to hold in contempt.

The peasants, again in theory, ranked next. As the primary producers of the essentials of life, they were to be honored above such nonproductive middlemen as tradesmen and artisans. In practice, their lot was hard. In the best of times, the rent collector left with a substantial share of the crop after harvest; in the worst, whole districts were virtually wiped out by famine. While the peasants managed, through family loyalty and the immemorial craftiness of the countryman, to survive and even to enjoy their kitchen fires and village festivals, their lives were oppressed and insecure.

The other two classes were the artisans and merchants, supposedly at the bottom of society. They were, however, the classes that came furthest, both materially and culturally, during the Tokugawa peace. Even without a significant import-export business, peace enabled population growth and security of internal transport which, together with a virgorous spirit of enterprise and rising expectations regarding the tangible attributes of the good life, made mercantilism prosper. Out of this milieu came the distinctive *chōnin* ("townman") culture that we have observed reflected in Chikamatsu's plays.

The townsmen loved, above all else, to see themselves reflected in art. The plays of Chikamatsu, the novels of Saikaku, the art of Hokusai and Hiroshige, all reflected the daily life or worldly dreams of the new class and the hedonistic *ukiyo* (floating world) life. The townsmen could also, however, be moved by romanticized visions of history and of the lives of their samurai betters; the popular Kabuki and puppet theaters alike presented thrillers of knightly valor.

By the time it entered the nineteenth century, the Tokugawa regime was creaky with age. Even given Japan's comparative isolation (though Western learning in science, geography, and other fields had crept in through the Dutch traders), change had been sufficient to make the *bakufu's* feudal concepts more out of touch with social and economic reality with each passing year. The periodic economic crises became more and more pronounced; the appeal of rival ideologies, such as the call for renewed direct imperial rule, became stronger.

The Unequal Treaties Outside incursion, however, gave the Tokugawa order its final push into extinction. After three centuries the Western world returned, demanding trade and missionary rights— and this time with a force that could not be fended off by a feudal regime's exclusion policy. After the coming of the American Commodore Matthew Perry's "Black Ships" in 1853-54, subsequent European and American traders demanded "Friendship Treaties" opening certain ports, in which foreigners would have privileges of extraterritoriality—the so-called unequal treaties. The *bakufu* found itself confronted by a situation beyond the power of its archaic institutions to handle. Apart from outright imperial rule from overseas as in India, or the humiliating subservience to foreign demands that was China's lot, the only possible solution was a wholly new government and social order able to stand up to the foreigners and to meet them on their own terms.

That was what Japan got in the Meiji Restoration of 1868, in another of the dramatically sudden turnings that mark its history. From a feudal fossil Japan became, within forty years, a modern military state able to defeat a major Western power on land and sea, and a showplace of modern education and industry, though less exemplary as a model of democratic values. Curiously, however, the Meiji Restoration (or better, Revolution) appeared to begin as a call to the nation to turn back the calendar drastically: to restore the primordial idyll of Shinto Japan ruled by divine sovereigns long before the contaminating introduction of Buddhism and Chinese learning, or at least to return to the Japan of the Taihō Code and the *Ritsuryō* state.

THE MEIJI PERIOD (1868-1912)

Xenophobia Trouble began in earnest for the *bakufu* in the 1860s. First, it became increasingly well known that the emperor in Kyoto, Komei, looked with disfavor on the government's temporizing accommodations with the foreigners; he preferred a policy of uncompromising resistance to them. As the rift between Kyoto and Edo grew, a basic weakness of the shogunal system, its potential for divided loyalty, became apparent precisely at a time when national unity was urgent. Those who favored a firm line against outsiders— and many did, with an emotional extremism that led to attacks on foreign envoys in the streets—justified themselves with the belief they were acting out of loyalty to the sovereign.

Scholars of the Kokugaku (National Learning) school had for some time been upholding a "high" view of imperial prerogatives and calling for a return to primordial Shinto; they hinted that something was wrong with a shogunal court that stood between the sovereign and his people. Their views were studied with new interest. Antiforeign, proimperial sentiment grew in feudal states like Satsuma and Chōshū (at the southern ends of Kyushu and

Honshu respectively), whose relations with the Tokugawa were rocky in any case. While the feeling was deep enough, support of the imperial house was also used opportunistically by those who, like the Satsuma and Chōshū leadership, had everything to gain from the fall of the beleaguered regime in Edo. The slogan *"Sonnō Jōi"* ("Revere the Emperor! Expel the foreigner!") was widely heard.

In 1863 and 1864 respectively, foreign ships bombarded the cities of Kagoshima in Satsuma and Shimonoseki in Chōshū in reprisal for violence against Europeans and their shipping. This bombardment increased tension still more. It was followed by a military confrontation in 1866 between rebellious Chōshū and the *bakufu*, in which the Tokugawa were worsted, to their further discredit. But the bombardment also impressed the Satsuma and Chōshū samurai with the military superiority of the West and the consequent need for Japan to modernize its forces. They did not forget that lesson, for all their apparent desire to return to the remote past of imperial legend.

New Leadership In late 1866 and early 1867 respectively, the shogun and emperor died within six months of each other, and new men were brought to the two thrones. The new ruler in Edo, Yoshinobu, was understandably reluctant to accept the troubled office and immediately set about to do what he clearly perceived to be necessary to relieve him of its burdens: to transfer power directly to the fifteen-year-old emperor newly installed in Kyoto, Mutsuhito, who was to become known by the name of his reign, Meiji (Enlightened Government). That transfer was completed in December of 1867.

The difficulties were not over, however, for shogunal loyalists remained who sought to save the old regime in spite of itself. Brisk fighting between factions broke out early in 1868, punctuated by violent outbreaks against foreigners. By April of 1869, however, peace had been generally restored by the triumphant imperial government, and in that month the sovereign and his court moved to Edo, renamed Tokyo (Eastern Capital), which was from then on both the imperial and administrative seat. Despite its antecedents, the new government was swift to mete out punishment to those who engaged in antiforeign violence.

That attitude anticipated more surprises to come. The new Meiji government, dominated by Chōshū and Satsuma men and their supporters from elsewhere, held two ideals: a desire to return to the symbols and structures of direct imperial rule and national integralism (symbolized by the "pure Shinto" ideal in religion); and a desire to modernize Japan politically, economically, and above all militarily, so that the humiliations of Kagoshima and Shimonoseki and the still-existent humiliation of "unequal treaties" with Western powers might be erased. The two ideals were not really consistent, and their juxtaposition was ultimately to lead to disaster. In the short run, however, they could be made mutually supportive. The stern authoritarian measures that modernization required could be defended by appeal to the emperor's divine and unquestionable will; the need for a strong central government and for powerful armed forces was justified by the state's duty to protect the sacred ruler and to enforce his commands.

Political Change Thus, in its inaugural years the new regime took the symbolically significant steps of restoring the ancient imperial rituals of the Ritsuryō era, of widely teaching the old myths of imperial divine descent, and of draconically separating Shinto and Buddhism. There was even an abortive attempt to suppress Buddhism as alien. But, at the same time, the Meiji Emperor in his so-called Charter Oath of 1868 had promised that "Knowledge shall be sought for throughout the world." Japanese of promise went abroad to study; foreigners in increasing numbers came to advise and sell; and before long the land of the sun-goddess Amaterasu and her descendants was spanned by railways and telegraph wires, hummed with industry, and was protected by an up-to-date army and navy.

Constitution of 1889 Although the old ranks, including the samurai, were abolished, most of the new rulers were ex-samurai, and their old autocratic attitudes did not die with the Tokugawa regime. Indeed, they were reinforced by the new centralism and the revamped imperial ideology. Conversely, considerable pressure for a liberal, constitutional state came both from overseas and from intellectuals in Japan who were awakened to progressive Western ideas. The mood of informed public opinion in Japan during the Meiji period swung cyclically between liberalism and reaction. The eventual compromise was the constitution of 1889, which made Japan a constitutional monarchy with parliamentary institutions. But the document made it clear that it was a gift from the throne, not based on inherent rights of the people, and the wording was carefully hedged to retain considerable power in the hands of the sovereign and his circle. Moreover, the electorate was initially little more than 1 percent of the population.

Nonetheless, a new day had dawned in Japan. The success of the Meiji transformation both in domestic renovation and in foreign opinion was evidenced by the termination of the "unequal treaties," by the defeat of China in a war in the 1890s, and above all by the successful war with Russia in 1904–05. These events resulted in Japanese annexation of the Ryūkyūs, southern Sakhalin, and (in

1910) Korea. Japan was recognized as a world power, and the Japanese Empire was well launched.

Meiji Culture   It was a new day in Japanese arts and letters too. Both at home and as they went in increasing numbers abroad to study, the Japanese were confronted on a massive scale with Western culture. The classics of the West, from Shakespeare to the great Russian novels, were translated; art and furniture in the Western style began to appear in Japanese salons. Inevitably, creative Japanese first imitated and finally assimilated the new wave from overseas, as they had long before imitated and assimilated Chinese culture.

Early Meiji novels and paintings were often emulations of the romances and impressionism then popular in the West. They were in the spirit of the Meirokusha (Meiji 6 [1873] Society), a group that published a magazine promoting enthusiasm for Western customs, dress, food, architecture, and such ideas as democracy, technology, and progress. But in the 1880s opinion swung back to a reaffirmation of the Japanese heritage. Novelists like Saikaku and poetic forms like the haiku were rediscovered and became widely popular.

Not until the 1890s did a mature modern Japanese literature, informed by both tradition and the West, begin to emerge. Some novelists who appeared first in that decade were of world stature, such as Ozaki Kōyō (1867–1903), who wrote in the style of Saikaku; Mori Ōgai (1862–1922), who had studied in Germany but who called for a return to the great literary standards of the Genroku era, and whose most famous novel, *Maihime* (*The Dancing Girl*) was significantly about an affair between a Japanese man and a European woman; and Sōseki Natsume (1867–1916), best known for his richly introspective *Kokoro* (*Heart* or *Feeling*). All these writers, and others like them, were basically realistic novelists, desiring to portray human life as it is. As did Sōseki preeminently, they combined the traditionally exquisite Japanese sensitivity to mood, nuance, impression, and feeling, the *mono no aware* of *Genji*, with the West's more advanced concepts of novelistic form and more wide-ranging realism than Japan had previously achieved.

Painting underwent a similar transformation. Somewhat surprisingly, in view of the immensely rich Japanese heritage in the medium, modern Japanese painting has not reached the same level of eminence as has writing and cinema. Early Meiji painting ran to slavish imitations of French impressionism, but later—partly under the influence of the American Ernest Fenellosa, who taught in Japan and greatly admired the Japanese artistic heritage—the native tradition was rediscovered.

The great Shinto-style Meiji Shrine in Tokyo, built in 1920, was dedicated to the Emperor Meiji, in whose reign Japan was so extensively transformed, and to his consort. (Courtesy Consulate General of Japan, N.Y.)

The New Ideology Even as Japanese arts and letters were becoming irreversibly free and expansive, other aspects of the culture were moving in other directions. The official imperial paternalism, not really modified by the new constitution, increasingly took on the overtones of an ideology inculcating a basically Confucian concept that loyalty and obligation to sovereign and state took priority over individual goals, and which was expressed through Shinto myth and rite. This was the burden of the famous Education Rescript of 1890, which until 1945 was hung in every school and was read and explained by all teachers to their students on stated occasions. The document taught loyalty, discipline, frugality, and acceptance of the imperial ideology.

Christianity Still another ingredient in the Meiji mix was Christianity. After the reopening of Japan, the missionaries came back. One surprising discovery they made was that in some isolated areas, the descendants of Christians converted in the days of St. Francis Xavier had secretly preserved their faith through two-and-a-half centuries of harshly enforced proscription. They had performed lay baptisms, taught their children texts like the Lord's Prayer, and concealed crucifixes within Buddhist images.

The number of Japanese converted to the cross never came near that of the earlier Christian era; over the past century it has probably never exceeded 1 percent of the population. But Christianity in Meiji and twentieth-century Japan has had an influence out of proportion to its numbers. Its health, educational, and social welfare institutions have been an indispensable part of modernization; especially in the Meiji period, some Christians were important public figures and articulate spokesmen for liberalism and democracy. In general, Christianity introduced new notes of moral seriousness.

The Meiji era was a complex mixture of progress and reaction, of freedom and autocracy, of expanding horizons and narrowing ideology. One thing is certain: few major societies have ever changed as extensively and irreversibly as did Japan in a mere forty-five years, the span between the Restoration and the emperor's death in 1912.

THE TAISHŌ
AND EARLY SHŌWA PERIODS (1912-1945)

The Meiji emperor was succeeded by Yoshihito, known by the era-name of his reign, Taishō. The new ruler's health, both physical and mental, was far from robust, and he was never more than a figurehead. His reign was an era of continuing change.

World War I Shortly after the inception of the First World War, Japan entered on the side of the Allies. That venture was wholly successful for the island empire: the serious fighting was far away, the war brought an economic boom, and Japan ended up with both a good image for having sided with freedom and democracy and a share of the spoils in the form of certain strategic German islands in the Pacific and outposts in China.

The war period and immediate postwar years were definitely benign for Japan. The economy prospered (save for a recession in 1920), industry rapidly expanded as the export market grew, and the trends seemed to be toward more and more liberalization of politics and society. The period has been spoken of as "Taishō democracy"; the characterization is not quite true politically but is accurate as a statement of the mood and the spirit of the flourishing popular culture. A labor movement gathered strength; the press was quite free and often irreverent; young people emulated Western "flappers."

But, beneath the surface, currents were running another way. Both the economy and Japan's position in world affairs were fragile; democracy was also fragile. In the twenties, tensions arose with Japan's erstwhile allies over the abrogation of Japan's alliance with Britain and Japanese emigration to the United States. The devastating Tokyo earthquake of 1923 added a further somber note. Japan's fundamental problem, though, was an expanding population in a small land area with very limited natural resources. This situation made the actions of the United States, Canada, and Australia to restrict or prohibit Japanese immigration particularly galling and led some Japanese to begin thinking of alternate solutions.

The death of the Taishō emperor and the accession of his successor, Hirohito, in 1926 marked the beginning of the Shōwa era. It had hardly begun when the Great Depression of 1929 and the increasingly unstable international situation, marked by the rise of fascism in Europe and of anticolonial movements in Asia, made the times seem ripe to those who favored alternate solutions.

Militarism The sort of thinking that led to military expansionism was centered among younger officers in the Army; of course, it was shared by many others who sought to profit, vent frustration, or fulfill ideological dreams through warlike adventure. The discontented junior officers were themselves largely from hard-pressed country families, and their zeal for the hard-pressed Japan with which they identified was coupled with rage against the profiteering *zaibatsu* (industrial monopolists) and their privileged cronies in the traditional ruling class. They demanded radical solutions—but radical solutions consonant with the conservative Bushidō values of which they felt themselves the custodians. They were quite prepared to accept, and indeed glorified, violent and military means. Extremist versions of the imperial ideology fitted the bill exactly, especially when they implied—as they had for the idealistic Meiji rebels—that the pristine imperial will was being hindered by traitorous counselors to the throne, who ought to be removed by whatever steps necessary. The corollary was that, once rid of timid placemen in the corridors of power, Japan would boldly seize by force of arms the markets, areas for immigration, and sources of raw materials it needed.

The faction that thought in this manner never completely controlled the government, nor even the armed forces. Some civilian statesmen and senior officers were always contemptuous of their ill-informed zeal and correctly foresaw disaster at the end of the road the militarists would have Japan travel. That the military extremists were nonetheless able to put Japan on that road was due to three factors. First, they did not hesitate to use assassination at home to terrorize their adversaries into weak-kneed capitulation. Second, military exploits, often unauthorized, forced the politicians either to accept the extremists' forward positions, or to face embarrassing withdrawals and difficult confrontations with popular field commanders. Third, insofar as the militarists did control, by advancement in rank or intimidation, the uniformed services—and they increasingly achieved this control throughout the thirties and early forties, especially in the Army—they could put insuperable leverage on the government as a whole. An unfortunate parliamentary provision held that the ministers of the Army and Navy had to be serving officers; if those services withheld consent for one of their officers to serve, a cabinet could not be formed. This provision gave the services an invaluable trump card for use in political infighting over policy.

The current of violence began in 1930, when a self-styled patriot shot the prime minister, Hamaguchi Yuko, after he had accepted compromises limiting Japan's sea forces at the London Naval Conference that same year. In 1931 military hotheads seized the Manchurian city of Mukden without prior knowledge of the government. The operation quickly spread. The Chinese, whose nation was in considerable turmoil, were unable to offer effective resistance, and within a year northeast China was Manchoukuo, an "independent" state under a puppet emperor protected by Japanese troops. The apparent benefits of the military victory to Japan were considerable: it gave the cramped island nation a vast Asian hinterland rich in natural resources, cheap labor, and investment opportunities, with wide expanses awaiting the colonizers who soon began to stream in from Japan. It also gave the extremists a heady confidence in their ability to achieve spectacular results by taking direct action without waiting for civilian politicians to make up their minds.

At home, assassinations of politicians and industrial magnates continued unabated, including another prime minister who was killed in 1932. The river of blood crested on February 26, 1936, when some 1,500 soldiers led by junior officers butchered several politicians and senior officers and seized a section of Tokyo, apparently in preparation for a coup d'état. Although the mutiny was suppressed and its instigators were hanged, the affair added its weight to the atmosphere of terrorism at home that accompanied expansionism abroad.

Expansionism was much abetted by the so-called China Incident of the next year, 1937, when fighting broke out between Chinese and Japanese troops in Peking and was followed by undeclared war. Again, the fighting was something that "happened" overseas rather than the result of government policy, but policy and patriotic sentiment quickly followed events. Soon enough Japan had occupied northeast China south of Manchoukuo, including most of its major cities, and a new prime minister, Prince Konoe, proclaimed that these moves had been made with a view to establishing a "New Order in East Asia." The principal consequence, however, was major, total war—and rapidly increasing tension with Japan's former allies, especially Britain and the United States, coupled with a corresponding rapprochement with the European fascist powers, especially Nazi Germany, which had similar designs for a "New Order" in its own sphere.

World War II By 1941 Japan, for all its conquests, was in a position of considerable difficulty. The war with China dragged on; embargoes by the United States and other powers trying to apply pressure had brought about a crisis in raw materials, especially petroleum; and Japan felt herself isolated and misunderstood. At the same time, alluring temptations presented themselves. French Indochina and the Netherlands East Indies, rich in the resources Japan urgently needed, lay under her nose, and the home countries, under German occupation, were in no position to defend their colonies. Britain and the Soviet Union, which also held territories in East Asia, had their hands full fighting Hitler. Only the United States, with which Japan was already engaged in acrimonious diplomatic feuding over the embargoes, seemed likely to challenge Japanese plans for the Orient. The military extremists convinced themselves that America lacked the will to fight a sustained war far from its homeland. They felt that the Americans would quickly come to terms if they were confronted by a knockout blow, followed by lightning conquests that would face not only Japan, but the world, with a fait accompli.

On December 7, 1941, the intended knockout blow was delivered to the American Navy at Pearl Harbor. Within six incredible months, the Japanese had taken the territories they wanted: Indochina (already partially occupied), Malaya, Singapore, Burma, the Philippines, and the East Indies. But the Pacific War, as the Japanese call it, was not yet over; in fact, Japan's enemies were only beginning to gather their strength.

Japan, on the other hand, was overextended and already at her maximum deployment of men and material. Attrition could only weaken her. That process was begun with the great sea battles of the Coral Sea and Midway, in which Japan suffered irreplaceable naval losses, and was continued by devastating Allied bombing of Japanese shipping and later of the home cities, coupled with "island hopping" reconquest of the occupied territories. By August 1945, when the atomic bombing of Hiroshima and Nagasaki finally forced Japan's surrender, the once-proud *gunkoku* ("military state") was a burning and starving ruin.

Cultural Life The culture of the 1912–1945 era was overshadowed by these momentous events, yet was not wholly dominated by them. While the hands of the censor and of the ideological police were sometimes heavy, Japan was never as culturally totalitarian as Nazi Germany or Soviet Russia in the days of "socialist realism." In contrast to those societies, significant independent, nonpolitical works of art and letters appeared all through the years of stress and war, save after 1940, when enforced conformity of all aspects of life to wartime goals, and national mobilization made any non–defence-related production impossible, and people were in a state of near exhaustion. Even so, during those dark days some writers kept working at manuscripts, which were published after the war.

The major writers of the period were Nagai Kafū (1879-1965) and Tanizaki Junichirō (1886-1965). Both explored areas of literary creativity other than the realism of the generation before them. They shared the attitudes of the European "decadents" who flourished in the days of their youth and of the worldwide intellectual disillusionment of the postwar twenties. The bizarre, the surrealistic, the nihilistic, the mood of intense nostalgia for the past are all present in their literary production. Both afford engrossing unconventional perspectives on the human scene; they delight in celebrating exotic sexual tastes and strange compulsions.

Tanizaki was much the more versatile writer. While Nagai remained predictable in his literary stance of nostalgia and alienation, Tanizaki was a zesty and thoroughly professional accountant of the whole human panorama. As such, he could combine in one career the leisurely, almost nineteenth-century study of fashionable Japanese society caught between tradition and modernity that is *The Makioka Sisters* (1943-1948), and the bizarre erotic tale *Diary of a Mad Old Man* (1965). Tanizaki was virtually a Poe and a Flaubert combined in one. What unifies his work and that of many others of the day, including some writers like Kawabata who began in the twenties and thirties but became most famous after the war, is the stance of the artist as outsider.

In an age of passionate covetousness alternating with passionate ideology, the most memorable modern Japanese writers are perhaps less bound by value systems—philosophical, religious, or political—than writers of any other society. Instead, they are observers—observers who believe little but see much. Not that they were dispassionate observers. Rather, the gaze of a Tanizaki goes to the core of human nature, and sees the insane dreams and passions beneath the surface. In our age, perhaps no one is more needed than the outsider whose eye does not shrink from craziness.

RECENT (POSTWAR OR LATE SHŌWA) PERIOD (1945-)

Before and during the Second World War, some outside observers took the propaganda of the militarists at face value and considered Japan to be the most implacably warlike nation on earth. They insisted that, even if defeated and occupied, the sons of the samurai would not lay down the sword until the last enemy of the Mikado was driven into the sea, however many generations it took. Instead, in another of the amazingly sudden shifts of Japanese history, no sooner had the emperor uttered his famous "endure the unendurable" surrender message to the nation, than that nation became seemingly another people. No guerillas appeared. Instead, the American occupation troops presided over a people who utterly renounced war, both in their new constitution and apparently in attitude; who harbored no bitterness for defeat, but seemed almost excessively eager to adopt the victor's ways; and who, as if they had never thought of becoming Asia's masters, were now wholly devoted to becoming its Switzerland, a democratic land engaged in the peaceful pursuit of industry and trade.

Time was to show that this idyllic picture was not quite 100 percent accurate. Japanese politics, while certainly far more democratic than ever before, had not changed as much from the prewar patrimonialist patterns, so deeply congruous with the structure of Japanese society, as appeared on the surface. The Cold War forced genuinely unwelcome modifications of Japan's idealistic early postwar pacifism in the direction of forming a paramilitary "Self-Defence Force."

Yet Japan was changed, profoundly so. The Allied Occupation (1945–1951) under General Douglas MacArthur gave Japan a constitution that, besides outlawing war, assured for the first time complete freedom of speech, religion, and political activity; completely separated the state from Shinto and from ideology; and brought about universal male and female adult suffrage. The Occupation also gave Japan a new dominant trading partner and a source of new cultural infusion: America.

Postwar Cultural Life Japanese cultural life flourished in the unprecedented freedom, soon made even more volatile by the unprecedented economic growth of the postwar era; Japan achieved one of the world's highest standards of living and most powerful industries in the sixties and seventies. But the culture was troubled by a lack of bearings and roots, and very self-consciously so. The Japanese veered wildly from one fad or one extreme to another, now enthusing over anything American, now preoccupied with the complexities of Japanese family life, now taken up with fantasy and science fiction.

The perennial theme of tradition versus Westernization and modernization was the bedrock of the postwar search for values, of course, but never had its ambiguities seemed more agonizing. Tradition was now not only the innocent enjoyment of No and Zen gardens, but also something that had been subverted to the service of the warlords who had led Japan into evil ways and so was discredited in the eyes of many, especially the leftists who now dominated much of Japanese education and letters. Modernization, however, was not only American democracy, but also seemed bound up with the grasping materialism that appeared to be the only value that interested most Japanese in those days of skyrocketing GNP. What does one say or do, intellectuals pondered, when the past is lost forever and, in any case, for all its humane beauty was too repressive? When the present is an unbearable desert of industrial pollution and roaring traffic wheeling pointlessly around a few crowded islands?

The postwar era started off idealistically. One of the great postwar cultural developments—though it had prewar roots—was the emergence of the Japanese cinema as a powerful artistic medium, and one much concerned with social statement.

The best-known director, Kurosawa Akira (1910-), produced a picture immediately after the war, *No Regrets for Our Youth*, which sums up eloquently the mood of the times. The story, based on an actual event, focuses on the daughter of a Kyoto University professor who was forced to resign in the early thirties because of his liberal views, an event that led to brutally suppressed student demonstrations. The daughter, Yukie, is at first a spoiled schoolgirl, but after the traumatic events she gradually discovers new passions within herself. Going to Tokyo several years later, she meets, after his release from prison, one of the leaders of the student protestors and lives with him. He is now engaged in activity against the high-riding militarists, and predictably is thrown into prison, where he dies. Yukie goes to live with his aging parents in a rural village, where they are cruelly taunted and harrassed by their neighbors as the family of a "spy." But at the end of the war her lover is suddenly seen for the hero that he was, and Yukie returns to the same village full of idealistic plans to work for improvement in the lot of rural women.

The passionate idealism of this 1946 film, suggesting the emergence of a new, morally concerned humanity in a new pacifist and democratic Japan, captures the mood of the first years after Hiroshima. It indicates the radical reversal of values in 1945, the postwar emancipation of women, the widespread feeling (especially among educators and labor leaders who had, like Yukie's father, long harbored privately more liberal opinions than it was wise to express openly) that the thorough disgrace of the old order would permit a new and far better society to be constructed from the ground up.

Inevitably, this idealism ran into ambiguities as Japan took charge of its own affairs after the end of the Occupation, grew wealthy again, and wondered what had become of the early postwar dream. A later film by Kurosawa, *The Bad Sleep Well* (1960), gives expression to these ambiguities. *The Bad Sleep Well* is about a young man who seeks revenge for the death of his father, who had been driven to suicide by a corrupt corporation executive with gangster connections. In order to insinuate himself into his enemy's household and to gather evidence of his corruption, the young man marries the executive's daughter. Although the marriage was only a ploy, he falls genuinely in love with his wife; he is vulnerable to his father-in-law and emotionally unable to proceed with his crusade. Thus the normal human act of falling in love, and the entanglement with another person and family it entails—involvements that fourteen years earlier had so nourished the idealism of Yukie—in this less innocent day is seen to stifle a young man's once uncompromising sense of right and wrong.

The film is almost a parable of the subtle seduction of idealism in a Japan once more dominated by *zaibatsu* conglomerates and a complicated social system based on hierarchy, family, and interpersonal relationships rather than on clearcut values. The idealistic young rebel may not now be, as was Yukie's lover, thrown into prison, but he is likely to find himself slowly becoming so entrapped in an invisible web of subjective and outer constraints that he cannot act; "Japan, Incorporated" wins in the end.

The postwar Japanese novel similarly reflects both the unprecedented opportunity for creativity in a free and prosperous society, and confusion as to direction. Kawabata Yasunari (1899–1972) was, in 1968, the first Japanese to receive the Nobel Prize in literature. But his lyricism and melancholic mood are traditionalist. His best-known novel, *Snow Country*, was begun in 1935 and finished twelve years later. It is about a prewar Tokyo aesthete, a characteristic artistic "outsider," who falls in love with a geisha in a winter resort area. Kawabata ended his life by his own hand, perhaps to exemplify his fundamental belief in the mission of art to enable one to accept and beautify death.

Even more contradictory and eloquent of the contradictions of modern Japan are the career and work of Kawabata's friend and fellow-suicide, the novelist Mishima Yukio (1925–1970). Mishima's first work, *Confessions of a Mask* (1948), is partly autobiographical and is set in the years of the war and early Occupation; yet the novel reflects little of those dramatic times. The hero-narrator is instead, in the best "decadent" and artist-as-outsider tradition, almost wholly preoccupied with his own obsessions—homosexuality, sado-masochism, and a limp love affair. Mishima's most widely read novel, *The Temple of the Golden Pavilion* (1959), is about a disturbed young man, caught between tradition and modernity and harried by overwrought subjective sensitivity; it is based on the life of the Zen novice-arsonist who actually set fire to the Temple in

1950. Yet Mishima could also write a lyric idyll like *The Sound of Waves* (1956), a seemingly straightforward love story set in a simple fishing village, and plays in the style of Kabuki and No. His last work, *The Sea of Fertility*, is a four-volume indictment of the emptiness of modern Japanese society, which he likens to the barren lunar sea of the title.

Toward the end of his short life, Mishima—who had failed to qualify physically for service in the Japanese forces during the war— became preoccupied with physical fitness, the samurai tradition, and the "shame" of Japan's defeat. He inveighed against Japan's imitation of the West, weakness, and loss of martial tradition. He organized a private army, the *Tate no Kai* (Shield Society), which shared his values and practiced his cult of physical fitness. On November 25, 1970, together with four members of the society, Mishima seized a Self-Defense Force general's office, gave a brief speech, and then disemboweled himself in the authentic samurai manner.

Kurosawa, Kawabata, and Mishima all reflect in diverse ways the power and paradoxes of postwar Japanese culture: its wealth of gifted creative people, its consummate accomplishments in the technical craft of cinematic or literary expression, its lack of any compelling sense of purpose or direction. Few Japanese accepted Mishima's reactionism; Kurosawa's early liberal idealism did not prevail; nor would most be content only with Kawabata's aestheticism. Postwar Japan has done well in holding up a mirror to itself, but has done less well in lighting new cultural dreams and visions.

Part Two
Eternal Waves:
Religion
and Philosophy

Ise is the site of the grand imperial shrine, the home of the goddess Amaterasu, where dwelt the imperial princess sent to serve her. The *Nihonshoki*, an ancient chronicle comparable to the *Kojiki* and compiled shortly after it in A.D. 720, speaks of Ise in these terms: "Ise, where roll in the endless waves, the eternal waves from the Other World."

In any civilization, religion and philosophy reflect the influx of such long-reverberating waves. Like the waves of the sea, their expressions are continually changing, rising and falling, swelling and breaking into foam. But they keep on rolling in, for something in the human spirit continually wants to give expression to that which is most ultimate, most eternal.

In looking at Japanese religion, we first examine Shinto, the religion rooted in prehistory that continues full of vigor and color today. Then we consider the successive waves of Buddhism and other religions that have swept into the islands of Japan from overseas. These religions are investigated in more historical terms than is Shinto, for Buddhism and its various denominations arrived and emerged in historical times, often in response to important historical circumstances and under the leadership of dynamic, historically important men. History and denominationalism, while not all-important to understanding Japanese Buddhism, provide a useful "handle" for comprehending it. Shinto, while it certainly has a history, has been less pervasively affected in its inner spiritual life by great events and great men such as Buddhism's Kōbō Daishi, Shinran, or Nichiren; it gazes back to the Divine Age.

Philosophy is even more a matter of personalities and schools, though like religion it also interacts with the social environment. As we shall see, Japanese philosophy in its several schools has certain common themes, above all that of finding intellectual ways to justify the meaningfulness of ordinary daily life and the political order. We begin with several great Buddhist thinkers. We then cite a number of individuals and schools of the Tokugawa period, both Confucian in that heyday of Japanese Confucianism, and those who reacted against Confucian thought and the society it was used to rationalize. Although numerous, they are all absolutely essential for understanding Japanese history and intellectual life in modern times.

Japanese religion and philosophy are important for the understanding of all Japanese civilization. Their deep themes break through in all its forms in sometimes indirect ways—in the Shintoistic divine dancer of the No drama or in the naturalness of Zen painting.

Religion: A Nation Secular and Sacred

Modern Japan is ostensibly a secular nation in which, if public opinion polls and surveys are any guide, religious belief is at a much lower level than in the United States. But casual visitors to Japan are likely, at least at first, to get a different impression. They will note a shrine or temple, sometimes large and impressive, sometimes tiny, on almost every corner of older communities and in the countryside. Moreover, these temples are not empty relics of the past; they give every impression of being well regarded. Clean, fresh offerings of flowers or food may grace the alters, and the more prominent will be thronged with visitors, worshippers, and tourists alike.

CHARACTERISTICS OF JAPANESE RELIGION

Relativism and Pluralism How are we to understand this situation? Obviously, religion plays a somewhat different role in Japanese society than in the West, especially America. Something of that difference is indicated by another poll. Shortly after the Second World War, a census of Japan was taken that inquired about religious affiliation; the results showed that the total number of members of religious "denominations" was half again the total population. Many Japanese, in other words, saw themselves as belonging to two or more religions simultaneously. In America one could not possibly belong to both the Roman Catholic and Baptist churches at the same time; in Japan, comparable plural affiliations with Shinto and Buddhism and perhaps one of the "new religions" are common.

Multiple religious membership in Japan is not considered to

indicate a grave lapse in logical consistency. Rather, most Japanese simply feel that different religions meet different needs and operate in different areas of life. Shinto, for example, is basically festive and concerned with the joys and deep relationships—family and community—of this life. Buddhism also expresses sociological ties but is considered to be more profoundly concerned with the ultimate mystery of existence and the ultimate destiny of people. Thus, it is quite common for marriages to be celebrated in Shinto shrines and funerals to be performed in Buddhist temples.

Deeper attitudes are involved too. Fundamental Japanese ways of thinking, reinforced by much of Buddhist philosophy, serve to strengthen religious relativism and pluralism. Relativism and pluralism are of a piece with the previously discussed tendencies of Japanese language and behavior to be situational rather than absolutistic and of Japanese art to be allusive, reticient, and marked by a deliberate asymmetry and incompleteness. In Japanese language, manners, and art the message is that no one setting or scenario can express everything; a single setting affords only one angle of vision, or one note in the concert of human experience, to be complemented by other times, other places. Japanese religion, by and large, delivers this message also.

Traditionalism Relativism and pluralism are kept from reducing Japanese religion to chaos by a counterforce that lends it firm structure: traditionalism and its related close links to family and culture. In a rapidly changing world, religion is seen by many as something to be treasured because it is stable and provides bridges to the past and to a people's "roots." Indeed, the ceremonial procedures of much of Japanese religion do change very slowly, if at all, and much religious ceremony is a showcase of the past. Shinto priests still dress in the formal court garb of the Heian era and start the fires for cooking offerings with an archaic friction device. Buddhist monks still enact the long, slow, chanted rituals of another era.

But religion is not just a museum. Not only is traditionalism appreciated for its own sake by many Japanese, but it is also bound up with a living function of religion: providing symbols of stable identity to people. Perhaps especially in a society where relativism and situationalism, a sense of unceasing flux and change, mark peoples' experience in the outer world and even in their own consciousness, symbols of "roots," of a sure identity, are important. These are afforded by the shrine and temple of the family, the original community, and (in feudal times) the lord, together with perhaps the altars of one's profession or work group. Family temples store the tablets bearing the names of ancestors, and family members return there on solemn occasions, even as the emperor himself reports major national events to his ancestral and patronal deities at the Grand Shrine of Ise.

Charismatic Leadership If Japanese religion were nothing but traditionalism, however, it would never change. In fact, it has been marked by remarkably dynamic movements, like those in the Kamakura period, which have partially changed its shape in a matter of a generation or two. This dynamism results from another important feature of Japanese religion, its production of powerful charismatic leaders.

The tradition of charismatic leadership goes back to ancient shamanism. In prehistoric times, deities were of two sorts: *ujigami* (patronal gods of clans), who represent the familial and traditional side of religion; and *hitogami* (man-gods), who were "outside" forces, wandering, visiting, exceptional, mysterious deities, often personified by shamans or controlled by them. Throughout history, more than a little of the shamanistic style has reappeared in the strong religious charisma of figures like Kōbō Daishi, Hōnen, Shinran, Nichiren, and founders of modern "new religions" like Nakayama Miki and Deguchi Onisaburō. These people have generally been extraordinarily vigorous, long-lived, and fearless prophets, unafraid of the whole hierarchy of church and state. They have become parent figures to their followings and have started movements that eventually became part of the fabric of tradition and the social role of religion.

Practice and Experience A final general characteristic of Japanese religion, after its pluralism, relativism, traditionalism, and charismatic leadership, is an orientation toward practice and experience rather than ideology. A religion like Shinto, for example, has little to compare with the great creeds, confessions, and doctrinal works of Western religion. Most Japanese, going to a Shinto shrine, have little concern for the exact nature of the *kami* they are worshipping. They are likely to experience a sense of peace, a nuance of heightened reality, in those hallowed precincts, and they find meaningful the traditional gestures of reverence and the traditional activities of *matsuri* and pilgrimage. For most people, Buddhism too is experienced in much the same way, though it does have a much vaster scriptural and intellectual heritage than Shinto; indeed, Buddhist spiritual masters tell us that, for all its intellectual content, the true experience of Buddhism is caught only by setting aside words and concepts.

We shall now explore the diverse world of Japanese spirituality, which has been called "a living laboratory of religion." We can accomplish this exploration by visiting in imagination a major center of each of its principal forms, most of them in and around the ancient cities of Kyoto and Nara.

SHINTO

In the world of Japanese religion, traditionalism and innovation under charismatic leadership have meshed together so well that, although new strata have continually been added right down to the twentieth century, nothing ever seems to disappear completely. In many places, one can find within a few miles of each other still-living prehistoric shrines to sacred mountains or waterfalls, medieval Buddhist temples, Christian churches founded by nineteenth-century missionaries, and edifices of the post–Second World War "boom" of "new religions." The new is superimposed but the old is not displaced, making for a continually more complex situation. This complexity is especially obvious in the relation between the two major religions, Shinto and Buddhism. Buddhism came to Japan at roughly the same time Christianity was prevailing in Europe. Instead of displacing the old faith, as did Christians in abandoning or converting to Christian use the temples of paganism, Shinto shrines continued to flourish alongside Buddhist temples, their *kami* or gods considered manifestations, guardians, or pupils of the Enlightened One. It is as though European temples to Zeus or Wotan continued in use beside Christian churches, and by and large the same people worshipped in both according to mood or occasion.

Shinto is fundamentally a religion of many gods of place and clan rooted in a worldview that, broadly speaking, is comparable to that of archaic Europe. The name Shinto, adopted to contrast this faith with Buddhism, means "The Way (*Tao*) of the Gods" or, in Ono Sokyō's term, "The *Kami* Way."[1] Shinto is, in other words, the spiritual path based on the rich diversity of Japan's native gods and shrines and customs pertaining to them.

Polytheism, as the distinguished theologian Paul Tillich once remarked, is not really a matter of quantity but of quality. Polytheists, such as Shintoists, are not set apart from monotheists simply in that they have numerically many gods, but because they experience religious reality in a quite different way. They experience a whole spectrum of finite colors rather than a single infinite white. Instead of emphasizing the unity of the all things under one sovereign, or as parts of one reality, polytheism emphasizes the experience of the universe as pluralistic, with different spiritual meaning behind every separate place and feeling.

Shinto, then, presents a pluralistic universe of numerous deities who usually work in harmony, though occasionally at cross-purposes, but who are not under absolute monotheistic rule. Shinto emphasizes the particularistic ties of each deity to determinate places, social groups, and roles. It is a religion that fits well a spiritual culture based on pluralism, relativism, and particularism in the role of the individual as largely determined by social roots and place in the social hierarchy.

The genius of Shinto is in its diversity. Each shrine has its own *matsuri* cycle and its own customs, from decorous processions in ancient costume to boisterous tugs-of-war at New Year's. There is no one representative shrine.

The Grand Shrine of Ise Even though it is unique as the Shinto "national cathedral" and sanctuary of the imperial ancestors, the Grand Shrine of Ise (Ise Daijingū, mentioned in connection with the priestess-princess) is a good introduction to the Shinto spirit.[2]

The Grand Shrine is composed of two main shrines, about five miles apart, and a number of related lesser shrines in the vicinity. The two main shrines are dedicated to Amaterasu, the solar goddess who is ancestress of the imperial line, and Toyouke, goddess of food. Each shrine is a smallish wood building, built in an archaic style based on the ancient granary, with clean and simple lines and a thatch roof. Within each, behind closed doors and encased in a box covered with many wrappings of brocade, is an object representing the presence of the deity; in the case of the Inner Shrine, or shrine of Amaterasu, the deity is represented by the mirror the great goddess gave her grandson as a reminder of her when he descended from heaven to earth to found the dynasty. No one in historical times has seen the sacred object; in Japan the divine, like homes and palaces, is characteristically hidden rather than ostentatiously displayed. The Ise shrines are surrounded by four palisades and a rectangle of white gravel, entered only by priests when presenting offerings. This assures alike the hiddenness and purity so treasured by the Shinto spirit.

The most important annual festival at Ise is the Kanname-sai (Harvest Festival) in the fall. Offerings of food are presented to the great deities twice during the night in two identical ceremonies. Food is presented with the slowness of ancient ritual to the main shrines and at the shrines of the *Aramitama* (Aggressive Spirit or Rough Spirit) of each deity, which are set on higher ground. At noon offerings of cloth and other goods from the emperor are presented by envoys from the court in ancient formal dress. These ceremonies are slow and archaic, yet strangely moving, whether the nocturnal ritual lit by flaring torches and accompanied by eerie and unusual music, or the noontime imperial rite with its brilliantly vested ministers.[3]

NARA BUDDHISM

The great outside influence in Japanese religion is Buddhism. As we have seen, Buddhism was first introduced from Korea around the early part of the sixth century and rose to its first cultural importance during the eighth century Nara period. The greatest work of that era was the temple of the Great Buddha of Nara built by the pious sovereign Shōmu.

Buddhism is the spiritual path inaugurated by Siddhartha Gautama (560–483 B.C.) of the Sakya clan, called the Buddha (Enlightened One). He is also called Sakyamuni (Sage of the Sakya Clan), rendered Shaka or Shakamuni in Japanese—a common Japanese appellation, especially in connection with works of art. The future Buddha was born a prince, protected from all sight of the suffering of this world. According to traditional accounts, he was led as a young man by the observation of an old man, a dying man, a corpse, and a wandering monk to consider how transitory and unsatisfactory human life is; he laid aside his princely robe in order to himself become a holy wanderer, questing for wisdom and self-transformation in the midst of the sorry world.

Some seven years after his departure from the palace, during which he explored the many philosophical schools competing for attention in ancient India and experimented with extreme yogic asceticism, the prince found that which he sought. Seated under an ancient fig tree on the night of his enlightenment, he fended off the temptations of Mara, a god who did not wish to see a human reach the exalted status toward which Gautama was moving. He then sank into deeper and deeper stages of trance. His mind slipped past all barriers to infinite consciousness and was silently filled with the wisdom that could lead others to the infinite.

In his first sermons, the Buddha explained the transcendent discoveries of that meditation. All life as it is ordinarily lived, he said, is full of suffering and frustration, because it is motivated by grasping at partialities: objects, concepts, ideas, goals, being and nonbeing themselves, the notion that one is a separate individual self rather than an expression of infinite reality. All these partialities are impermanent and incomplete, incapable of delivering the surety they seem to promise. Pursuit of them, based on ignorance, leads only to frustration and despair in the face of old age, sickness, and death. Grasping after partialities predicates and produces endless rebirths, each time a separate ignorant self doomed to suffering, because through karma one gets what one's state of mind entails.

There is a way out, the Buddha taught: the syndrome of suffering and grasping can be stopped by ceasing to grasp. How does one do that? By following the Middle Way, which aims at equilibrium between indulgence and asceticism, grasping this and grasping that, life and death, being and nonbeing. In the Middle Way one is in equal relationship to all things, having no special attachment to any, and so one overcomes partiality and shares in the Buddha's unobstructed clarity of mind and vision.

How does one align oneself with the Middle Way? The royal road to transcendence, the Buddha said, was through meditation or concentration, the culmination of his Eightfold Path. Meditation stills the activity of mind and therefore cuts off the sensory and fantasy inputs that keep one fixated on elusive partialities. For the Buddha, meditation was not escapism or lethargy; it was a hard but rewarding discipline by which one slid out of the toils of finite, desire-ridden mind into attunement with the unbounded. By this transcendent concentration one could ultimately attain Nirvana, the opposite of all the "conditioned reality" experienced by the desirous mind. One best set foot on that infinite way by taking the Triple Refuge: the Buddha, as the supreme exemplar of the goal; the Dharma, the Buddha's teaching or gospel; the Samgha, the order of monks inaugurated in his disciplines who teach and, ideally, exemplify his path.

By the time the Three Jewels or Triple Refuge came to Japan, the Dharma and the great spiritual empire founded upon it had spread throughout much of south, central, and east Asia and was already a thousand years old. It had developed as much as had Christianity between the time of Christ and the Crusades. The version of Buddhism that prevailed in China, Korea, and Japan was Mahayana, the "Great Vehicle." It was, it is fair to say, true to the essence of the Buddha's insight, but expressed it in novel and subtle ways.

Mahayana was less interested in the historical Buddha, Gautama, than in the ultimate nature of the universe his teaching and experience unfolded. That is a universe in which everything is relational and nothing absolute, empty but marvelous, free and unbounded save for the mind-forged shackles we make for ourselves. Its essence, realized by the Buddha in his inward leap to freedom, is everywhere; every human being, every blade of grass is a Buddha already, and needs only to realize it.

That realization can be obtained in meditation, the method of the well-known Zen school of Mahayana. But meditation is not the only way. Ultimately one's teacher is not a human Buddha, but the cosmic Buddha, the universe itself, who teaches not only through books but through every breath of wind and every blade of grass, and who has a unique path for every pupil. Indeed, Mahayana teaches that methods are highly relative; to seize upon one method absolutistically would be a form of the attachment one is trying to surpass. Mahayana depends not only on meditation, but also on faith, chanting, magical evocations: anything that enables one's ordinary stream of consciousness to be suspended long enough to afford another vantage on the universe than that distorted by the false perspective of egocentricity.[4]

The Kegon Sutra   Nowhere is the Mahayana worldview set forth in more breath-taking plenitude than in the Avatamsaka (Garland) Sutra, called the Kegon Sutra in Japan. In it the whole universe, infinite in space and time, is portrayed as made up of an endless series of worlds and systems of worlds. Each is a Buddha-world, for the essence of each is the universal empty-but-marvelous essence perceived by a Buddha in enlightenment; each is taught by its own Buddha, who is a reflection or emanation of the cosmic Buddha, the universe itself in its pure and absolute aspect. This supreme Buddha personifies the universe as the unfathomably deep meditation of an unlimited mind out of whose thought all things flow, but which also sees the cosmos as unobstructed, for to it nothing has reality of itself. Rather, each entity is like a reflection in an endless series of mirrors; the picture in each is an image of the whole universe from a particular perspective, different from any other.

This Garland Sutra was popular in China during the T'ang dynasty. It is said that the master Fa-Hsien once demonstrated its point to a T'ang empress, who was having difficulty understanding its subtleties, in the following manner: He placed an image of the Buddha on a small table and put a lamp behind it. Then he completely covered the walls, ceiling, and floor of the room with mirrors. When the empress entered the room, she gasped in amazement, for she saw the Buddha reflected in all the mirrors—not once, but reflections of reflections of reflections, an infinite lineage in each of the countless glasses. Then Fa-Hsien took from his sleeve a crystal ball, held it up—and lo! the process of infinite multiplicity through reflection was repeated in miniature on its surface. The empress smiled; she understood.

The Tōdaiji   The Kegon school was one of the first introduced to Nara, Japan, and it is the school to which the Tōdaiji, the temple at Nara housing the Great Buddha, pertains. That massive sculpture expresses well the profound teaching of the sutra and of Fa-Hsien's

The Great Buddha inside the Tōdaiji in Nara was cast in bronze between 745 and 749 A.D. *The Daibutsuden (Hall of the Great Buddha) that shelters this Buddha-image is the largest wooden structure in the world. (Courtesy Japan Air Lines.)*

room, not on paper or in mirrors, but in bronze. In the temple's center is the huge image, not of the historical Buddha, but of Vairocana or Birushana, Dainichi or "Great Sun" in Japanese, the Buddhic personification of the infinite universe. This infinite Buddha-essence of the boundless cosmos is flanked on either side by attendants representing infinite space and infinite compassion.

Behind and arching over the Great Sun Buddha are numerous other enlightened figures, smaller but similarly seated in cosmic meditation: the contemplative rulers of the endless Buddha-worlds. The observer feels deeply Vairocana's still inward gaze amidst countless aeons and universes.

The Hokkedō The active side of the Buddha-nature is displayed in a temple on higher ground above the Tōdaiji, called the Hokkedō or Sangatsudō, whose principle image is of the immensely popular bodhisattva, Kannon. The concept of the bodhisattva is characteristic of Mahayana beliefs. A bodhisattva is a transcendent Buddhist figure who has mastered all the deep secrets of the cosmos and who could enter into a Buddha's supreme nirvanic meditation beyond being or nonbeing. Out of compassion for all sentient beings, he has vowed not to enter nirvana until all those beings have realized their Buddha-nature. Motivated by sublime wisdom and compassion, the bodhisattva can take many forms and perform many acts—symbolized by the multiple arms often displayed by the most popular, Kannon—to help people and succor them along the long road to final enlightenment. Kannon represents, then, the active interface between the transcendent Buddhist realities and common clay.

Perhaps the most striking monument to Kannon devotion in Japan, though, is the Sanjūsangendō (Hall of Thirty-Three Bays) temple in Kyoto. Founded in 1164, this Tendai temple contains 1,001 gold statues of Kannon, lined up rank on rank in a most imposing display. Each has ten tiny heads atop the main one, the eleven representing the bodhisattva's omniscience in all directions. Each has twenty-one pairs of arms holding various symbols of mercy and salvation; they represent 1,000 arms because each can save twenty-five worlds. Kannon can change into thirty-three different forms to further his work of compassion; therefore the 1,001 figures actually represent 33,033. The Sanjūsangendō well expresses the imaginative and artistic opulence of Kannon devotion.

SHINGON

The complex interface between the world and Buddhist transcendence is revealed in all its intricate glory in the Tōji temple in the southern part of Kyoto, a temple of the Shingon sect. The Shingon school was the most esoteric of the two denominations dominant in the Heian era, Shingon and Tendai. It was founded by Kūkai (773–835), called Kōbō Daishi, a brilliant monk sent by the court to China to study, and who brought back much learning.

Shingon centers on Vairocana, the universal Great Sun Buddha present everywhere, a secret reality beneath the world of appearances. It teaches equally secret ways of realizing reality, especially the "three secrets" of gestures, chanting, and evocational meditation. But Shingon also puts great stock in more outward forms, such as art and ritual, for these forms reveal explicitly the hidden Buddha within a piece of wood or a human being. For all its esotericism, therefore, Shingon had a powerful impact on the development of art and, through the presentation of vivid Buddhist images for those unable to read, on the popularization of Buddhism.

Equally important in this respect was the parallel between archaic shamanism and the intense evocational meditations of esoteric adepts, who were not content merely with calm contemplative states, but who wrestled with the universe of their minds to conjure up visible cosmic Buddhas with whose enlightened state they would then identify. Shingon had not just one universal Buddha, Vairocana, but rank on rank of such entities born from infinite mind, reborn from the mind of the adept. Each represented an aspect of universal consciousness, and they could be arranged in patterns called mandalas, usually with Vairocana in the center, which together mapped the inner dynamics of cosmos and mind. Shingon has two basic mandalas: the Diamond, representing the cosmic Buddhas in their absolute wisdom aspect; and the Womb, representing them as outward-looking, engaged through the active bodhisattvas in compassionate work in the world.

The Tōji Temple This complex splendor is manifested in the incredible Kōdō hall of the Tōji; it was erected for the protection of the nation in the Heian period and was reconstructed in the Momoyama era. In this rectangular hall, twenty-one fine Buddhist images are set into a great three-dimensional mandala: the inner esoteric universe made visible. In the center is Dainichi (Vairocana), surrounded by four great cosmic Buddhas; this mandala will be familiar to readers of the popular *Tibetan Book of the Dead.* On the right, a mandala centered on Kongo-Haramitsu (Vajra-Prajña-paramita, Diamond Essence of the Perfection of Wisdom) represents compassion actively working in the world. Before him are five bodhisattvas. On the left, a mandala represents the Myōō (wondrous kings), a sort of "fierce" bodhisattva concerned—also in the name of wisdom and compassion—more with aggressive attack on error and illusion than with works of mercy. That mandala is centered on Fudō, much worshipped in Japan, a sword-bearing, fire-encircled expression of this order.

At the same time, gods from Hindu mythology were imported with Buddhism; at the four corners of the Tōji mandala were guardian deities such as Brahma, and "deva kings" to protect the Buddhas. As we have already suggested, Shinto also became part of Shingon's (and Tendai's) comprehensive construction of the cosmos. In the development called *Ryōbu Shintō* (or *Honji suijaku* in Tendai), the Shinto *kami* were viewed in turn as manifestations of the cosmic Buddhas. The grounds of major shrines, with their outriding lesser shrines, thus also became mandalas and pilgrimage centers.

Some of the rich Shingon pantheon, from bodhisattvas to the imported deities of India, stepped out of the mandala, so to speak, to become the quasi-independent gods of folk religion. Thus Shingon, more than any other religious force, constructed the popular Buddhist-Shinto symbiosis that for many centuries was the prevailing spiritual climate of Japan and the backdrop against which other movements acted and reacted.

TENDAI

Hardly less important than Shingon was the other great Heian sect, Tendai. Both Tendai and Shingon had vast mountaintop monasteries and temple complexes that were their headquarters; Shingon's was Mt. Kōya and Tendai's was Mt. Hiei, located atop a high peak just to the northeast of Kyoto. Because the temple at Mt. Hiei, called the Enryakuji, was much closer to the capital, its priests had a greater political effect.

Tendai, the Chinese T'ien-t'ai, was named after the mountain on the Chinese mainland where it originated; the sect was brought to Japan by Dengyō Daishi (762–822), called in his lifetime Saichō. According to its teaching, the Lotus Sutra contains the fullness of truth that descends like sun or rain on the world. Though actually not written till several centuries after the historical Buddha's life, the Lotus Sutra is considered doctrinally to be his culminating expression, and all other sutras are ranked beneath it; they are considered to be on various levels of partial truth for the accommodation of those not yet ready for its supreme articulation. Thus the Lotus is for Tendai an expansive umbrella, allowing for countless varieties of faith and practice to meet the needs of people on all stages of the Buddha's way. In fact, most of the later sectarian or popular-devotional styles of Buddhism in Japan, such as Pure Land, Zen, and the widespread worship of the bodhisattva Kannon as "goddess of mercy," began as one of the many optional varieties of Tendai piety.

The Enryakuji The templed top of Mt. Hiei is a Buddhist panorama. Amid its deep meditative woods and rushing streams are set numerous temples, each representing a different path to supreme enlightenment. There is one to Amida, the honorer of simple faith; for the philosophically profound, a shrine to Dainichi; for those aligned to prayer and mercy, a sanctuary of Kannon.

Today, the Enryakuji only hints at what it was before it was razed by Nobunaga in 1571. Then it was a monastic metropolis of more than 3,000 temples; now only a few score can be found. While

nothing can really justify such callous destruction, one can understand that a harsh warrior like Nobunaga would see Hiei as a citadel
to be leveled, for medieval Hiei was much more than a contemplative
hermitage. Its abbots were powerful politicians concerned with
their own interests and those of their allies; moreover, their policies
were backed by an army of *sōhei* (soldier monks), rough men of
indifferent background, who, in troubled times, had taken refuge
in the cloister but whose chief talent had been, and remained,
for brawling. The *sōhei* of Hiei would fight with similar brigades
of other temples and also would not hesitate to demonstrate in
the capital in order to impose Hiei's will on the government. Not
surprisingly, when Oda Nobunaga found this colorful but hardly
spiritual force plotting with his enemies, he felt it necessary to put
an end to the temporal might of the Tendai monastery once and
for all.

Never again did the sacred mountain affect the political affairs
of the nation. But Tendai temples are still common throughout
Japan. The sect's immense historical influence can never be erased,
and a morning's walk through the lovely, haunted woods of that
summit, with its scattering of rebuilt temples, is well worthwhile
for those for whom the religion and violence of Japan's past still
lives in memory.

JŌDO

The Kamakura era brought new popular Buddhist movements
based on the teachings of charismatic prophets, who each offered a
single, simple, sure key to salvation. Usually that sure key was a
devotion drawn from the treasure-house of Tendai, separated out
from its ponderous synthesis to become the center of a simple,
streamlined faith.

An excellent example is Jōdo (Pure Land) Buddhism. It was
originally brought in from China, and as taught by Tendai, became
increasingly popular as the Heian era advanced. Pure Land said that
Amida (Amitabha, originally the Buddha of the West in the cosmic
mandala of Vairocana) had vowed out of compassion that all who
called upon his name in simple faith would, upon death, be brought
by him into his Pure Land or Western Paradise—the "Buddha-
heaven" that surrounded this mighty being like an aura. Borne into
paradise on lotus blossoms—recall the reference in Chikamatsu—
the faithful would find themselves in a place of idyllic beauty, from
which final release into Nirvana would be easy.

Pure Land is obviously a different sort of Buddhism from that
founded upon austerity and meditation. Its chief devotional act

was simply repeating, with faith, the chant *Namu Amida Butsu* ("Hail Amida Buddha"). But it is no less profound that the older Buddhisms, for it suggests even more than they that the universal Buddha-reality, which Amida quickly came to represent, really is present everywhere and accessible to everyone.

Hōnen   That was the message of Hōnen (1133–1212), a monk of Hiei and the teacher under whom Pure Land became an independent movement. He said that he had read all the sutras five times but found no peace in them. Then, hearing of the Amida way, he tried it and discovered that in its very simplicity it worked. Hōnen divided Buddhist practice into two types: *Shōdō* (holy paths), by which one saves oneself through denial and meditation; and *Jōdo*, the Pure Land way, by which one depends on the grace of another. Shōdō practices are all right if one can do them, but for most people they are hopeless. This is especially true, Hōnen like other preachers of his day emphasized, in the present *Mappō* (the degenerate last period of the Buddha's teaching). Kamakura Japan believed widely— a belief greatly reinforced by the disasters of the civil wars—that it was in the last and worst of three thousand-year periods after the time of the Buddha, which humankind could be saved only by faith, if at all. (Paradoxically, though, this belief also made Buddhism more popular; salvation by faith alone makes religion accessible to everyone, however occupied or unlearned, not just to priests and monks with opportunities for elaborate spiritual exercises.)

The Pure Land path, Hōnen taught, was not only more accessible than the way of the holy man; it was also even more profoundly Buddhist, for dependence on *tariki* (the help of another) requires a negation of egotism likely to elude the adept who strives self-centeredly to pull himself into nirvana. This teaching was immensely popular in the tumultuous age of the samurai, when the religious laity was beginning to come into its own.[5]

The Chionin   A central temple of Jōdo-shu, the Pure Land denomination that follows Hōnen alone, is the Chionin in Kyoto. Erected on an eastern hill in 1234 by Genchi, a disciple of Hōnen (though the present buildings are mostly Tokugawa), this temple has huge grounds and gardens and affords a spectacular view of the city.

To enter the Chionin, one first passes through the Sanmon, widely considered the most impressive temple gate in Japan, which is saying much. Going up a flight of steps apparently built for giants, one approaches the Miedō (Hall of Images), the main temple hall. In its center an extremely ornate altar suggests the fairytale splendor of the Pure Land itself. Metallic streamers fall from the ceiling like golden cascades, and an orchard of fantastic plantlike creations shields the inner sanctuary. Around the exterior of this hall the *uguisu* (warbler) corridor, on which each step taken makes the pleasant sound of that bird, suggests the outer precincts of paradise. An image of Hōnen himself graces the central altar. He is invisible behind closed doors, as though the founder of the faith centered in this temple had now himself slipped out of view into the paradise he preached.

To the west of the Miedō is the Amida-dō (Amida Hall), which contains a huge but fairly austere image of Amida, the golden lotuses of paradise on either hand. This hall contains many tiny drums, which worshippers may beat to accompany their chants; the steady drumbeat of devotion can often be heard all around the temple. The famous guest rooms of the Chionin, containing not Buddhist art but the gold-backgrounded trees and birds of Momoyama taste, suggest the impact of history more recent than the days of Hōnen on this venerable religious institution.

Shinran Hōnen had a disciple named Shinran (1173–1263), who was even more radical and even more successful in propagating Pure Land than his master. He insisted that even one utterance of the *Nembutsu* (the "Namu Amida Butsu" chant) was sufficient, since salvation according to Amida's "original vow" did not depend on one's merit or works, but only on the Buddha's grace received by faith. This faith, in turn, was all that was needful; like Martin Luther, Shinran gave up his monastic garb, married, and had a family when he realized the full meaning of a religion of inward faith rather than outward works.[6]

Jōdo Shinshu The large denomination that follows Shinran's interpretation of Pure Land is called Jōdo Shinshu. It is headquartered in Kyoto in two large temples only a few blocks apart, the Higashi Honganji (Eastern Temple of the Original Vow), and the Nishi Honganji (Western Temple of the Original Vow). The denomination was divided into two administrations by the Tokugawa, in a typical divide-and-rule move, for in the days of civil war they too had their sectarian armies.

The Higashi Honganji, the largest wood-roofed building in the world, is a very imposing structure. Inside, however, the edifice is austere enough, a sea of straw mats with low altars to the front. The only images in the sanctuaries of this movement are of Amida and Shinran, the father in faith. These altars themselves are ornate in a way characteristic of Japanese Buddhist temples: all is gold and black lacquer, with offering tables, golden lotuses, and large picturesque drums to accompany chanting. Here also, from time to time, one can hear priests leading large groups chanting the *Nembutsu*. Many will be holding a *juzu* (Buddhist rosary). The chant of faith in the Buddha of the original and infinite pledge becomes a low murmuring, like the voice of a vast and restless surf. In the corridor between the two shrines is a part of a black rope made of the donated hair of believers to haul timbers when the present sanctuary was built in 1895—surely a remarkable expression of devotion.

NICHIREN BUDDHISM

No important temple of Nichiren Buddhism can be found in Kyoto. In 1536 the soldier-monks of Hiei—themselves to be decimated by Nobunaga less than forty years later—destroyed its hated prominence in the city's religious life by the typically violent means of leveling all twenty-one of its temples and slaughtering priests and believers in the thousands. Curiously, the best known Nichiren temple in Kyoto today, the Honnōji, now tucked behind office buildings in the heart of the city, is famous as successor to the temple where the leveler of Hiei, Oda Nobunaga, was murdered, though it is not on exactly the same spot. Nichiren Buddhism survived to become, in the twentieth century, the seed of an explosive new spiritual growth.

Nichiren   This stormy history fits the mood of the faith's founder, Nichiren himself, a fiery and militant prophet in a violent age. Nichiren (1222-1282), the son of a poor fisherman, was an intelligent youth haunted by religious questions. He wanted to understand the spiritual meaning of the bloody events of his time, and he wanted to know how one can have certainty of salvation. These questions he shared with Hōnen and Shinran. If an age can sometimes be more profoundly understood by the questions it asks than by the answers it gives, one can observe that the fundamental anxieties of the Kamakura Buddhist reformation (as of the Reformation in Europe) were: Is there a simple, sure way I can be positive I am saved? and, How can I understand spiritually the seeming degeneration of society into chaos and violence? Heian Shingon and Tendai, in contrast, asked (like the medieval philosophers of the West), How can all the phenomena of the universe and all human experience be integrated into a vast, complex, but comprehensible system?

Nichiren asked much the same questions as did others of his time, but his answer was distinctive. He studied at Hiei, and, though he broke with Tendai, he was convinced that its supreme scripture, the Lotus Sutra, was the answer. But Nichiren, with a simplifying zeal typical of his day, was not satisfied to see it just as the cornerstone of the vast cathedral of pieties. Rather, the Lotus had to be the one and only scripture for this age; faith had to be exclusively related to it. In 1253 the prophet began a vigorous national mission declaring that, unless the country turned exclusively to the Lotus, the calamities plaguing the country, signs that the Last Age had arrived, would continue. Nichiren predicted that to the disasters would be added foreign invasion; he claimed to be vindicated by the Mongol invasions of 1274 and 1281. His life, as might be expected of the life of one devoted to proclaiming without fear or favor what he perceived to be truth, was eventful; once he was even about to be executed but was reprieved at the last moment.

For all his medieval zealotry, Nichiren was in important ways an early example of a modern type of man and a maker of modern Japan. First, he made much of national corporate life and of the historical destiny of the nation, both ideas in advance of his time. Second, he stressed the unity of all reality and all planes of existence in the here and now, an affirmation suggesting the modern emphasis on life in this world. Moreover, he emphasized that spiritual causes, such as devotion to the Lotus Sutra, can produce material effects, and vice versa; the inner and outer, the material and spiritual, are one.[7]

This faith has come into its own in prosperous modern Japan. Sparked by the lay Sōka Gakkai organization, the Nichiren Shoshu denomination grew at a remarkable rate in the 1950s and 1960s, until it now claims a third of the nation's households and is unquestionably the most lively religious movement in the country. Nichiren Buddhism has also spread overseas.

The basic practice of Nichiren Buddhism is chanting the *Daimoku*, the words "Namu Myōhō Renge Kyō" ("Hail the marvelous teaching of the Lotus Sutra"). The words can be chanted at any time, but in formal devotion are said before a *Gohonzon* (a sheet of paper containing the names of leading Buddhas and bodhisattvas from the Lotus Sutra), which is usually enshrined on an altar. In its earlier stages, the Sōka Gakkai–led modern Nichiren revival stressed the power of the *Daimoku* to produce concrete results, such as success in business and healing of disease. Now more emphasis is put on the *Daimoku*'s spiritual value, and on the movement's role as the beginning of a new civilization, foreshadowed by its many social and cultural activities.[8]

The Shōhondō The most appropriate temple to commemorate Nichiren and his still-vital movement would be the Shōhondō near Mt. Fuji, completed as the central temple of Sōka Gakkai and Nichiren Shoshu in 1972. It is a large, neotraditional building designed by a leading architect, with clean, graceful lines. The concave suspension roof over the main sanctuary (which has capacity for 6,000 people) makes it one of the major achievements of modern construction. The object of worship therein is a great *Gohonzon* said to have been inscribed by Nichiren himself; it is ordinarily kept behind huge doors and a gold screen, typical of the Japanese inclination to veil that which is most sacred.

ZEN

The Ryōanji Old Kyoto is embraced by a serene empire of great Zen temples. The inner city is dominated by Shingon and Pure Land; Tendai gazes down from cloud-touching Mt. Hiei; the pleasant suburbs belong to Zen. The austere Nanzenji and the elegant Ginkakuji lie to the east; the Chinese-styled Mampukuji or Obakusan keeps watch to the south; the mountainous Tenryūji guards the west; the spacious, many-wondered Daitokuji has its seat in the north. The penchant of Zen for broad estates on the urban fringes is due to its preeminence in the tumultuous Ashikaga and Momoyama periods. Most of the Kyoto Zen temples were originally properties of noblemen, which passed into the hands of monks in those days as the spoils of war or of uneasy consciences, as we have seen was the case in Ashikaga Takauji's donation of Tenryūji to placate the shade of the emperor he had driven from the throne.

The greatest Zen concentration is to the northwest. Here is situated the dazzling Kinkakuji, built as a retreat by Ashikaga Yoshimitsu, the hushed and rewarding gardens of Myōshinji, and the much-celebrated Ryōanji with its world-famous arrangement of rocks on dry gravel. The Ryōanji was built on the estates of Hosokawa Katsumoto, one of the leaders in the Ōnin War, who died in the course of that conflict in 1474. Shortly after his death the estate became a Zen temple. The garden was built about 1500; its designer is not known, though many feel it must have been Sōami, the most famous painter and garden architect of the time.

The Ryōanji rock garden beside the monastery is surrounded by beautiful landscapes complete with pond. The rock garden— in Japanese, *kare niwa* (dry garden)—is a rectangle in which are set nothing but its fifteen rocks and five natural rock islands surrounded by a little moss, all on an expanse of white, carefully raked gravel. The rocks are set in no discernible geometric pattern, yet somehow the simple, subtle arrangement has a deep contemplative effect. The observer feels drawn into its abstract stillness, until a sense of formless transcendence is induced in his or her mind. Like the gardens of the Gold and Silver Pavilions, the Ryōanji represents one of the greatest human monuments to calm beauty against a background of savage violence.

The fifteen rocks in the Ryōanji Temple rock garden are placed in such a way that all cannot be seen from any one spot. The Zen garden is famous for its stark simplicity. (Courtesy Japan Air Lines.)

Principles of Zen What is the Zen Buddhism that inspired this achievement? We have already discussed its principles to some extent in conjunction with Yoshimasa's Higashiyama culture. The word Zen is a transliteration of the Sanskrit *dhyana* (concentration or meditation). Zen, then, is the form of Mahayana Buddhism that emphasizes meditation as the royal road to enlightenment. Meditation is preparation for a total life of direct, immediate seeing of the universal Buddha-nature in all things; the ordinary rational, cognitive mind has to be transcended. Meditation does this, but Zen also uses such devices as *koans* (the enigmatic Zen sayings like "What was your face before you were born?") that express deep points of Buddhist thought in ways that bring the rational mind up against its limitations. Koans may be the basis of interviews between students and *roshi* (master) that may include silent gestures and even blows. Zen is not dependent upon a single method; to Zen all scriptures and methods are a finger pointing at the moon, not the moon itself. They are all devices to induce *satori* or *kenshō* (sudden awakening), when the mind breaks through to a surprising, wondrous new awareness.

What is realized? One's true nature, which is the "unborn mind"—the universal Buddhic essence. Even this statement should not be taken as a Zen "answer," for realizing one's true nature may be simply the release of an ability to question in a deeper, more uninhibited, more joyously spontaneous way. In a Kyoto Zen garden, I once saw a modern poster displaying a young woman in Zen meditation, and the words: "What is human life? I think human life means asking, 'What is human life?'" Fresher, simpler, more spontaneous, more basic than surface "reality," true nature is that nature brought out in the wonderfully direct and free vision of Zen art and personality—a style of both art and life splendidly above all artificiality or pretence. Yet its sense of unfeigned immediacy, we must always remember, is the product of a hard discipline. One of the more common subjects of Zen painting is Bodhidharma (Daruma in Japan), the half-legendary master who is said to have brought Zen from India to China. He is usually portrayed as a roguish old fellow with a twinkle in his eyes, whom one would sooner expect to see telling a juicy tale over a convivial glass than in a monastery. Yet this same gentleman is reported to have meditated for nine years facing a brick wall and to have sat in the Zen meditation posture until his legs atrophied. The combination of heroic self-discipline and colorful personality somehow bespeaks the essence of Zen.

Whatever the historicity of Bodhidharma, the style of Buddhism that became Zen began forming in China in the early centuries A.D., when the Indian faith met the indigenous outlook of Taoism. The Zen method of meditation was brought to Japan by Tendai in the Heian period, but attracted little notice until brought again in the Kamakura era by two great masters who studied the two major Zen schools that by then had emerged on the mainland. Eisai (1141–1215) imported Rinzai, a school that later, especially under the influence of the great master Hakuin (1685–1768), made great use of the koans and an aggressive quest for *satori*. Dōgen (1200–1253), a major Buddhist philosopher, brought in Sōtō, a school that uses the koans and other confrontational means but little and emphasizes instead just "quiet sitting."[9]

Zen and Art Zen had an immense impact on Japanese culture. The direct, spontaneous Zen vision was captured in paintings, poems, and gardens. The Zen self-discipline that could produce a selfless and free person paradoxically appealed to samurai who wished to stand on the field of battle unafraid and to hit the mark with their swords or arrows with the same economy of effort as the Zen painter wielding his brush.

Finally, we may note that probably no other aspect of traditional Japanese culture has had more influence worldwide than Zen and its related arts. This influence is in no small part due to the numerous books and lectures of the modern Zen advocate, D.T. Suzuki (1870–1966). As the Pulitzer Prize–winning American poet Gary Snyder, himself a serious student of Zen, once commented,

Suzuki has undoubtedly affected world culture more than any other single Japanese, by what he brought of Japan to the world.[10]

NEW RELIGIONS

In the last two centuries, a number of "new religions" developed that combined old, often shamanistic or Buddhistic, motifs with new revelations that were sometimes obvious responses to the traumas of the modern world and to its optimistic possibilities. The new religions are diverse in doctrine and practice. Tenrikyō (the Religion of Heavenly Wisdom) teaches attractive sacred dances that symbolically sweep away dust and reenact the creation of the world. Perfect Liberty, believing that "Life is Art," instructs its members to integrate their lives in perfect works of art, emphasizes sports, and endeavors to build golf courses on the grounds of its churches. The Church of World Messianity offers "johrei," a rite in which the "Divine Light of God" is "channeled" through the upraised, cupped hands of one who administers it. Seichō no Ie (House of Life) teaches that "All is Perfect," and, while its doctrine was considerably influenced by the American "New Thought," "Positive Thinking" tradition, realizes its doctrine through a method of meditation probably based on Zen.

Nonetheless, the new religions have much in common. All have had strong charismatic leadership, often female, in the shamanistic tradition. In reaction to the unprecedented events of Japanese history in the nineteenth and twentieth centuries, they have all emphasized the coming of a new age, of even greater changes to come than what has already been seen. They have also been this-worldly; like modern Nichiren Shoshu, they have stressed benefits in this world. They have all been tightly knit groups, which, at least in the first generation, people joined out of deliberate choice rather than family tradition. They have all emphasized healing and solving personal problems more than traditional religion does in practice. Finally, most of them have constructed lavish centers, often entire cities devoted to the faith. This not only gives members a focus for pride and pilgrimage, but also offers a foretaste of the paradisal new world the believers expect will soon emerge in the world.[11]

Tenrikyō A good example is Tenri-shi (Tenri City), the town near Nara that is the sacred center of Tenrikyō. The founder of this faith was Nakayama Miki (1798-1887), a farmwife. When she was forty-one, she served as medium for a *yamabushi* (one of an order of shamans and healers related to esoteric Buddhism, formerly common in the countryside) in an endeavor to cure her son. While she was in trance, the voice of the supreme God seemed to speak through her and said he wanted to use her as his vessel in the world. From then on, her life was entirely changed. She healed, delivered many revelations, and saw the emergence of a faith around her. The heart of her teaching was that there is one supreme God, "God the Parent." She offered a new account of his creation of humankind, which commenced at a site in the yard of her home. Miki's followers in time built a pillar there called the Kanrō-dai, and were taught a dance to perform around it that acted out the creation.

Now the Kanrō-dai is set in the midst of a vast temple complex, complete with residences for pilgrims, schools, a university, a world-famous museum, and the administrative offices of a large institution. Pilgrims come from all over Japan, and from overseas, on the occasion of the sacred dance. As the paradisal new age begins, they believe, dew from heaven will fall on this pillar.

Christianity Finally, Christianity in Japan, though not a new religion in the same sense as the others, must be mentioned again as a major influence in the last century as well as in the sixteenth. Christian churches, schools, and hospitals are common in modern Japan. Although the number of Christians is small, the influence of Christianity, through its institutions of social welfare and the impact of a few influential missionaries and converts, has been considerable.

Philosophy: Thinking about Ultimates

5

Philosophy is systematic thinking about the ultimate principles of the universe, of thought, of human life, and of the proper ordering of society. Philosophy differs from religion in that it is generally derived from what the human mind can work out for itself on these matters and depends less on revelation or mystical states of consciousness than does religion. The term philosophy also refers to intellectual ideas themselves, whereas religion refers as much or more to their expression in art, worship, ritual, and sociological configurations.

Some have asserted that Japan is weak in philosophical thought, but this statement is misleading. To be sure, Japan has not been the homeland of such great philosophical workshops as those of ancient India, China, and Greece. But philosophical thinking has not really been so much behindhand in Japan as less visible to the superficial observer of the nation's culture. Philosophy, like most other facets of Japanese life, is less isolated from the stream of ordinary cultural and spiritual life than in some other places. Like art, it tends to have a *fūryū* face.

Indeed, the conclusion Japanese philosophers often reach is that true reality is simply ordinary life and ordinary things, and that truth is relative to time and place. As we have seen, this belief is also expressed in art, literature, religion, and social convention. The vigorous battles of philosophy, religion, science, and the social order of the West have partially been avoided in Japan, but at the price of making less apparent the distinct identity of each of these contenders for the human spirit.

BUDDHISM

Premodern Japanese philosophy has had two main sources, Buddhism and Confucianism. Japan's Buddhism has been dealt with in Chapter 4. Much of Buddhist thought is inseparable from the practice and monastic life that makes this great spiritual way a religion, and many of the Buddhist concepts that had so much influence in Japan originated elsewhere.

Two Buddhist philosophers in Japan do, however, deserve special attention. Even though—because of Japan's position on the fringe of Asia—they had little premodern influence outside Japan, they made remarkably profound original contributions of a philosophical nature to Buddhism and had an inestimable effect in their homeland. They are Kōbō Daishi, the bringer of Shingon to Japan, and Dōgen, the importer of Sōtō Zen.

Kōbō Daishi Kōbō Daishi wrote much on the principles of esoteric Buddhism; he emphasized the presence of the Absolute in all things and the possibility through Shingon's methods of becoming a Buddha in one's present body and lifetime. His most important treatise, however, is the *Jūjū shinron* (*The Ten Stages of Consciousness*). In this work of around 800, which could make a strong claim to being the first systematic comparative philosophy of religion in the world, Kōbō Daishi surveyed and ranked in order all the spiritual paths known to him—Confucianism, Hinduism, and the many types of Buddhism—and showed the benefits and limitations of each. The second highest was Kegon, with its unparalled vision of the Buddhist universe; the highest was Shingon, which was able not only to picture reality but also to provide the tools for realizing it inwardly. Shingon's emphasis that one could become a Buddha in this lifetime, however elaborate and otherworldly the process, in the end reinforced belief in the oneness of the Absolute and ordinary life.[1]

Dōgen Dōgen also urged the oneness of the ordinary and the essential. His first emphasis was on the unity of practice and enlightenment—and by practice he did not mean only Zen meditation, but also the whole life of the Zen practitioner, including eating, sleeping, working, and recreation. Buddhist enlightenment, in other words, is nothing exotic or otherworldly, but simply living ordinary life. But it is living in a unified state of mind: for the enlightened person mind and body are in unity (typified by Zen meditation); the wonderful and the ordinary are not distinct; self and universe are not set against each other.

Dōgen also said that being and time are one; his discussion of this point has attracted the attention of modern existentialists and philosophers of relativity theory alike. All existence means existence in time; to have time some form of existence must be manifested. All being is time, according to Dōgen, for absolute being is found only in its motion, which is time. It is time, also, that makes distinctions, for different objects are, as it were, different times.

Time itself, however, has no substance or continuity; every moment of time stands beside all others, self-contained. Thus, paradoxically, though only time exists, we know it only as a present moment that simply *is*, complete in itself, having no relations to past or future save those built by the desire-ridden clingings to memory and the fantasy of our minds. The point of Zen is to eliminate these relations to past and future and to live wholly unified in the present.[2]

CONFUCIANISM

Confucian philosophy starts from quite different concerns and perspectives than Buddhist, though—partly under Buddhist influence, to be sure—it has ended up with outlooks not as different from the Indic faith as might have been supposed. In China and Japan, Confucianism too has come to a celebration of the ordinary as the real substance of life. It has, however, continued to make political thought a sphere of special attention, one which Buddhism has generally neglected.

Confucianism is named after the Chinese philosopher Kung Fu Tzu (551–479 B.C.), whose name is latinized as Confucius. In a sense, however, Confucianism is a misnomer; it might better have been labeled, in Harlee Creel's term, "Sinism"—the "ism" of China. Confucius never saw himself as a philosophical innovator, but as a transmitter of the traditional values of his people, in his own day fallen somewhat into disarray. He did not write the "Confucian classics," but at best only edited and interpreted those from before his time and inspired followers such as Mencius and the authors of *The Great Learning* and *The Mean* to extend his vision further.

The core of all Chinese thought is the notion that human life should follow the *Tao*—the Way, the Great Course down which the universe is moving. Following the Tao means getting aligned with the true nature of the universe and also with one's own inner tao or true nature, an inward reflection of the great Tao. According to Confucianism the supreme human good is a good social order, for people are by nature social beings; one's inner tao is fulfilled only through right relationships with others. Supreme good is achieved through *te*—virtue, sincerity, selflessness—which in turn derives from "rectification of names," truly living out who one is in the web of social relationships. Confucius spoke of five basic relationships: sovereign and subject, parent and child, husband and wife, older and younger brother, friend and friend. If one rightly "becomes who one is" in all these relationships, then one is living rightly; if everyone in society would do the same, then the society would achieve perfect harmony. Societies can achieve harmony through turning the hearts of those within them by means that include music and ritual. The great importance of *li*—propriety, ritual, courtesy, formalism—in Confucian thought and society is based on the idea of lifting society through *li* from a "jungle" state of individual grasping to something like a great dance, in which everyone would act out, and in time internalize, his or her proper role.

Political Orientation The stress on social virtue made Confucianism politically oriented. Its highest ideal is the selfless, magnanimous statesman who sets an example of sublime virtue for his people. The rituals and ethics are primarily for the civil service elite, for Confucianism holds that if they are attuned to virtue and Tao, the rest of society will follow virtue as naturally as water running downhill.

Confucian thought came to Japan as early as Buddhism, if not before. It is given prominent place in the "Constitution" of Shōtoku Taishi, and during the Heian period the government sponsored a Confucian university. The Confucian concept of bureaucracy and civil service is reflected in the government institutions borrowed from China and in the rhetoric used to explain both the edicts and the Shinto rituals of the state.

Through such means as these Confucianism pervasively affected Japanese values and especially the language in which the values were rationalized and expressed. Confucian ideals such as loyalty to parents and rulers almost imperceptibly merged with and interpreted traditional clan values. They also affected literary form, as can be seen in the great importance given exemplary historical writing from the *Kojiki* on down. In the Heian spiritual potpourri, Confucianism shared influence with Buddhism, Shinto (whose state rituals could be interpreted as the "rites" important to the Confucian state), and Taoism—the last not represented by its best philosophy so much as by the divination, directional taboos, and deities of popular religion in China.

In the Middle Ages Confucianism took a back seat to the popular Buddhist movements. It nevertheless influenced some important quasi-philosophical works, such as the *Gobusho* (*Five Books*) of Ise Shinto, a medieval movement that attempted to put Shinto on a firmer theoretical basis than before. It also appeared in the important writings of Kitabatake Chikafusa (1292-1354) defending imperial legitimacy, even though he stopped short of the Chinese Confucian idea of a movable "mandate of heaven"; he stressed instead the unique superiority of the Japanese monarchy, with its unbroken succession of emperors legitimated by their possession of the imperial regalia (mirror, sword, and jewel) bestowed by Amaterasu.

Neo-Confucianism

In the meantime, new developments were taking place in China. A new school called Neo-Confucianism was giving the thought of the old master a more metaphysical bent, making it a means of internal transformation; one could become a sage embodying moral principles and participating in the work of nature. Through self-discipline and contemplation of the principles of things (*li; ri* in Japanese), one transcends ordinary self to work on the larger scale of heaven, earth, and society. The perspective is well illustrated by this passage from Yeh Ts'ai's commentary on the works of Chu Hsi (1130–1200), the dominant Neo-Confucian figure.

> The mind of Heaven and Earth is to produce and reproduce. The sage participates and assists Heaven and Earth so that all things will fulfill their nature and destiny correctly. This is to make up one's mind for the sake of Heaven and Earth. To establish the Way for living men is to establish and make prominent moral principles and to support human relationships and cardinal virtues. To continue interrupted learning means to continue the transmission of the Way. If great peace is inaugurated, whenever a true king arises he will adopt the system as a model, and benefit ten thousand generations.[3]

Here we see that the sage understands and works with nature, yet the greatest object of his mystic labors is moral and political; the supreme study is humankind, and its purpose is the regulation of the ideal society whose sovereign is a utopian ruler, both king and sage.

The philosophers sought to work toward the goal of ultimate social transformation by transforming themselves, "making up one's mind" by means of serious, contemplative study of the nature of things. According to Chu Hsi, everything has its own *li*, and there are supreme *li* of heaven, earth, and humankind from which all else derives. The *li* are known by intuition induced by concentration and are expressed in proper ethics and rites. According to the most important Neo-Confucian philosopher after Chu Hsi, the idealist Wang-Yang ming (1472–1529), the *li* are themselves actually in the mind of the observer, so that intuiting them is really knowing the nature and essence of mind.

However metaphysical, Neo-Confucianism would clearly have substantial social and political ramifications when taken seriously. It envisioned a coherent cosmos in which the nature of ultimate reality is manifested in the social order and in which a rightly attuned society facilitates realization of ultimate reality. Thus Neo-Confucianism combines study, meditation, and moralistic politics in the life of its ideal, the sage.

Neo-Confucianism was brought to Japan, chiefly by Zen monks, in the Middle Ages but did not come into its own until the Tokugawa period. The Tokugawa regime found its moralistic conservatism, support of the education needed by an increasingly complex society, and rationalization of social regulation wonderfully suited to its objectives. But other currents were moving in the intellectual life of that superficially stable yet inwardly fermentive age.

TOKUGAWA PHILOSOPHY

The Tokugawa regime adopted Confucianism, interpreted by Neo-Confucianism, as its official ideology; its firm and stable ordering of society was said to be an expression of Confucian ideals. But the period was infused with a yeasty intellectual life of many styles.[4]

Orthodox Philosophy The orthodox philosopher was the court teacher Hayashi Razan (1583–1657), whose family became hereditary heads of the Confucian academy in Edo. His school, Shushigakuha, taught a close following of Chu Hsi. Hayashi said that *li* is inherent in nature, yet must be cultivated; when this is well done, then society would create itself properly with freedom. A truly free society would be one whose institutions allowed expression only to the true *li* of each person and class and of the state as a whole.

This position was countered by the Ōyōmeigakuha (Wang Yang-ming school) of Nakae Tōju (1608–1648), which said one should act by mind or will (*shin*) and its intuitions; the principles are not external but come into being through their perception.

Kogaku School Neo-Confucianism as a whole was challenged from several directions. One was the Kogaku (ancient studies) school, which advocated going back to more primordial Chinese sources of the time of Confucius or even before. An early spokesman for the school was Yamaga Sokō (1622–1685), who is also supposedly the author of a systematic code of Bushidō, the way of the samurai or warrior, founded on *giri*, the Confucian-based idea of ineluctable obligation.

Another Kogaku thinker was Itō Jinsai (1627-1705), who taught that the universe is basically kinetic energy and that all is in a process of change and action. All is then naturally good, for action is good and death is the only evil. Death does not really exist, for the universe is a living being; what is called death is only a transition in a tiny part of that immortal life. The supreme virtue is humaneness, characterized by love.

Ogyū Sorai (1666-1728) took a more pessimistic stance. He claimed to go back to ancient sages even before Confucius; his position was somewhat comparable to that of the early Chinese school called the Legalists. He stressed discussion of how to control society rather than how to let it be free to follow *li*. Sorai believed that the Tao is not natural but was invented by the ancient sage-kings; in other words, it is a social construct. History rather than philosophy, he said, is the way to truth, for we learn what is socially good through practice and the lessons of the past, not through speculation. (Sorai ridiculed the quiet contemplation of certain philosophers.) His thought had both conservative and utilitarian overtones.

Kokugaku School A different school, which was to have far-reaching impact at the time of the Meiji Restoration and after, was the Kokugaku (Japanese Learning, literally National Learning) School. Its leading lights were Kamo Mabuchi (1697-1769), Motoori Norinaga (1730-1801), and Hirata Atsutane (1776-1843). It favored a rejection of everything foreign, including Buddhism and Confucianism (which, despite their exclusion policy, set Kokugaku at odds with the Tokugawa government, which made much use of Confucian ideology and Buddhist social institutions). Instead, the Japanese Learning scholars favored a return to the ancient ways of the *Kojiki* and the archaic rites, including direct imperial rule. Perhaps influenced by Taoism, they felt that with a return to primordial simplicity and sincerity, virtue would come of its own, without the need of Confucian-type ethics; this was the ancient Japanese way, the way of Shinto. These scholars made immense contributions to Japanese philology and antiquarianism through study of classical texts. In their promotion of a nativist, Shinto, and proimperial ideology, they laid much of the foundation (without intending the results) of the Meiji Restoration and subsequent nationalism.

Rangaku Another interesting movement was Rangaku (Dutch Studies). As we have seen, despite the Tokugawa exclusion policy, one Dutch ship was allowed to land at Nagasaki for trade each year. Among its goods were books and scientific devices from Holland. Certain Japanese learned the Dutch language and became familiar with Western science, particularly geography. Because the government did not encourage the importation of Western books on philosophy and religion, the reflections of the Rangaku scholars were largely secular. But they were adventurous and free spirits, straining at the bonds of a cramped social order, who helped prepare the way for the subsequent modernization of Japan.

Popular Philosophy Finally, mention should be made of popular Tokugawa philosophies. The new bourgeoisie, and even the newly self-conscious peasantry, like their counterparts everywhere, welcomed intellectual statements that reinforced the virtues of community loyalty and hard work upon which their lives were grounded. Several popular philosophies, which had an immense effect on popular culture then and after, accomplished this task in appealing ways.[5]

Shingaku (Heart Learning or Mind Learning), founded by Ishida Baigan (1685–1744), was typically eclectic. It promoted worship at Shinto shrines, but its ethics were based on Zen and Neo-Confucian concepts of cultivating the original purity of the heart. It taught due respect for the social order and its laws and saw them as an expression of the natural moral order of which human nature is a part.

Ninomiya Sontoku (1787–1856) was another popular teacher, who became known as the "peasant sage." He was a vigorous advocate of rural welfare who did much to improve the quality of life in the impoverished countryside through his instruction of peasants in how to budget, plan, and cooperate. He was also a philosophical teacher; his basic idea was *hōtoku* (returning virtue), a concept of obligation that emphasized the individual's dependence on nature and human society. Life is a process of cooperation, of returning good in gratitude for what is received. At the same time Ninomiya believed in the value of hard work and the dignity of labor; he gave farmers a sense of pride in their occupation and a desire to follow his example of industry for the good of all. While not a radical reformer, he helped induce a desire for a more equitable social order in which those who labor would be given a fair portion of respect and reward.

MODERN PHILOSOPHY

Since 1868, Japanese philosophy has understandably been under the heavy influence of the West. At first the models were British and American but later, German philosophy, especially idealism, phenomenology, and existentialism, held the field, as it has in many other places.

Thus, at the turn of the twentieth century, Inoue Enryō tried to combine Buddhism with Western ideas. He saw Kegon and Tendai as the highest expressions of Mahayana and wrote that in them pure reason or spirit in the Hegelian sense is the essence of reality. About the same time, Takayama Rinjirō, following the Hegelian T.H. Green, taught that realization of the self is the ideal (compare Confucianism); he saw Nichiren as the ideal superman in the Nietzschean sense.

The best known modern Japanese philosopher is undoubtedly Nishida Kitarō (1810-1945). He was influenced by the pragmatism of William James and by Zen. The fundamental reality, he said, is "pure experience"—the direct awareness of things as they are. All oppositions, like subject and object, must be transcended by pure experience, which alone leads to whatever reality there is.

Since 1945 Japanese philosophy has been swept by most of the same movements as has Western: phenomenology, existentialism, and logical positivism. Marxism has been very popular with educators, social scientists, historians, and political activists and has deeply colored much work in these areas; however, it has been on the wane, at least as a dogmatic ideology, since the 1960s. Few Japanese philosophers, however, have attained world stature since the end of the war, though the work of D.T. Suzuki as an interpreter of Zen for the West and the important work of Nakamura Hajime on intellectual history must be cited.[6]

Part Three
Still Mirrors:
Sculpture, Painting,
and Other Visual Arts

The *Kojiki* and *Nihonshoki* tell us that the lovely Amaterasu, hiding in the rocky cave of heaven in sorrow over Susa-no-o's depredations, was lured out by a mirror after she opened the cavern door just a crack. A deity held a mirror before the beautiful goddess's face; struck by the bright beauty of her own reflection, she drew closer to it and so was led back into the world. When her grandson was sent down to the islands of Japan to establish the imperial throne, she gave him this mirror to remember her by. It is now one of the three imperial regalia and is said to be enshrined in the Grand Shrine of Ise.

Like a mirror held for a moment to a divine face, an immortal painting or statue captures an unforgettable meaning in a single gesture or expression. It seizes the awesomeness or mercy of a god, the transitory grace of a bird on a branch, or the glory beneath the surface of ordinary daily life. Indeed, it creates that grace and glory, so that after seeing the painting we may see actual birds or people in a new and brighter light.

In Japan, the eye of the artist for the vitality of his subject has always been especially keen. His still mirror has seldom been without the aura of frozen life. In the first chapter of this section, we trace the story of Japanese painting and sculpture. The approach is historical, since the various periods of Japanese history have each evoked some very distinctive responses from the wielders of brush and chisel. At the same time, some distinctive emerging themes will appear: a sense of unique personality in each human subject and an ongoing movement from Buddhist to natural subjects—though nature is no less sacred when interpreted by the Zen hand.

The second chapter of this part discusses certain other arts that, though they might be regarded as minor in some cultures, are traditionally taken very seriously in Japan: architecture, gardens, the tea ceremony, and flower arrangement. All have been deeply influenced by the Zen spirit and especially by Higashiyama culture. All reveal much about Japanese aesthetics, especially its delicate interweaving of skill and nature. Even though made of natural materials, the Japanese garden or flower arrangement is also a still mirror that captures nature on the wing.

Sculpture and Painting

In this chapter we survey Japanese painting and sculpture up to the present. This is an art of remarkable richness and technical skill, yet its angle of vision is somewhat different from that of much Western art.

CHARACTERISTICS OF JAPANESE ART

Classical Japanese art is never truly abstract or surrealist. It portrays the visible world with carefully and splendidly executed attention to detail. At the same time, it lacks the geometric perspective discovered by the Renaissance masters of the West. The Japanese painter is able to combine realistically conceived details on a flat, undistanced surface in a way that expresses his subjective perception of patterns rather than photographic realism.

For example, *byōbu* (screens), which often provide invaluable records of historical events, were particularly well developed in the Momoyama period. A series by Kanō Naizen, the *Namban Byōbu* (*Southern Barbarian Screens*), records the arrival of Portuguese traders and the conversion of Japanese by Jesuit and Franciscan missionaries. In one example, at the bottom a street scene is painted, in which vividly characterized foreign priests, monks, and merchants mingle with natives; the background is a shop and pine grove portrayed without depth, partially covered by the golden mists that the period favored as background. The mists half-veil the foreground as well, as though busy scenes like this one pop into view from time to time as the aureate haze of eternity parts. Above a bank of golden cloud is another scene; whether it is simply another structure on higher ground, or something from another dimension lowered down to near proximity with the street scene, is not clear. On the upper level a Catholic priest is saying Mass, attended by three or four Japanese worshippers, before a baroque altar incongruously placed in a Japanese building. This painting, with its brilliant golds and perceptive eye, magnificently captures the spirit of its age—Momoyama pomp, Japan in a curious and expansive mood, the colorful sixteenth-century meeting of East and West—through a typically unobtrusive yet technically sure combination of realistic detail, abstract background, and interpretive juxtaposition of large blocs. The diverse garbs, the Franciscans' beards, even the number of beads on the Christians' rosaries, are accurate; the Mass, seemingly suspended in midair or mideternity, interprets the spiritual meaning of events on the shop-lined street below.

Japanese sculpture, too, displays an effective combination of technical precision with interpretive freedom. One of the most famous Japanese statues is the portrayal of the priest Kūya by the early Kamakura-period sculptor Kōshō. Kūya, a popular Pure Land Buddhist characteristic of his period, wandered about the countryside simply saying joyously the *Nembutsu* and teaching it to high and low. The statue shows him in vibrant detail realism walking with his staff, beating a gong to attract attention, wearing the simple cloth of an itinerant monk—but, in a brilliant gesture, out of his open, chanting mouth proceeds a row of six tiny images of Amida Buddha, to represent the six characters and syllables of the chant that was always on Kūya's tongue and in his heart.

ANCIENT ART

The striking combination of technical skill and interpretive freedom is as old as Japanese art. The earliest known representational art, the Jōmon figurines, with their strange slit eyes and disproportionate anatomy, combine these unreal features with considerable psychic power.

Haniwa Figurines The famous *haniwa* figurines of the Kofun period also display indigenous Japanese genius, untainted by heavy continental influence. They show already the Japanese artist's use of simple, even austere, concepts, executed with sureness of touch, a deft sense of motion, and the intangible quality that gives great art an unmistakable sense of life. Above all, the *haniwa* figurines, with their ovals for eyes and tiny, barely expressive mouths, possess an odd timeless, immortal quality, archetypical in their performance of ordinary—though perhaps sacred—activities. Dancers, shamanesses, warriors, and animals are given a primordially fresh and naïve life, achieved through sure grasp of artistic technique and rhythm, a quality approaching the *yūgen* later to be so celebrated.

This ceramic haniwa *figure from the fifth or sixth century* A.D. *is of a young girl holding a cup. (Courtesy Museum of Fine Arts, Boston, Edward S. Morse Memorial Fund.*
© *Copyright 1979. All rights reserved.)*

Even in the late Yayoi and Kofun periods, continental influence was making its impact, chiefly through Korean trade and immigration. Some authorities think that, however original the *haniwa* figures may be in execution, the idea of human and animal grave figures was inspired by China. More evident of continental models are the bronze bells (*dōtaku*) modeled on those of China's magnificent Bronze Age. While inferior to those of the mainland, these bells—more ornamental than functional—are paneled with scenes of hunting, agriculture, and animals that provide interesting insights into the life of the times.

Early Buddhist Art   The formal introduction of Buddhism in the sixth century opened up the explosive new artistic developments of the Asuka and later periods. Buddhism, as we have seen, was far more than just a new religion in a narrow sense. It was an overwhelming social and cultural force that provided a means of unifying the nation under a "neutral" imported ideology and inspired hitherto undreamed of heights of creativity in virtually all cultural media.

The preponderance of sculpture is of the human form. Why make an inanimate image of a human being? Certainly not simply to show what a human looks like, which can be ascertained by more direct means. Rather, the sculptor makes some sort of statement about what a human *is* beyond mere appearance, though that being-ness may be mediated through the nuances of appearance. So great Buddhist sculpture brims over with the religion's founding discovery, that the supreme human attainment is a state in which infinite peace, wisdom, and love are conjoined.

The greatest early Buddhist monument is the Hōryūji near Nara. Among its notable works of art is the Shakamuni Triad (the historic Buddha with two attendants) of Kuratsukuri no Obito Tori, a gifted sculptor of Korean-Chinese immigrant background. The Shakamuni Triad, famed for the "archaic smile" lighting the face of the Enlightened One, is quite Chinese in form, showing the influence of the late Northern Wei styles. Yet one senses even here just a hint of the vigor, even tension, that was to give later Japanese Buddhist sculpture its particular "feel." Beneath the calm hieratic gesture is life that surfaces in the heavy sensual lips and the determined concentration of the brow.

Also from the time of Prince Shōtoku are two representations of Miroku, justly praised as among the most marvelous wood images in the world. One is located at the Chūgū temple near the Hōryūji, and the other at the Kōryūji in Kyoto. Nearly identical, they follow Korean models. The unknown creator of these images—undoubtedly one of the many Korean craftsmen then resident in Japan—has cre-ated a sense of warmth, tenderness, lightness, and poised tranquil strength through incomparable mastery of the medium. There is a humanness, an almost playful charm about these future Buddhas as they sit cross-legged in light meditation, fingers of one hand raised to the chin, that points toward the lively future of Japanese art.

The oldest surviving oil paintings in the world come from Tamamushi shrine near the Hōryūji. These are murals on the life and previous incarnations of the Buddha. While derivative, these works have a rich sense of movement and charm.

NARA

In the Nara period the Japanese cultural assimilation of Bud-dhism reached a new level. It focused on a great city, modeled on the T'ang capital Ch'ang-an; Nara was full of temples that served as supreme examples of Buddhist art and centers of its dissemina-tion. In the religious art of Nara, the combination of Chinese and Japanese inspiration found its greatest fulfillment; actually the best remaining examples of sculpture in the T'ang style are in Japan, as is the case with T'ang dynasty music and dance.

At the same time, Nara produced a fresh Japanese self-confidence in art that augured well for the future. Already one sees a sure sense of movement, of sensuality, and of humanness in its subjects, however exalted. The "archaic smile" is gone. In its place is the startlingly boyish, clear-eyed, level gaze of an *asura* (low-ranking Buddhist guardian deity) in the Kōfukuji. In the Hōryūji is the early Nara Yumetagae Kannon, a small bronze figure standing with right arm raised in blessing. Yet, though the gesture is conventional, the image is neither hieratic nor stiff. Rather, the figure seems to sway with life without losing dignity, to flex the knees and waist ever so slightly, to bow the head subtly toward the worshipper, as though possessed of a divine life more warm and maternal than mysteriously exalted.

Portrait Sculpture   The tradition of portrait sculpture, especially of distinguished priests, was begun in Nara. These works achieved from the beginning a convincing realism and sense of unique personality so compelling as to seem almost un-Buddhist! For example, the portrayal of the blind Chinese immigrant priest Ganjin (finished in 763) is a splendid representation that shows the eminent monk in a pose of pious meditation; from the firm yet kindly turn of the mouth and the hint of a crinkle in the corners of his unseeing, nearly closed eyes, we receive an immortal impression of a distinctive and appealing human being.

Buddhist Art In the Buddhist art of Nara, religious faith drew forth the best skill of artists. Some later Japanese Buddhist art gave way to sentimentality or overstriving for effect through lavish halos and the like. But in the great Nara work, faith was still fresh and deep, and brilliant technique was considered to be the hand-maiden rather than the subverter of piety. However, in the end, the almost-breathing humanity the Japanese hand imparted was to prevail over Nara's iconographic model of Buddhist sacred art. To some degree it prevailed even against Buddhism, for the humanness even of Japanese sacred art is not, in fact, far from the secular and skeptical side of the Japanese mind that has never wholly made its peace with Buddhist asceticism.

The new humanness of Nara Buddhist art was partly inspired by the rich T'ang style, introduced in the late seventh century, which was more sensuous and monumental than the exquisite early Buddhas. Japanese artists developed the mode further, merging native instincts with T'ang inspiration. They imparted a life-giving Japanese sense of surface and texture, already evident in the Miroku, where the grain of the wood is blended into the contours of the face to make the wood itself seem almost to rise and fall with holy life. Naturalness of artistic pose and rhythm suggested that even a many-armed figure, as some were, need not be wholly dehumanized and made only into a sacred archetype. Above all, each separate figure has a distinct personality. Even the masks made for the *Gigaku* dances in the Nara period combine godly or demonic power with personality and humor.

The treasure-trove temples of Nara are too numerous to mention all of them. The most imposing, of course, is the Tōdaiji, which houses the great Buddha. Not far from it is the Shōsōin, a wood building containing the magnificent contents of the Emperor Shōmu's household, presented to the temple after he became a monk. Miraculously preserved through more than twelve centuries, this repository contains not only fine Japanese works, but treasures from China and elsewhere.

Apart from such artifacts, Nara offers relatively little secular art. Some talented but derivative secular painting, based on Chinese examples, does not compare with the magnificent Buddhist wall paintings of the Kondō hall at Hōryūji, executed about 710 and tragically destroyed by fire in 1949.

Nara was a great age of religious art, of art sacred in both subject and inspiration. We shall find that Japanese art loses none of its skill down the centuries, but it does gradually lose this sacred combination. First, in Zen-related art of the Muromachi period and after, explicitly religious subject matter gives way to nature; religious inspiration remains, for nature is seen with the eye of enlightenment. Finally, by the Momoyama and Tokugawa periods, the mainstream of Japanese art is secular in both subject and inspiration, though no less magnificent.

HEIAN

In the Heian period, the new cultural waves that most affected the visual arts were esoteric Buddhism first, and finally Pure Land Buddhism. Great art continued to be predominantly religious and Buddhist, even though some interesting statues from the Heian era are of Shinto deities, and an increasing number of nonreligious paintings appear.

Shingon and Tendai Buddhism, with their vast pantheons of heavenly hosts, opened up awesome prospects for the artist. The great three-dimensional mandala of the Tōji temple in Kyoto bespeaks esotericism's vast range of subject matter.

Equally important was the artistic feeling that esotericism evoked. The Shingon of Kōbō Daishi, in particular, carried with it a profound and influential artistic theory. Art, like ritual, is a means of bringing out the Buddha-nature already present in all things; to make a piece of wood into an image of the Buddha is to show what it really is. Moreover, this act is a spiritual exercise, much like the effects of ritual or meditation on the human body and mind. The artist must prepare for it inwardly and must wield his scalpel or brush with reverence. This attitude toward art has spread beyond the circles of esoteric Buddhism and is still widely felt in Japan, reinforced by a comparable Zen attitude.

Buddhist Sculpture Early Heian Buddhist sculpture has a feel of mysterious power, of vigorous but ponderous and unearthly activity, like that charted in the mandalas. While technically skillful, sometimes the vibrant humanity that marked the best Nara work becomes lost amid the complex iconography of the esoteric schools. Transcendence appears to be suggested by nothing more subtle than solemnity and size.

Perhaps for this reason, one of the most satisfying of early Heian works is the small, simple wooden image of a Shinto goddess in the Matsu-no-o shrine in Kyoto. Only the location of the piece reveals its sacred nature; the sculpture shows a quiet, matronly woman, seated and dressed with simple and elegant taste in the court garb of the day. Yet rarely has the medium of wood been more perfectly mastered by an artist or have its own qualities been integrated more finely into the texture and rhythm of the image itself than in this example. The natural grain of the wood flows with the folds of the garments and the curve of the cheeks; the long, straight hair hangs with a fullness, yet a lack of weight, that well-rounded wood quietly communicates.

In general, however, the late Heian period (sometimes called the Fujiwara by art historians) was more productive in painting and sculpture. Sculpture is dominated by Jōchō (d. 1057) and his school and by works relating to the rising Pure Land movement. The centerpiece is the image of Amida carved in wood by Jōchō himself for the Byōdōin in Uji, the temple built by Fujiwara Yorimichi (992–1074) out of a villa built by his father, the great Michinaga, whose Hōjōji attempted to replicate the Pure Land; the Byōdōin is the best surviving Heian temple. Jōchō's Amida set new standards; it is relatively small and light, yet has an ethereal charm intermingled with calm, the former suggested by the almost sensuous lips, the latter by the half-closed meditative eyes. In his restrained delight, this Amida seems a merry yet wise child. Around him on the upper walls and ceiling is something very rare: a troupe of high-relief bodhisattvas spinning, wheeling in joy, dancing and playing musical instruments. In this place, one is led to feel, the rapture of the Pure Land can hardly keep from breaking through on earth. Indeed, the descent of Amida to meet the faithful is the subject of the celebrated paintings on the walls of this chamber;

A scene from the mid-thirteenth century by Heiji Monogatari Emaki depicts an event from early in the war between the Taira and the Minamoto. Here, Minamoto troops have forcibly abducted the retired emperor, Go-Shirakawa, who was mistrusted by both sides. Accompanied by a princess, he rides in the carriage, surrounded by a well-armed escort. (Courtesy Museum of Fine Arts, Boston, Fenollosa-Weld Collection. © Copyright 1979. All rights reserved.)

they are also the oldest existing examples of the next genre to be discussed, the *yamato-e* (Japanese painting).

Yamato-e Raigō-zu (paintings of Amida descending to meet the faithful), often designed to be hung before the eyes of the dying to assist them in their final devotions, were common, and many were of good quality. The same can be said of the more lively *emaki* (scrolls) on Buddhist subjects; these tended toward such colorful if gruesome subjects as the hells and the hungry ghosts. Both types of Heian painting represent the emergence of *yamato-e*, named in contrast to Chinese painting. The scrolls were devoted to Japanese scenes, literature, and sentiments; out of them came the special Japanese sense of accurate detail and interpretive juxtaposition of blocs of material on a flat surface.

The *yamato-e*, being Japanese in inspiration, are more often secular than Buddhist in subject matter. The most famous is the late Heian scroll of *The Tale of Genji*, showing scenes from that celebrated novel. A striking example is the *Chōjū Giga* (*Frolicking Animals*) of Kakuyū (1033–1140). The artist, though a priest, used cartoon-like animals to parody the Buddhist clergy.

Though its greatest work is undying, the visual arts of the Heian era do not quite equal the splendor of its literature. Its significance is chiefly as a time of assimilation and transition between the brilliant Hakuhō-Nara creations and the subtle Muromachi and Tokugawa work that was to follow. It was an era when sculpture became more and more naturalistic, and when native styles of painting with secular subjects came into their own.

KAMAKURA

The keynotes of the Kamakura era were transfer of power to warlords of the samurai class and the rise of the new Buddhisms. Appropriately, an important form of art was decorative swords and armor, many exquisitely crafted. Although Kamakura is, like the Heian, essentially a transitional period rather than one in which an artistic wave reached its consummation, it produced significant work.

Realism The dominant trend was toward greater realism in both sculpture and painting. Works in both media were often related in style and subject to the popular new Buddhisms, with their desire to make faith accessible to the common man. We have already discussed the famous statue of Kūya, the tenth-century "saint of the streets" and forerunner of Kamakura Buddhism, who wandered the highways and byways to chant and teach the grace of Amida. This work was by Kōshō (d. 1237), the fourth son of Unkei (fl. 1175–1218), founder of an important school. Both the subject matter and the striking naturalness of the pose, with the priest striding down the road, legs apart, as the tiny Amida figures proceed from his lips, suggest mature confidence in the Japanese interest in humanity, as well as mature technical skill.

The age of Kōshō was in fact the last great period of Japanese sculpture. With the rise of Zen to prominence in cultural influence, Buddhist sculpture declined; Zen made little of the artistic merit of the images on its altars, and indeed of explicitly religious art in general. But painting advanced; portraiture was popular in this age of powerful personalities both secular and religious, as also were *emaki* telling stories or the traditional histories of temples and shrines.

MUROMACHI

In the wartorn world of the elegant Ashikaga shoguns, Zen monks were the main custodians of culture, even as were the Benedictines in the Dark Ages of Europe. Their values, together with the cultural values they had helped import from China, shaped a new aesthetic. In art, its major form was the *sumie* or *suiboku* (ink on paper with use of *haboku* or splashed-ink wash) landscapes inspired by Chinese masters, especially those of the Sung dynasty.

Landscapes *Suiboku* landscapes followed certain conventions. They were highly vertical, showing steep craggy mountains and deep basins with lakes and canyons. The rises had three levels, perhaps separated by space or cloud banks, that were reminiscent of the three forms of the expression of the Buddha-nature: the *nirmanakaya*, or Buddha-nature in this world, in the form of humans and their teachers, such as the historical Buddha; the *sambhogakaya*, or heavenly form of expression, that of the many Buddhist paradises that, like the Pure Land, perhaps ultimately represent the inner world of dreams and the sources of artistic creativity; and the *dharmakaya*, the "clear light of the void" that is the absolute essence of reality. Thus the lower level of the painting reflects artifacts of

A Japanese artist paints a traditional suiboku *design on rice paper. (Courtesy Japan Air Lines.)*

the ordinary earth and the realm of humans: low land, a lake, a hermit's hut, and perhaps a beached boat or even a traveler or two. On the middle level appear jewel-like structures suggesting the turrets of paradise: a temple or pagoda. Finally, on the highest plane looms only the icy purity of mountain peaks, a transcendence beyond the human level and beyond even the conventional heavens.

Shūbun and Sesshū   These themes were developed in Japan by two painters of especial merit, both priests of the Shōkokuji Zen monastery in Kyoto: Shūbun (d. 1450) and Sesshū (1420–1506). Shūbun's work, while meritorious, is highly Chinese in style and thus rather derivative. But Sesshū is considered by some to be the greatest of Japanese painters. He not only painted landscapes of brilliant originality even while observing the conventions but also explored a variety of other topics: portraits, studies of birds and flowers. He Japanicized Chinese models, supplying through sharpening contrasts of tone and more use of space that peculiar life-giving tension that infuses the best of Japanese art.

Among Sesshū's best-known paintings is the *suiboku* "Winter Landscape." This striking work offers the conventional three levels: a temple sits beneath the jagged cloud-lost peaks, and near the base a traveler in a broad-brimmed hat, dwarfed by the immense landscape, gingerly makes his way. But what immediately strikes the viewer is not convention but the novelty of the style. The black-

and-white painting is composed of a tangle of short, ragged, restless lines; a seeming division trailing down the center gives it an electric energy. Here is no mystical softness or overrefinement. Rather, Sesshū's Zen eye sees nature as harsh, sharp, yet tremendously alive with nervous energy. He strips it to its twitching geometric bones, and yet, with his celebrated use of empty space, saves room at the top for this quivering mass to dissipate into vagueness, and finally into the whiteness of infinity.

MOMOYAMA

The short Momoyama era was an important one in Japanese art, just as it was in the political development of the Japanese state. Like the Renaissance in Europe, it was a time of munificent patrons, such as Hideyoshi, who would spare nothing to proclaim to the world their wealth, power, and—what was even more important to them—their refined taste and exquisite connoisseurship. If their taste was not actually as delicate as Yoshimasa's, the new men who made it to the top did have a love of art and artists. They decorated their castles with the lavish paintings with gold backgrounds that are a hallmark of the era, which portrayed often life-sized trees, flowers, birds, and animals. The greatest exponent of this Momoyama style was Kanō Eitoku (1543-1590).

Momoyama art was eclectic. Chinese and Japanese influences mixed in single paintings. The rich colors and baroque subject matter of the *Namban* or "Southern Barbarian" screen shared place with a work like "Shrike" by Niten (1584-1645), a Zen-like ink drawing. It is mostly white space, broken only by a single reed drafted with just a few soft, deft strokes, upon which sits a single tiny bird, executed with a few strokes and a smear of wash.

The monument that best expresses the flavor of Momoyama culture is the great Nijō castle in Kyoto, even though it was not started until 1603. This massive edifice was built by Tokugawa Ieyasu to be the shogunal residence in the imperial capital. It is the best example of the period's taste in interior decoration, for the good reasons that the new regime had most other castles torn down and possessed the wealth to decorate their own with the work of the most prestigious artists of the day. These were painters of the Kanō school, a family that produced talented artists for a remarkable seven generations, from Momoyama to Meiji. Their work was sometimes a bit too academic, but at its best both captured the sensibility of the age and was of timeless beauty. The Nijō screens and walls are characteristically gold, with pine branches running from one to another. The arboreal scenes are enlivened by splendidly wrought birds and animals. The temper of the work is quiet and restrained, and often subtle; the only artistic indicator of the armory or the doors behind which the shogun's bodyguards hid in his reception room is that on them the graceful animals under the eternal pines are birds and beasts of prey.

The Momoyama was a vivid, tumultuous period of many conflicting values, each one of which seemed to offer a different cultural future to Japan. What is remarkable is that most of the options, in chastened form, managed to find a foothold in the quite different Tokugawa world that succeeded it and so became a part of the complex Japanese culture of recent centuries.

TOKUGAWA

Tokugawa painting has left two main heritages: the famous *ukiyo-e* (floating world pictures), wood-block prints depicting the life and personalities of the lively entertainment world of Edo; and "mainstream" painting in the Chinese-influenced tradition of earlier art like the Muromachi and Momoyama landscapes. In Tokugawa Japan, and indeed into the twentieth century, the popular art of the "floating world" was considered hardly worth the attention of serious appreciators. Now, thanks as much to Western as to Japanese discovery of them, so much attention is given to the block-print artists Moronobu, Harunobu, Utamaro, Sharaku, Hokusai, and Hiroshige that we are inclined to forget that other very excellent art also appeared in the seventeenth through nineteenth centuries.

Kanō School The Tokugawa period started off inauspiciously so far as painting was concerned. It was dominated by the celebrated Kanō school. Kanō Eitoku (1543-1590) was the great Momoyama artist who decorated the palaces of Nobunaga and Hideyoshi. The school's leading exponent in the first Tokugawa century, however, was Kanō Tanyu (1602-1674), whose ambitious landscapes and scrolls tend to be imitative. Nonetheless, the Kanō school enjoyed so much fashionable prestige that its members were widely patronized by the shogunate and leading aristocrats. Scrolls like the *Namban emaki* (c. 1600) depicting the arrival of the "southern barbarians," were also done by Kanō painters, indicating that some artists had a certain flourish and interest in current events and ordinary people as well as in classical studies.

Sōtatsu, Kōetsu, and Kōrin Splendid art in the traditional aristocratic mode was also produced by another school, that of Tawaraya Sōtatsu (d. 1643), his close associate Honami Kōetsu (1558-1637), and a later master of the same school, Ogata Kōrin (1658-1716).

They were of merchant class and were chiefly patronized by wealthy persons of the same rank. These clients favored the rich decorative scrolls and screens in which these artists specialized. Sōtatsu, renewing the *yamato-e* tradition, produced large-scale screens of the *Genji monogatari, bugaku* dancers, and seascapes. He also did a series of scrolls, the "Saigyō monogatari emaki," on the life of the priest-poet Saigyō.

Kōetsu represents another strand of Japanese fine arts. He was a sword appraiser by profession but did his creative work in calligraphy, pottery, and lacquerware. The importance of these media for the artistic life of Japan should not be underestimated, and Kōetsu was among their most consummate masters. He was a close friend of several distinguished tea-masters, and his pottery shows their influence; the deliberately rustic and irregular shapes, combined with luminous undertones in the finish and subtle colors that seem to glow from within the bowl itself, reflect the most refined Japanese taste. His lacquer work, in contrast, displays delicate designs that contrast markedly with the rough-hewn force of the tea vessels. Products in both media show his interest in decorative calligraphy.

The art of writing has long been a more important artistic vehicle in East Asia than in the West, understandably in view of the greater variety and potential of the thousands of characters compared to the twenty-six Roman letters. Great calligraphers are as widely known and highly honored as top artists in any other medium, and distinguished calligraphy is as likely to grace a wall or *tokonoma* as is a landscape. Moreover, writing is apt to be an integral part of other works; the short poems that grace many paintings, particularly landscapes of the Sung tradition, are not attachments to the paintings but a living part of them, whose placement has been governed by the harmonies of the picture and whose orthographic style suits the subject and style of the work. Kōetsu's use of calligraphy shows his close relationship to Sōtatsu, considered one of the great calligraphers of his age; he possibly placed the writing on some of Kōetsu's pieces.

Ogata Kōrin brought the decorative tradition to a lavish apex during the elegant and lively Genroku era; his work reflects both its boldness and its taste. His manner of life was equally sumptuous as he became wealthy from his brush; this brought him the disapproval of the shogunate, since show was not considered appropriate for those of his mercantile class. Kōrin's most celebrated work is his iris screen, based on a passage in the *Ise Monogatari*. It shows only a row of iris in three colors—green leaves and flowers in two shades of purple—against a gold background. The effect of the rich colors combined with detail realism and utter simplicity of concept is stunning; it seems to epitomize both an age and a way of life.

Kōrin's brother Kenzan, a potter, was a more subdued, Zen-influenced artist. His work is less pretentious than much other of the age, but pleasing in its own way. For example, his "Flowers in Baskets" shows three tumbly wicker baskets done with rough, bold, dark strokes, almost like a child's; flowers and grasses pour out of them. The poem that dominates the upper part of the sheet is scrawled with a flowing hand that picks up the rhythm of the blossoms and baskets. It reads:

> Flowers, even wild flowers,
> Are enticing,
> Bewitched by their color and fragrance
> The mist of the field emulates them.[1]

Pictures of the Floating World

The term *ukiyo* (floating world or transient world) was originally a Buddhist expression referring to the passing-away of all conditioned things and the sadness of attachment to them. Yet in the Genroku era and after, it acquired a brave, cheerful tone, suggesting delight in the gay world of fashion and entertainment not darkened but only enhanced by the thought of its changeableness. Part of the fascination of the human parade is that it never fails to provide something new and fresh and compelling—and the *ukiyo* folk were always alive to the latest slang, the latest gossip, the latest fad, the latest tips on what is "in" and what is "out." Far from venerating the old and nostalgic with other Japanese aesthetes, for these early moderns the best recommendation for an actor, artist, or style of dress was that it was the latest thing.

Ukiyo-e This world, and the world of daily life and work that swirled around it on the streets of the great cities, was captured by the ukiyo-e (pictures of the floating world) blockprints; the denizens of this world, and merchants intrigued by the demimonde and the daily scene, bought them. The pictures were earthy and were not done with any pretense that great art was being created; not a few blockprints of the day were frankly pornographic. But the best have become recognized as powerful and innovative work in the great tradition of Japanese art.

Moronobu The form was virtually created by Hishikawa Moronobu (1618–1694). He moved from Kyoto to Edo in the 1660s, when the shogunal capital was being rebuilt as a more modern city after the great fire of 1657 and the national cultural center was beginning to move north from the Kansai region of Kyoto and Osaka.

Moronobu was the first to discover that, by using wood-block printing methods already developed for book illustrations, he could manufacture albums of separate prints and large picture sheets that he could sell cheaply enough to command a large market. Many were hand colored. Moronobu drew lively street scenes of priests and samurai on their rounds, of fishermen selling their produce, flower viewing, scenes of the Yoshiwara pleasure district.

Kabuki Prints A favorite topic of ukiyo-e was Kabuki actors, those idolized stars of a disreputable but wildly popular entertainment. Several leading masters of this genre were members of the Torii school of Torii Kiyomasu (ca. 1720–1763). Their work has been regarded and appreciated as "primitives" of the ukiyo-e world for their bold, dark lines and simple, almost expressionless faces. But the swirling, curving lines of the gestures and costumes offer a majestic power; we sense the actor becoming a stage character with his or her gamut of intense, simple emotions.

Sharaku The greatest portrayer of Kabuki actors, and in the opinion of many the greatest of all ukiyo-e artists, was Tōshūsai Sharaku (fl. 1794–95). Virtually nothing is known about this mysterious genius, except that in the year 1794–95 he produced a series of incomparable Kabuki pictures. Why he stopped, what he did before and after that short spurt of brilliant creativity, how he came by his sure and highly individual style, have all been topics of much speculation but no information. We can now only appreciate the results of his one productive year.

The heart of Sharaku's power is his control of facial expression. With a few lines and circles, he created mouths and lines that capture superbly the actors' emotional moods. The actors are usually shown in the strong, clear-cut, set emotional poses of Kabuki drama, splendid and much appreciated masterpieces of the actor's craft: rage, triumph, feminine coyness enacted by *onnagata* (male actors who played female roles). The heavy makeup is colored in with broad strokes that almost recall the smell of the theater. In all, Sharaku manages to communicate unforgettably the combined force, artificiality, and excitement of the theater he obviously loved, and with it the exaltation and sadness of the actor's life.

Portraits of Women Another favorite topic of ukiyo-e art is beautiful women. Their most famous depictors are Suzuki Harunobu (1725–1770), noted for his willowy young ladies decorously whispering secrets or wading in a stream, and Kitagawa Utamaro (1755–1806), whose beauties exude a more languid and sensuous air. None-

This woodblock print shows the Kabuki actor Shigemaki as onnagata, or male actor playing a female role. The artist is Torii Kiyomasu. (Courtesy Museum of Fine Arts, Boston, Spaulding Collection. © Copyright 1979. All rights reserved.)

theless, these women are often engaged, though in a curious and charmingly passive manner, in the ordinary business of a woman's life: cooking, caring for children. Others of his most famous pictures are set poses of elegant courtesans of the Yoshiwara.

Hokusai and Hiroshige

The art of the final decades of the Tokugawa regime was dominated by two print artists, Katsushika Hokusai (1760–1849) and Ichiryūsai Hiroshige (1797–1858), who brought that medium to its highest pitch of versatility and mastery. They carried printmaking considerably beyond the ukiyo-e in range, making it an art form virtually as effective as painting. Like many Japanese artists and writers, they confusingly used several names in the course of their careers but are generally known now as Hokusai and Hiroshige.

Both were late enough to be influenced by the Western art in-

"High Waves off Kanagawa" is one of the famous thirty-six views of Mt. Fuji by Hokusai Katsushika (Courtesy Consulate General of Japan, N.Y.)

troduced by the Dutch traders at Nagasaki. Both were interested in the lives and work of ordinary people, as were the ukiyo-e artists, but they favored the scenic countryside and peasant villages over the metropolis. Both are most famous for landscapes, but generally the landscapes included people at work or travel; Hokusai is particularly noted for studies of such laboring folk as carpenters, spinners, and weavers.

Hokusai is the more varied and original of the two. His genre studies, like those of daily work, are of unfailing fascination, and his landscapes are striking in their control of composition and use of unusual angles of vision. His views of Mt. Fuji, including the world-famous view through a curling wave of the great peak that is virtually Japan's trademark, show that he does not so much copy nature as remold it to fit the requirements of drama and geometry.

Hokusai's great volume of work has risen and fallen in critical favor. When Japanese art first began to make a major impression on European painting after the opening of Japan, Hokusai's influence in this cross-fertilization was second to none. Later, partly because of poor reproductions of his prints, his importance was downgraded. Now, once again, his originality and masterful control of line are being appreciated, as well as the great humanistic and social-historical value of his scenes of traditional life—a way of life that passed away sooner than anyone in his time would have expected.

Hiroshige's art is more subdued and restricted in topic than that of the flamboyant Hokusai. Much of his work is landscapes, in which people usually appear as small detail figures, as though overwhelmed by the immensity of nature. His rain and snow scenes, marvels of mood and of the juxtaposition of blocks of grays and whites, are his most famous work; quiet and atmospheric rather than flashy, they show a mastery of light and subtle harmony. Hiroshige produced a remarkable number of prints; one estimate is 5,460.

MODERN ART

Like everything else, art was thrown into confusion by the opening floodgates of the Meiji period. Suddenly the Japanese past seemed cramped and isolated, and the European models newly available in all their diversity were an almost overwhelming challenge. Some Japanese continued to paint or make prints in traditional manners, but their work lacked confidence and seemed merely derivative. Others sought to paint in the current European styles, especially French impressionism, but their art, while often technically impressive (especially considering the artist's alien background), is generally imitative and does not quite attain first rank.

A break in the hapless situation of artists caught between two worlds was achieved partly under the influence of the American orientalist, Ernest Fenollosa, who taught at Tokyo Imperial University from 1878 on. A well-informed appreciator of East Asian art, Fenollosa vigorously encouraged Japanese artists to maintain pride in their tradition and to allow Japanese art to develop in ways continuous with the tradition, rather than to imitate European styles.

Nonetheless, both European (chiefly French) and Japanese art has continued to be produced. Perhaps the most impressive recent Japanese art has been seen in revivals of traditional forms in which modernistic and cosmopolitan influence is visible in the use of cubistic and other nonrepresentational forms, basic colors, and various motifs of the changing avant-garde world. Examples are the calligraphy of Morita Shiryū and the wood-block prints of Munakata Shikō. Inhibiting tensions between cultures still exist, however. Perhaps that is why, though it has produced extremely gifted exponents of certain genres and secondary media, modern Japan, despite its powerful artistic heritage, has yet to produce a great painter of truly international stature.

Architecture, Gardens, and Other Arts: Miniature Paradises

In this chapter we examine several arts—architecture, gardens, the tea ceremony, and flower arrangement. Although they may seem "minor" to some outsiders, they have played an important role in the traditional Japanese way of life and afford incomparable insights into its spirit. If space allowed, still other crafts and regional arts of real artistic merit could be discussed. Books have been written on Japanese pottery, fabrics, the famous dolls, and even on the lovely and interesting traditional ways of wrapping various objects for transport or sale—for even to this day in Japan, if nowhere else, the package will often be as much a work of art as the contents.

ATTITUDES TOWARD ART

Two basic interlocking attitudes underlie the special meaning that such arts have in Japan. The intellectual background of the attitudes is complex, and includes the Shingon view of art as bringing out the Buddha-nature of the material, Taoist and Confucian attitudes toward following a "way" in what one does, Taoist and Buddhist ideas of paradises, and the immemorial Shinto attitude toward special "pure" places and the beauty of simple, clean, natural objects or handicrafts that mark them. These attitudes can be thought of as aspects of the Japanese spirit, understood (if not always practiced) by virtually all Japanese.

The first is the concept that any meaningful skill or accomplishment to which one applies oneself—such as the mastery of a musical instrument, or the tea ceremony, or flower arrangement, or calligraphy, or painting—is a *dō* (a *tao* or way) like *chadō* (the way of tea). The concept of *dō* adds to these crafts a wealth of spiritual overtones.

They are each not merely a skill, however perfect, that one has attained, much less just a way of making a living. Rather, for the master of tea or flower arrangement, his *dō* becomes, in a phrase much overused but that fits nicely here, a way of life. What one does in the tea hut or with flowers expresses a whole relationship to oneself and the universe and creates attitudes toward existence and nature that ought to permeate one's entire life. At the same time, the time and place devoted to the craft becomes a sort of sanctuary, a place where tension is eased and the universe experienced on a deeper level in those miniature expressions of it.

The second major attitude toward these arts is one that explains the perfection and tranquillity that is sought in them: they create a miniaturization of the universe, in which the universe becomes paradisal harmony. The garden, the tea hut, even the flower arrangement, are not just beautiful—they are beautiful in a special way that gives them cosmic significance. The traditional canons governing their creation indicate that, as in the Sung landscape paintings on which the Japanese garden is in fact based, all the major components of the universe are to be symbolically placed—the masculine and feminine *yang* and *yin* forces, land and water, upper and lower, and so forth. This is done with a *fūryū* rather than an ostentatious hand, and the sense of balance is deliberately diffused by the Japanese eye for tasteful assymmetry; yet the ideal of making a paradisal universe in a backyard garden or even a flower vase remains.

The Japanese place of beauty will be relatively small; this in itself is a characteristically Japanese expectation. Visitors to modern Japan often have difficulty reconciling the people's manifest love of beauty with the widespread ugliness of the modern industrial nation, and with the violence of so much of its past. The secret is that beauty in Japan is essentially seen as a personal rather than a public thing, made by oneself to be enjoyed in one's own way almost as a private therapy, alone or in the company of intimate family or friends.

Today some priceless treasures like temple gardens are open to the public, but their mood is still far from that of the public beauty expressed by the great parks and monuments and proud boulevards of the West. Modern Japanese attempts to emulate the latter have not been very successful aesthetically, for something in the national spirit does not quite grasp them. Traditionally, beauty (like the sacredness of shrines) has been enclosed, walled in. Even imperial palaces are not impressive from outside; they present only forbidding walls to the street. One does not expect to find beauty, unless that of honest labor, on the highways; avenues and buildings are where one goes to make a living, but they are not really *seen*, except for the scroll or flower arrangement even the humblest shop or office is likely to have in a quiet corner. To the Japanese, beauty is seen, but ugliness is not; it does not matter so much how dirty is the factory or littered is the street outside the precincts of loveliness. One sees it no more than one sees the black-robed set-shifter in Kabuki or the puppet-manipulator in Bunraku.

ARCHITECTURE

Architecture in Japan is definitely related to this concept of beauty, for its basic aesthetic function has been to create small private paradises, either for a family or, in religious buildings, for a *kami* or Buddha. Thus, the best examples have striven, unlike much Western architecture, not for the outward, public grandeur of an imposing facade or setting, but for the total control of aesthetic and even subjective environment of the interior space.

The traditional Japanese house, with its straw-mat floors, its sliding-screen walls, its virtual lack of furniture, creates a living space of extraordinary simplicity, even austerity. In its very simplicity this house dominates the lifestyle and suggests a total philosophy of life for those who live in it. Removing one's shoes upon entering suggests decisively transition to a different place from that of the workaday world. Within, one lives a life close to the straw floor upon which one sits and sleeps; the flimsy screen walls seem on the one hand ill-designed for human comfort, for they offer minimal protection against nature. Yet, on the other hand, they make the house a vehicle for flexible expression of human mood in a way that may seem startling to the Westerner caught in rigid walls of wood or stone. The rooms themselves and the light, spare furniture can be shifted with ease; in winter the family huddles under quilts around the faint heat of the charcoal brazier; in summer a whole wall can be opened to the garden, and the lines between indoors and outdoors, between the human and nature, are nearly erased. The word *ma* can mean both an interval of time and a demarcated space like a room; this feature of the language suggests a philosophy of life in which a place and the time one spends in it become a single unity, the nature of the room and the nature of one's activities in it forming each other. Whatever discomforts are endured, they are more than compensated for by the delights of the *ofuro* (the hot bath), whether public or private.

Shinden Style   The peculiarities of traditional Japanese architecture, particularly its incongruity with the temperate climate, are thought to indicate its southern provenance. The earliest known

The thatch-roof houses and trim rice fields of this country village suggest the simplicity and quiet continuities of Japanese life. (Courtesy Japan Air Lines.)

style is that of Ise and other ancient shrines. These buildings have a thatch roof, held down by an exterior ridge pole and short cross pieces, and have high crossing beams called *chigi*. The entire structure is set off the ground on large pillars. Nearly identical buildings can be seen in Indonesia today. Probably such structures were granaries while shrines were still out-of-doors, hence the need for elevation to insure dryness. The same general style was probably also used for homes, at least for important people, in ancient Japan. We may recall that the notion of the home, as well as the granary and shrine, as relatively impermanent is very old and goes back to the days of this thatch and wood building. Shrines were often only temporarily set up in fields at harvest; the Ise shrine is rebuilt every twenty years; and, until the establishment of Nara, the imperial palace and the capital were relocated after the death of each sovereign for reasons of purity.

By Heian times, however, the people "above the clouds" wanted something more lasting and imposing. The *shinden* style was created under continental influence, but expresses well the Japanese desire for architectural "lightness" and rapport with nature, combined with a subtle but total control of the environment by the edifice. No residential examples of *shinden* remain, but it is represented by the Byōdōin temple and in numerous illustrations. The main house of the family faced south, the auspicious siting according to Chinese geomancy; lesser buildings, connected by covered corridors, went around the other three sides. Within those square walls, which excluded sight of anything distasteful, was a small paradise. There would be an artificial lake with streams running into it and islands reached by arched bridges in its center. Memorable parties would be held in the garden, with "verse capping" contests and wine cups floated down the streams. In the main house would be the high screens through which elegant but bored women of high society conversed with friends and behind which they received especially favored guests—often, if the literature of the period is any guide, with compromising results.

Shoin Style During the Muromachi period, a new style, inspired by the Zen temple and specifically by the abbot's quarters, was introduced. Called the *shoin* (literally, writing room) style, it is the basis of the traditional Japanese house today. The *shoin*-style main room is centered around a floor-level writing desk, with a *tokonoma* (alcove) containing *ikebana* (arranged flowers), and perhaps a *kakemono* (hanging scroll) in a corner. The floors are covered with *tatami* (straw mats), and the walls are *shōji* (sliding paper doors and screens).

The supreme examples of the *shoin* style are undoubtedly the main buildings of the Katsura imperial villa on the edge of Kyoto. These light and well-proportioned buildings, set amid hills, gardens, and lakes, have numerous sliding walls that, when opened, each afford a view of unique beauty. Favored rooms exist for such traditional contemplative activities as moon-viewing and snow-viewing. The Katsura retreat fulfills virtually to perfection the *shoin* architectural ideal of combining aesthetically pleasing shelter with as much openness as possible to the even greater beauties of nature.

GARDENS

Virtually any album of the beauties of Japan will give prominent place to photographs of the traditional gardens of the island nation, especially those austere yet somehow unforgettable rock, moss, and gravel landscapes that are the pride of certain great Zen temples. Like most traditional arts of Japan, they have both aesthetic and spiritual meaning. Also like most traditional Japanese arts, they have two sources, native and Chinese.

The idea of a special set-apart place with gnarled old trees and large stones can be traced back to ancient Shinto. Though it is misleading to call Shinto "nature worship" as is often done—the *kami's* role as patrons of clans and families was and is more important than their relation to particular natural phenomena—it is true that its shrines often hallow sites of great natural beauty. These are places where, for both spiritual and aesthetic reasons, one would come to breathe an atmosphere of purity and rejuvenation. Countless Japanese—and foreigners—have felt this atmosphere in the classic gardens of Zen temples and imperial villas.

The transition from outdoor shrine to Zen garden, however, required a massive infusion of Chinese culture. The Chinese garden, most faithfully reproduced in the landscaping of the Heian *shinden*, endeavored to reproduce the islands and grottoes of the immortals of Taoist mythology or of the Buddhist Pure Land. The gardens were sited by geomancy and gave appropriate place to *yang* and *yin* elements. A high *yang* boulder was counterbalanced by a *yin* pond; lines were curved rather than straight; waterfalls were introduced to represent life and bamboo to symbolize strength.

In the garden of the Taizōin the Myōshin temple in Kyoto, one of the most pleasing and philosophical of Zen gardens, the visitor enters by passing between two rock gardens representing respectively *yang* and *yin*. One then proceeds through paradisal landscaping to a lovely pond, where benches allow one to sit and meditate. One can imagine that the pond stands for the great Tao itself, the unity beyond all polarities of *yin* and *yang.*

In the Ashikaga period, under Zen influence, Japanese gardens became more abstract. They strove to reproduce the elements of the Sung landscape painting and so were really imitations of Chinese art rather than of Japanese nature. Because of their association with the meditative Zen way, they were intended to be objects of contemplation rather than places for strolling. In the new Muromachi gardens were no obvious signs of human presence, no benches or wine cups in the streams. No showy flowers dominated these gardens; they presented nature in the abstract, nature embodied in rock and moss symbolizing its internal principles. The epitome of the abstract garden were the *kare sansui* (dry landscapes) of Zen monasteries, such as the Ryōanji of Kyoto, built about 1500. These gardens have no ponds or streams, but only white gravel neatly raked to resemble waves and eddies washing against scattered moss-lined rocks. As at Ryōanji, the dry rock gardens are usually in a rectangular enclosure that is itself surrounded by broader and greener landscaping, as though to suggest an austerely mystical essence of nature at the heart of its lush and varied outer manifestations.

Attempts have been made to explicate the symbolic meaning of these waterless waves and randomly scattered stones, but the real meaning of these gardens seems to transcend meaning in the ordinary sense. As one looks at these islands breaking their sea of whiteness, the world turns over and they become clouds scudding across an endless sky, or galaxies hurtling over the rim of the expanding universe. The abstract garden is finally not nature, but the Void.

TEA CEREMONY

Discussion of the famous *chanoyu* (Japanese tea ceremony; literally, hot water for tea) logically grows out of talk of gardens, for the tea rite ideally takes place in a traditional garden. In a tea garden, the tea house is the one obvious human artifact—or rather, the transcendent viewing place for contemplating the landscape. The tea house is set at the back of a deep mossy garden and is reached by stepping stones called the *roji* (dewy path).

The house is a very simple structure of bare wood and plaster with shoji screens in the windows, but all is of the highest quality; today, a proper tea house is an expensive investment. The door is low, so that guests must stoop to enter. The only ornaments within are a *tokonoma* flower arrangement and hanging scroll.

While the tea ceremony may include a light repast and several kinds of tea and other drinks, its essence is the graceful making and serving of whipped green tea, a frothy liquid with a fresh astringent taste. Each guest takes in turn the large cup in which it is served, swallows two sips, wipes the rim of the cup, turns it and passes it on, and comments on the aesthetic beauty of the bowl. Inevitably, the service is elegant in the old, cracked, asymmetrical manner of the *fūryū* spirit and is lovingly held by host and guests.

Indeed, the tea ceremony can virtually be regarded as a Zen sacrament, or at least as a sacrament of traditional Higashiyama culture. Several of its major vehicles quietly combine in the rite: garden, flowers, tea, and the *suiboku* painting or calligraphy that probably graces the hanging scroll. Above all, as there was about Yoshimasa's Silver Pavilion, an unspoken and perhaps inexpressible Zen quality lingers in the air when the ceremony is well executed.

The livelier ghost of Hideyoshi, the enthusiastic afficianado of tea and the other bequests of the Ashikaga, is also present. Until they finally had a falling-out, Hideyoshi richly patronized Sen no Rikyū, the greatest of all tea masters and protagonist of *wabicha* (poverty tea), a performance of the rite that emphasized absolute simplicity and ordinariness in its accoutrements. For all that, the newly rich Hideyoshi and his associates embraced the tea rite with a virtual orgy of conspicuous consumption, paying immense sums for museum-quality services, many from China, and sparing nothing in mounting great public tea parties.

The tea ceremony, here shown out-of-doors in a garden, commemorates the fūryū *aesthetic of Zen. (Courtesy Consulate General of Japan, N.Y.)*

FLOWER ARRANGEMENT

The smallest and most abstract of gardens, the ultimate miniaturization of paradise, is the garden indoors, the *ikebana* (flower arrangement). Its practice is another *dō, kadō* (the way of flowers), with its own traditions of refined aesthetics, its hereditary teachers, and its schools. Its masters have devoted their lives to perfecting what might seem to outsiders a relatively trivial matter, the arrangement of cut flowers. But their craft is not seen as trivial in Japan, where perfection in anything is admired and where the traditional Zen-related arts of Higashiyama culture are regarded as sure hallmarks of cultivation.

Every traditional home, like the tea house, has a *tokonoma* calling for ikebana to bespeak the taste and skill of the household to guests. More elaborate arrangements form the centerpieces for banquets and nowadays add a touch of color and tradition to offices and department store showcases.

The principles of ikebana are those we have encountered in related arts: simplicity, asymmetry, and form more important than color (even as the most refined gardens had no flowers and *suiboku* was considered more subtle than palette painting).

A mother instructs her daughter in ikebana, *the traditional art of flower arrangement. (Courtesy Consulate General of Japan, N.Y.)*

Like Nō, ikebana at its best hints of mysterious meaning, whether in the very old and elaborate *rikka* (standing) style or in modern constructions that are often very free and highly imaginative, the floral equivalents of surrealism. Most popular and conventional is the Tokugawa period *ten-chi-jin* (heaven, earth, man) style, which is supposed to contain three elements, one high, one low, and one in the middle on the opposite side from the low branch. While the structure is determined, the artist can employ nature's endless bounty of flowers, grasses, leaves, sticks, and stems to create the age-old pattern in a fresh manner.

Part Four
Dance before
the Cave:
Literary, Musical,
and Dramatic Arts

In the *Kojiki* we are told that when Amaterasu hid in the rocky cave of heaven after her brother's outrages, the heavens and the earth were darkened, and the myriad *kami* met in the celestial riverbed to decide what to do. After a time, a goddess arose to do a brazen, hilarious, and shamanistic dance. The parliament of gods burst into divine laughter. Amaterasu, lovely and eager, stuck her head out to see what the revelry was all about, and she was lured on by a mirror, originally part of the dancer's headdress.

Those arts that portray serial events and require unfolding in time—whether they are read, heard, acted, or danced—may be compared to the performance before the cave. Beautiful in themselves, they seek to evoke light within the dim caverns of the psyche and call forth mysterious beauty. The four chapters of this part endeavor to explore the dance before mystery and light as represented by drama, poetry, prose literature, and the modern world's entry in this everlasting quest, cinema.

We begin with an impressionistic account of a famous No play that captures not only the essence of that sublime art but of all Japanese literature, which perennially seeks the distilled essence of whatever motion or scene it ventures to create. We then look more systematically at other forms of dance and drama, beginning with the ancient Shinto *kagura* (sacred dance), a backdrop for all the classical Japanese stage arts. We consider Japanese music and its varied instruments, because music in Japan is inseparable from poetry and drama. We finally examine more historically No, Kabuki, and modern drama.

In subsequent chapters we trace the splendid heritage of poetry and literature, from ancient song to modern novel. Finally, we look at the world-famous Japanese cinema, a new art in which certain ancient themes of the old culture are revivified.

Dance, Music, and Drama: The Past in the Present

The shrill tones of a flute pierce the still air. Hand drums beat out a complex rhythm, and a chorus dressed in traditional formal male kimonos begins a recitation like an eerie atonal chant interspersed with what seem—to Western ears—to be bizarre yelps and yells. An imposing figure emerges down the long runway leading into one side of the wooden stage from a curtained antechamber. He is, in this case, dressed as a portly Buddhist priest of the Middle Ages—black mitre, golden stole, extremely wide white pantaloons. Walking with impressively slow and deliberate steps, he comes to the center of the stage, which is bare save for two upright evergreen branches on low tables. He speaks in a strange, strangled-sounded tone, and begins an equally strange tale.

The priest, a character in the No play *Tsunemasa* by Zeami, tells us of the Taira scion of that name who was exceptionally fond of the lute and who was killed, along with the rest of his house, in a great sea battle. The Emperor has asked that a lute, which he himself had given Tsunemasa, be presented to a temple built in the warrior's memory; the priest has now come with an assembly of musicians to dedicate that sanctuary.

Then, as a break in the thus-far unremarkable action, comes a ghostly voice from offstage:

> . . . but I, because I could not lie at rest,
> Am come back to the World for a while,
> Like a shadow that steals over the grass.
> I am like dews that in the morning
> Still cling to the grasses. Oh pitiful the longing
> That has beset me!*

*From *The Nō Plays of Japan*, Arthur Waley, trans. (New York: Grove Press; London: George Allen & Unwin Ltd., 1957), p. 82. Reprinted by permission.

No drama is enacted on a traditional stage with the orchestra in the background. (Courtesy Consulate General of Japan, N.Y.)

The company, gathered for its sacred task, remarks that a mysterious human shadow seems to be falling in its midst. The audience sees a brighter vision: down the runway comes a figure in the brilliant court dress of a samurai, his face frozen by a small white mask bearing a subtle smile. It is the revenant of Tsunemasa, restless in the Other World where, because he died in battle, he must expiate his sins by continually doing battle with demons. He is drawn back by the mention of his name in prayers and above all by the lute that he loved. The lute is struck, and the ghost briefly, yearningly recalls the joys of fleshly life by dancing. It is, on the No stage, a slow hieratic dance whose movements are only suggested by the actor's slight, infinitely skillful and controlled gestures as he slowly progresses around the stage. The dance climaxes as the hell-condemned warrior, still accompanied by the tuneless yet fast-paced and oddly haunting music, draws his sword, thrusts, and then strikes himself with it. He laments that the horrible passion of his grim otherworldly warfare is rising within him, and he can no longer stay amongst the music and revels of earth. He vanishes, and the chorus, like the audience deeply moved by this pathos-laden apparition, sings of the iron fate of one whose real love was song rather than sword.[1]

The No is the classic theater that represents a culmination of traditional music, drama, and dance; we can perceive in it something of the essence of all three as they have developed in Japan. No is comprised of short plays lasting only about an hour, in which music and dance are abstracted to the simplest tones and sparest gestures, corresponding to what haiku is in poetry—that essence is very finely distilled indeed. But for that reason No represents a pure form in which music, dance, and drama can be well studied.

THE ROLE OF THEATER

Consider the meaning of No as drama. No has been rightly compared to a strange combination of Greek tragedy and Christian high mass. That is to say, a No play is often one which, like *Tsunemasa*, has all the earmarks of tragedy; yet it is enacted in a peculiarly liturgical manner, with vestments and stylized, symbolic gestures. The No play, like worship, embodies a society's deepest values and the worldview of its religion. This is a role that music, dance, and drama have played in Japan from prehistoric times until the partial adoption of certain Western attitudes.

In the West music has, perhaps, had as central a role as it has in Japan. But, apart from liturgy itself, we tend to think of dance and drama as entertainment. Although the entertainment may be rich, cultivated, therapeutic, and valuable to the soul, the forms are not central to the cohesion or ultimate meaning of the society as a whole. We consider plays and ballets as expressions of the visions of individual writers and artists rather than of the common worldview. In fact, both have also been suspect for religious reasons by forces as strong as Protestant puritanism.

In Japan, in contrast, *kagura* (sacred dance) is absolutely integral to Shinto; its heavy steps, splendid costumes, and hieratic movements are seen as primary ways in which the gods themselves are made manifest to humankind. *Kagura* is said to go back to the dance that the goddess Ame no Uzume did when Amaterasu hid herself in the mythic cave. The relation of the No plays to the Zen that their original Ashikaga patrons espoused has been much discussed. But a more popular or literary Buddhism than pure Zen comes through in such themes as fate (karma) and hell-suffering in *Tsunemasa;* the Shinto background of No should also be recognized. Not only is the stage modeled on the porch of a shrine where *kagura* is performed, but both the music and the dances of No have *kagura* provenance. Moreover, the common No themes of gods—sometimes transmuted into the ghosts of departed mortals—who appear in dancing form owes more to Shinto, and even to the bits and pieces of Hinduism that came with Buddhism, than to Zen.

Japanese Attitudes

However, the distilled-essence acting style of No is certainly in the spirit of the coeval Zen culture. Another important feature of Japanese music, dance, and drama is simply that they are *theater*. In other words, the stage, the masks and makeup, the highly unconventional voices—all that makes the enactment obviously a *performance*—are not minimized or eliminated as they might be in the drama of "realism" but are enhanced to extremes. This is true not only of No, but also of *kagura*, of Shinto and Buddhist liturgy, of Kabuki—of all premodern Japanese stagings. The attitude is also receiving a brilliant revival, after some unmemorable experiments with Western naturalism, in the symbolism and surrealism of such contemporary playwrights as Abe Kōbō.

The Japanese attitude is that truths deeper than ordinary knowledge can be revealed precisely through actions that show that the stage is no ordinary space or time and the actors no ordinary persons. Because they are stylized, even the faces perhaps concealed by enigmatic masks, the actors and dancers of the Japanese stage become universalized, and their rage or sorrow or celebration becomes everyone's. They represent ranges and depths of universal feelings not everyone has consciously explored. The actor not only brings them to the surface but also magnifies them. Then, every nuance of feeling and every ampere of buried intensity can be thoroughly explored. Even the appearing gods and ghosts of No can be, and often have been, regarded not so much supernatural as dramatic manifestations of the archetypes and shadows of things past sunk like depth charges in everyone's psyche. Thoughts like these—and the shuddery feelings they evoke—are superbly stimulated by the sorcery of traditional Japanese performance with its non-natural enhancements.

In Japan the actor's craft is generally very highly regarded, and in turn the actor brings to it a consummate professionalism. Japanese theater is basically actor's theater; the performances of master actors, rather than story or setting, is what Japanese theater-goers respond to most, and the demanding mastery of No or Kabuki leads requires a life-long commitment. Traditionally, the acting profession and serious *kagura* as well have been the business of certain theatrical families, in which training begins very young.

DANCE

Kagura We have observed that dance has been a major part of the spiritual culture of Japan from the world of the *Kojiki* to that of today. At most larger Shinto shrines, the visitor can see *miko* (graceful maidens in red and white) who perform dances as parts of offerings or festivals. More rarely, lavishly bedecked male *kagura* dancers can be seen. These shrine dances are generally slow, harmonious, and given to aesthetic poses.

A different sort of *kagura* is the performances of the semishamanistic *yamabushi*, mountain ascetics who practice rites of possession and healing after initiation. Rarely seen today, *yamabushi kagura* begins slowly and builds to an incredibly intense climax of whirling and gyrating to indicate the possessing presence of the deity.

Another form is *sato kagura* (village sacred dance). These folk dances are considerably more lively than shrine *kagura*, and often good-naturedly obscene elements appear; these derive in part from magical gestures intended to promote the fertility of the fields. These dances would be performed at the village *matsuri* as part of the festivity.

All *kagura* have a twofold sacred meaning; some sources emphasize one side and some the other. The sacred dances are offerings to the god, like the offerings of food, presented for the deity's pleasure; they are also viewed as manifestations of deity through human impersonators, and their vigorous rhythms, extraordinarily slow or fast, represent divine activity. One of their ultimate origins undoubtedly is shamanism; like the *yamabushi kagura*, they were thought to be the actual performance of a god inhabiting temporarily a human body.

Japan has many other forms of folk dance besides *kagura*. Traditionally, dance was an important part of agricultural work. The backbreaking labor of rice planting, transplanting, and harvesting was made easier by rhythm and song and dance-like steps, which were then carried over into colorful dances representing these chores. We have already mentioned the Ōbon dances by which returning ancesters were greeted in this midsummer festival. New Year's has also had its share of popular dances, some enacting colorful *marebito* (mysterious visitors) who in some districts go from house to house at that season demanding favors, like American trick-or-treaters at Halloween.

Bugaku   At the other end of the scale are the fascinating and important *Bugaku* (court dances). These dances are performed to ancient music called *Gagaku*. Among the oldest living music and dance forms in the world today, they ultimately derive from folk dances of mainland Asia and were prominent among the ceremonial performances of the T'ang dynasty court in China. They were imported to the Japanese court early in the Nara period. Although

Bugaku and *Gagaku* died out completely in China and elsewhere, these forms were never lost in Japan. They are still performed at the imperial court in Tokyo and at a few major shrines.

Bugaku costumes are extraordinarily colorful. Although ponderous, the dances have a vigor and archaic atmosphere of their own. All dancers are male, and typically four perform in each dance. Some dances are military, enacting ancient arts of war; some interpret the rejoicing of gods; some perpetuate their obvious folk background by choreographing a snake hunt or the dances of the monkey-king.[2]

Dance is an art that eminently suits Japanese culture from village to court. Japan's is a culture with strong Apollonian strands emphasizing form and style. It has a deep sense of grace and control and can appreciate the subtleties of slight but polished gestures. For all of this the dance is an ideal form of aesthetic expression. At the same time, Japanese society has strong communal sensitivity. The traditional village knew itself to be a community of shared lives and shared values in a way that most moderns, both East and West, have lost. This communalism was the matrix of folk dance—in turn the ultimate mother of more formal dance—for communal dance creates and expresses community even as it amuses and manifests the community's gods. Both Japanese aesthetics and sociology, then, have conspired to make Japan a land in which dance is a very highly developed art, and one that has easily merged into its performance-oriented theater.

MUSIC

Even though it is nonverbal, music often seems almost as hard to translate from one culture to another as poetry. The traditional music of Japan is as subtle and skillful as that of any other culture. Yet, to the average Westerner, it is likely to appear to be an assemblage of strange, deceptively simple-looking instruments, and to sound more like the exciting but random notes of nature than the tunes of a Schubert or a Victor Herbert. The listener may grant that the strong percussion has its intoxicating quality and the flute-like instruments their ghostly charm, but he will miss the melodiousness that to many Westerners *is* music. (The more knowledgeable critic, however, will recall that both medieval and contemporary Western music resemble more the oriental notion of what music can be than does European music of the "classical" period.)

How then shall we understand Japanese music? Two fundamental historical facts may help to set its enduring characteristics in perspective. First, one major ultimate source of traditional Japanese music is the Shinto *matsuri*, with its vibrant dancing and its oracular shaman songs sung to a zither ancestral to the modern *koto*. In this setting, music is not produced chiefly to enjoy a tune or listen to a performer. It is, rather, intended to induce the "participation mystique" of a community acting together and to alter consciousness in a way that stories come alive and the listener is sensitive to divine activity. Music is, in other words, a communal matter instrumental in the creation of a special time with a different "feel" about it than the ordinary. The same quality can be sensed today in the unmelodious and unearthly drums, flutes, and voices of No, Shinto worship, or Buddhist chant.

Second, let us consider the close relation of music to story. Traditionally, no story was properly told unless half-chanted and accompanied by at least such a simple instrument as a pair of wood clappers to keep up the rhythm and entrance the listener into a receptive state of mind in which the dream-like world of fox-spirits or samurai heroes could become real, even as the Hollywood movie today has its background music. The music of *Bugaku*, No, and Kabuki is of the same order. Vocal expression, whether in narrating or acting, is central to Japanese music. All the major instruments developed basically as accompaniments to the human voice or the dance, or as background to a cultivated party. They are, in other words, aids in the weaving of a magical world of which the human tongue or gesture is the prime creator. This accompaniment rather than concert nature of traditional instruments explains much about them: their apparent simplicity, their lightness of tone, and also the iridescent range of feeling of which they are capable in the hands of a master, for stories have many moods.

When instruments are played simply for their own sake, the performer is likely to be shamanistic or playful in expressing a mood or spontaneous series of moods. Japanese and other oriental music has much less than Western the compulsion to "go somewhere," to develop a systematic melody and structure. It treasures more the capacity, rediscovered in Western jazz, to follow the music's own inner voice, to repeat what seems right with perhaps nuanced shadings, to introduce variations without worrying where they lead, to simply enjoy or exploit the tone and texture of the instrument. All of this, of course, really works only in the hands of a master with years of musical discipline and experience. But in such hands, an instrument does not need a well-tempered symphony or concerto; each trill of the *shakuhachi* or twang of the *samisen* is in itself a story or mood out of old Japan.

Musical Instruments

Although a stringed zither-like instrument comparable to the modern *wagon* or *koto* is portrayed in one of the clay *haniwa* figurines from prehistoric times, most Japanese instruments were imported from the mainland. During the Nara period court music and dance were dominated—as were most of the more skilled crafts in the sixth through eighth centuries—by Korean and Chinese artists who played music from the elegant courts of their homelands. Thus *Gagaku*, the musical accompaniment to the *Bugaku* dances, brought in several styles of drums, stringed instruments that are ancestral to the *koto* and *biwa* (lute), and wind instruments such as the doubled-reed *hichiriki* (flutes) and the *shō* (a set of seventeen reed pipes placed in a cup-like circle and blown through a mouthpiece).

The *biwa*, like the Western lute, has a romantic history. Heian literary sources like *Genji* present it as an instrument used to accompany popular songs in courtly settings. In the Middle Ages, a class of blind priests, whose lays were originally thought to exorcize evil spirits, were wandering minstrels who accompanied their songs with the *biwa*. In the Kamakura period, they rendered long narrative recitations to this instrument; the *Heike Monogatari* originated in *biwa* epics.

Hardly less romantic is the *shakuhachi* (Japanese flute). An early form of this flute was among the ancient *Gagaku* instruments, but it was not until the Muromachi period that it came into its own, when it was adopted by other wandering beggar priests. Early in the Tokugawa era, it was taken up by a new kind of wandering priest, the *Komusō*. This colorful religious order was actually comprised of *ronin* (masterless samurai), whose lords had been on the wrong side in the bloody wars leading up to the Tokugawa triumph. Many had been Christians before the persecution of that faith. With some cause, given the tenor of the times, they feared that the new masters of Japan might not yet have finished in their dealings with erstwhile foes. Thus, one group of such desperate men sought what sanctuary temple and cloth might afford, and as an added safeguard the *Komusō* covered their heads with large straw baskets that completely concealed their identities. From beneath this basket-hat protruded a *shakuhachi*, played to solicit alms for the order. Bending with the times, the *Komusō* also arranged, in the course of their Edo-period wanderings, to serve as spies for the government.

Komusō can still be seen occasionally on the streets of modern Japan, and the *shakuhachi* is a traditional instrument that has never lost popularity. Its Edo associations and its soft, plaintive tones make it, for many, the very spirit of old Japan. It is one traditional instrument for which there is a small but exquisite body of concert music, both solo and duet; public performances are frequent today, and the body of amateur enthusiasts of the instrument is not small. Related types of flutes are used in the No orchestras and in Shinto and Buddhist religious music.

Two stringed instruments, the *koto* and *samisen*, also have powerful associations with the "old Japan" of the Edo era. The *koto* and the related *wagon* are mentioned in connection with highly romantic situations in the *Genji*. All through medieval literature, woman are known—and sometimes their hiding places are discovered—by the beauty of their *koto* playing. The slow, languid music of the instrument has also been used by shamans to induce trance. The *koto* has a considerable literature of artistic music that transcends its romantic and "floating world" linkages, however; this makes its acquaintance one of the graces of traditional cultivation and has led some to suggest that the *koto* may have a brilliant future in the hands of fresh composers who are able to break out of traditional styles of expression.

Much the same can be said about the *samisen*. Introduced from the Ryūkyūs in the sixteenth century, this banjo-like instrument also has rich ties with the old-fashioned entertainment quarters but is much more as well. It is basic to the music of Kabuki and the Bunraku puppet theater, is a mainstay of party music, and is as essential to folk music in Japan as the fiddle—more recently, the guitar—is to American folk music. There is also a body of art music for the *samisen*, though its main genre is as accompaniment for recitation, song, and dance. The most important forms are called *Gidayū* and *Nagauta*. The former is the music of Bunraku, narration done to the accompaniment of the instrument and capable of a truly amazing range, from low rumbles to high squeaks, which reflects an emotional power well complemented by the hard, crisp tones of the *samisen*. *Nagauta* (long song) is the heart of Kabuki music and best expresses the lyrical possibilities of the *samisen*, possibilities also explored in various popular ballads and lyrics. Standard *nagauta* have six sections, each with its own emotional tone; each is reflected on stage by appropriate song or dance advancing the story.

Instruments other than the *samisen* are used in the Kabuki ensemble; in fact, a remarkable range of drums, bells, and clappers is available for special effects. But the *samisen*, its fast-paced melodious clacks exactly right for enhancing the unfolding excitement of drama, reigns supreme.

Two stringed instruments little played at present but of some historical importance should also be mentioned: the *kokyū* and the *kokin*. Both are played with bows like the violin and produce comparable sounds, though they have less range than the violin. For that reason they have been generally replaced by it, except as curiosities.[3]

Western Music in Japan Although Japan has a rich native musical tradition, modern Japan is also a stronghold of classical and popular Western music. The first important Western influences were the military band music and missionary-brought Christian hymns introduced in the Meiji period, and traces of these forms can still be heard in Japanese popular music. But Japan soon took the great tradition of Western music to heart as well. Traveling orchestras generally play to full houses in Tokyo or Osaka, and Japanese artists, such as the well-known conductor Seiji Ozawa, have attained international reputations. Education in Western music is now regarded as one of the essentials of cultivation, as accomplishment on the *koto* once was; walking of a quiet Sunday morning through the more stylish residential districts of any Japanese city, one can hear novice piano or violin attempts on Schumann or Chopin from virtually every other house. The passion of Japanese youth for international jazz and rock is well known and may be witnessed in the thousands of coffee houses that enliven the Shinjuku district of Tokyo.

Music is part of the soul of Japan. Like dance and drama, it is experienced as a natural way of being alive—not as something exotic, but as something that humanizes.

NO

No, the first great classical theater, had many origins. The *Bugaku* dances imported from the continent at the beginning of the Nara period certainly influenced it. So did *Gigaku*, a more lively dance entertainment brought from China as early as 612; *Gigaku* now survives in the lion dances popular in many village festivals. Both these dance forms centered on masked portrayals of gods and heroes and a supernatural atmosphere. The masks of *Gigaku* are worthy of special mention. Unlike the more archetypal visages of *Bugaku* and No, they are lively and, whether fierce or humorous, have a hearty flavor of individuality and personality.

No's most immediate antecedent, somewhat surprisingly, was a quite boisterous circus-like entertainment originally imported from China, known as *sangaku* or *sarugaku* ("monkey music"). It featured such crowd-pleasing but not terribly elevated acts as juggling, acrobatics, performing animals, and satirical skits. We have only the titles of *sarugaku* playlets, but little imagination is needed to summon up the slapstick and raucous laughter of plays called "The Head Clerk of a Temple Slips on the Ice and Loses his Trousers" or "The Country Bumpkin's First Visit to Kyoto." No performance still retains a reminder of its ancestry in *sarugaku* in *Kyōgen* (*Wild Words*), the humorous interludes usually staged between the major No dramas of an afternoon or evening program.

However, during the Middle Ages *sarugaku* absorbed new influences and expanded its repertoire to include solemn or aesthetic moments as well as tumbling and broad humor. One was *Dengaku* ("field music"), the folk dances that by the fourteenth century had become a rage. Elegant performances of these popular musicals, embellished with elaborate costumes and poetic songs, were mounted by great lords. Another influence was *Ennen* (*To Prolong Years*). Originally a prayer ceremony for the longevity of a distinguished patron, *Ennen* came to be enacted by traveling troupes and included dances and plays with appropriately elevated language.

Nor should the origins of No in native Shinto *kagura* be overlooked. The oldest No play—and also the most frequently performed even today—is *Okina* (*The Old Man*). Of unknown authorship, it is said to derive from an occasion when an old man was observed dancing under a spreading evergreen tree at the Kasuga Shrine in Nara; the ancient one turned out to be the god of the shrine. That tree, the Yōgō Pine, is painted on the backdrop of every No stage.

Kannami and Zeami During the shogunate of Ashikaga Yoshimitsu in the late fourteenth century, *sarugaku*, *dengaku*, and *ennen* troupes were playing in courts and communities alike and were borrowing each other's acts. In 1374 a climactic event for the development of No occurred when Yoshimitsu, only seventeen but already an accomplished connoisseur of culture as well as master of the country, attended the performance of a *sarugaku* troupe founded by one Kannami, who danced the lead in *Okina.* Yoshimitsu was immensely taken by the power and possibilities of the old man's acting and that of his son, Zeami. The shogun extended his patronage and friendship to both.

With this august support and the freedom it gave them to develop No in accordance with its own genius, Kannami and the even more brilliant Zeami produced a new dramatic form that, from its first unshackled moments, possessed an astonishing maturity and depth. The mysteriously appearing ghosts and gods were no mere dramatic effects, but voices from out of the furthest reaches of human experience, telling poignantly of universal pathos stretched to the highest pitch—of love, beauty, joy, and sorrow, and of how their substance eternally eludes our grasp, save in dreams and memories.

Zeami, as important for his theoretical writings on No as for

This No mask was created by an artist of the seventeenth century; this is the style used to portray a leading female character. (Courtesy Museum of Fine Arts, Boston, Bigelow Collection. © Copyright 1979. All rights reserved.)

his plays, discussed the inner meaning of No. He compared *monomane* (the "imitation of things" type of acting), good and important in its place, with *yūgen* (acting that has a transcendent charm that suggests the ineffable ultimates of beauty and meaning). The quest for *yūgen* and how best to express it in No was carried on by Zeami's successor and son-in-law, Zenchiku, upon whom Zen influence was marked. It led him to the final extremes of bare stage, minimal props, and understated acting.

Still later, Muromachi, Momoyama, and Tokugawa No plays — most of which are much less frequently acted today than are the original plays of Zeami and his immediate school—reverted to greater dramatic excitement. No did, however, have a colorful history in those centuries. The flamboyant Hideyoshi lavishly patronized No and acted in the plays himself. He particularly favored plays about his own heroic achievements, and in these he would play himself with a flourish.

In the Tokugawa age, with its official Confucian ideology, No came to be well endowed, and also rigorously controlled, by the government as a Japanese equivalent of the "rites" and "music" required in the well-tempered state ruled according to the teachings of the ancient sage. Careful performances of No on state occasions were thought to affect mystically the welfare of the entire realm. Under such conditions innovation was scarcely possible. But highly skilled schools of No performers were maintained; they preserved the art, and so made possible the modern enthusiasm for No both in Japan and abroad, an enthusiasm that—despite the decline of other traditional arts around the world—continues unabated in the late twentieth century.[4]

Characteristics of No   What, then, are the characteristics of No? We have already suggested the general features of the austere stage: the walkway, the pines, the musicians, and the chorus. The action, more like a tableau than a dramatic plot in the Western sense, centers on two principals. The *waki* appears first. His speeches set the background. Very often he is a priest or traveler bound on some mission, as in *Tsunemasa*, that recalls haunted memories from the past. He then encounters a strange character, masked and splendidly garbed; this is the *shite* (the main performer). The *shite* plays one of five types of beings—a god, a hero, a woman (usually deeply enmeshed in hopeless love), a contemporary grandee, or a demon—depending to which of five traditional categories this play belongs. Gradually, the *waki* realizes that the mysterious visitor is a ghost or otherwise supernatural figure, drawn to this place and time by some deep power or attachment. During the last part of the play, the *shite* dances, with very decorous, symbolic motions in which a step can represent a long journey. As he dances the deep meaning of his appearance is made more and more manifest, and the sense of *yūgen* the episode induces is increasingly intensified.

Nonomiya   As an example, let us examine the play *Nonomiya* (*The Shrine in the Fields*), a "woman play" ascribed to Zeami. It is related to the scene from *The Tale of Genji* presented in the first chapter of this book and is another in a series of examples related to the Saigū institutions. The choice of *Nonomiya*, however, requires no apology, for it is one of the most powerful of all No plays.

The Nonomiya, we may recall, was a shrine-like residence at which the princess destined for duty as priestess at the Saigū at Ise underwent purification. In the earlier selection from *Genji*, we observed that the Prince had visited the Nonomiya to see the Lady Rokujō, whose daughter was preparing for Ise.

In the harsher days of the medieval civil wars, Heian peace and magnificence was a glory departed forever. An itinerant priest, the *waki*, opens the play by visiting the ruins of the Nonomiya— symbolized by the single prop, a simple wood *torii* set up on a stage.

This masked No actor could be the protagonist of Nonomiya. *When worn by a true artist, the mask itself is said to become alive and expressive. (Courtesy Japan Air Lines.)*

As the holy man muses and prays, a girl appears singing to herself these lines:

> Shrine in the Fields
> Where I have lived with flowers . . .
> What will be left when autumn has passed?

And:

> Each year on this day,
> Unknown to anyone else,
> I return to the old remains . . .
> What remains now to recall
> The memories of the past . . .*

The priest and the girl speak to each other. She tells him that each year on this day, the day when Genji visited the place and slipped a gift to the Lady Rokujō (here called by her title Miyasudokoro), she returns—unknown to anyone else—to sweep and consecrate the shrine. She asks the priest to leave so that she can be alone in this task. Finally we learn that she is herself the shade of Miyasu-

*From *Twenty Plays of the Nō Theatre*, Donald Keene, ed. (New York: Columbia University Press, 1970), p. 184. Reprinted by permission.

dokoro, drawn back to this world by her undying attachments and memories.

A *Kyōgen* interlude follows, in which "a villager" typically gives the Miyasudokoro story in plain language, enabling less well read members of the audience to gain the necessary background for understanding the action of the play.

The priest then determines to offer prayers for the repose of this disturbed spirit. As he does so, his visitor appears again, now in gorgeous court dress that fully reveals her as the highborn lady of the past. She sings and dances, recalling bittersweet memories of that past—that is, from *The Tale of Genji*. She relates her love of the Shining Prince, the painful episode at the Kamo Festival when her carriage was pushed aside to make way for that of the Princess Aoi, Genji's wife. She tells us that the agony and attraction alike of those bygone days make her return again and again in suffering and delusion, and she begs to be made free of it. The play ends on a somber note, with these lines:

> I, whom he visited,
> And he, my lover too,
> The whole world—turned to dreams,
> To aging ruins;
> Whom shall I pine for now?
> The voices of pine-crickets
> Trill *rin, rin,*
> The wind howls:
> How I remember
> Nights at the Shrine in the Fields!*

This autumnal scene is the very essence of No: the sense of yearning, of beings haunted by the past and caught between worlds in a many-wondered universe, even as our own minds are caught by the haunting movement and poetry.[5]

KABUKI

Two important new dramatic forms appeared in full-bloom in the Tokugawa period: the Bunraku or *jōruri* puppet theater, immortalized in the work of Chikamatsu, and Kabuki, the famous popular theater of the new townsmen. We have already discussed the puppet theater and Chikamatsu in chapter 1. We must now

*From *Twenty Plays of the Nō Theatre*, Donald Keene, ed. (New York: Columbia University Press, 1970), pp. 190–191. Reprinted by permission.

turn our attention to Kabuki, the theater of another era, which—like No—has continued to inspire the loyalty of both Japanese and foreigners.

Actors and Acting

Kabuki owed much to No and *Kyōgen*, both in stories—many of the most famous Kabuki plays were adapted from the No stage—and in the stylized manner of acting. Like No's, Kabuki's direct antecedent was much less reputable. The word was first used for a troupe of female dancers who performed in Kyoto around 1600. Although based on the folk-Buddhist *Nembutsu* dancing, these Kabuki performances also included highly suggestive farcical skits, and the women's reputations both on and off stage were not the best. But the act was very successful and led to many imitations. The new Tokugawa government, informed by a puritanical Confucianism, responded by outlawing female Kabuki performances. When handsome young men were substituted, the repute of the genre did not improve. After 1652 actors were required to be adult males or youths whose forelock was shaved so that they appeared adult. From then on Kabuki developed into a true art form and a theater with it own reigning families, colorful traditions, and thespian styles. Its position with the government was still sometimes precarious, but, despite its unsavory character in the eyes of the authorities, its role as an emotional safety-valve was not unappreciated.

At its highest development, Kabuki was supremely actor's theater. Its stories were unabashedly melodramatic, of little worth save as vehicles for the talents of actors who were able to give the roles the exaggerated but intensely moving treatment idealized by this theater.

The stage itself was constructed, under the influence of No, so as to emphasize the centrality of the actor. At one side the orchestra was seated, dressed in gray and black kimonos. Down the other side, stretching nearly the whole length of the theater, was the *hanamichi* (flowery way) on which the lead, perhaps in samurai garb, would enter slowly and deliberately, striking powerful heroic poses at nearly every step.

The special quality of Kabuki acting and dancing, especially the *aragoto* style favored in Edo, must be appreciated. It emphasized greatly the force of the hero and the evil of the villain by extremes of dress and gesture. Elaborate, fearsome makeup is a part of *aragoto* as well. At its very heart are the strong, highly theatrical poses hero and villain assume as they circle, half-dancing, about each other in combat.

Equally at the heart of Kabuki, though, are the *onnagata*

A scene from the Kabuki drama Musume Dōjōji *shows the lavishly costumed lead in the foreground and the orchestra of drums and samisen in back. (Courtesy Consulate General of Japan, N.Y.)*

(woman-actor's roles). Since actresses were forbidden on the Kabuki stage, female roles had to be taken, as in No, by males. The greatest *onnagata* actors have become legendary in their ability to capture to the slightest nuance the rhythm of feminine walking, speaking, and fluttering of fans; with white makeup, elaborate coiffures, and rich kimonos they are indeed an impressive sight and a triumph of the actor's art.

Some Kabuki plays have been built around *onnagata* roles. One of the most popular is *Musume Dōjōji*, based on an old legend about the beautiful daughter of a lord. Apparently in cruel jest, her father told her that she was betrothed to a certain priest who stopped at their home. She made advances toward the celibate, who, fearful for his salvation, escaped and hid inside a temple bell. The maiden pursued her love, undeterred by floodwaters; changing herself into a serpent, she crossed a raging torrent and coiled herself around the bell. The bell melted from the heat of this serpentine embrace, and the reluctant priest perished.

Several Kabuki versions of this story have been staged. All clearly give expansive opportunity for colorful settings, changes of costume, and above all dances that were an *onnagata* speciality, representing several different "feminine" moods—love, joy, despair, and rage.

Kabuki plays drawn from No became especially popular in the Meiji period. An example is *Tsuchigomo* (*The Ground Spider*), based on ancient legends of giant spiders that can take human form. The story tells of a sick nobleman who is visited by a Buddhist high priest at midnight. Ostensibly the prelate is on a mission of mercy, but in fact he is a spider in disguise and seeks to kill the hero by sorcery. The nobleman manages to draw blood, and the spider withdraws, leaving a crimson trail. The hero and his retainers pursue, and after a lengthy battle they slay the monster. This play affords incomparable opportunities for dramatic dance, makeup, and special effects. The spider tries to ensnare its adversaries in its web, which is represented by long paper streamers on stage; its demonic face is painted with terrifying power.

The supreme technique of the Kabuki actor came to be known as *mie;* the word has passed into ordinary language to mean seeking a dramatic effect or "playing to the galleries." The *mie* is actually the rigid pose that the actor strikes at the climax of his passion—the pupils of his eyes dilated with emotion, fingers outstretched, head slowly turning toward the audience—as wooden clappers in the orchestra beat rapidly to heighten the tension.

Kabuki, for all its staginess, is superb theater. The skills of its great performers are the achievements of a lifetime. To attend Kabuki today is not only to move delightfully into the world of classic Japanese culture of the Tokugawa era but also to see acting unexcelled anywhere for technical skill.[6]

MODERN THEATER

Shingeki (modern theater of the Western sort) has had a mixed career in Japan. Before the Second World War, plays, such as those of Ibsen, were performed in translation in Japan, as were Western-style "realist" works by Japanese writers. They were not highly successful or influential, however, partly because they were out of touch with the expectations and genius of Japanese theater, and partly because *shingeki* tended to propagandize for ideologies that were increasingly uncongenial to the nationalistic state.

After the war the situation changed somewhat. The nontraditional stage theater still has only a limited appeal, now because people of innovative theatrical talent have largely been drawn to the far more brilliant and successful world of Japanese cinema. However, some playwrights have succeeded in reviving the traditional Japanese use of the exaggerated and bizarre in the theater to illumine hidden subsurface aspects of the human condition by casting them in the mold of modern Western avant-garde, surrealistic drama. Here Japanese theater has managed to break free of both its own culture and didactic realism to achieve true international importance.

Nonetheless, playwrights have usually also been novelists and script writers, for the nontraditional theater is simply not large enough, apart from translated imports, to sustain many independent authors. Sometimes the combination of media has been very creative. Perhaps the best known contemporary author who has written for the stage is Abe Kōbō (1924-). The author of the novel that lay behind the celebrated film *Woman in the Dunes*, Abe's dramas are no less original and striking.

In *The Animal Hunter*, for example, Abe pictures an ordinary household to which is unexpectedly delivered a large cage containing two creatures, to all appearances humans clad in animal skins, which are incapable of speech beyond yips and whines. They are a remarkable new kind of pet that a company is offering to them on a trial basis. The resultant confused reactions and discussion among the family provide remarkable insights on what we assume it means to be human and how those assumptions are shaped in turn by social expectations.

Japanese theater, ancient and modern, has at its best been characterized by its ability to probe, through breathtakingly fantastic but telling images, to the very roots of social form and the deep-seated loves and fears that shape the individual. At the same time, it is very conscious of what the theater is, what its unique skills and possibilities are, and how it works. For these reasons it is, in every sense of the phrase, a theater of the world.

Poetry:
A Nation of Poets

In few cultures is the enjoyment of reading, reciting, and composing poetry a more common occupation than in Japan. In the modern West, unfortunately, reading and writing poetry is often considered to be a rather precious pastime.

In Japan the situation has always been quite different. There, poetry books, magazines, and newspaper columns are immensely popular. Now, as in the Nara and Heian periods, drinking parties are not complete without the recitation and spontaneous creation of verse for the occasion, and games involving the "capping" or identification of poetic lines are enjoyed by all classes. Moreover, millions of ordinary Japanese—stationmasters and shopkeepers as well as "literati"—not only take pride and pleasure in writing verse, but publish it in countless local or national poetry magazines.

Yet, despite its impressive popularity, the traditional styles of Japanese poetry (excluding for now the poetic character of No and Bunraku drama) that account for most of the enthusiasm show, by Western standards, a remarkably limited range of theme, mood, and technique, though the depth and versatility of Japanese poetry within its self-imposed limits is second to none. True, the works of both the earliest poets and of modern writers since the Meiji era have shown more flexibility than the long centuries of "classic" verse; over the last century, cosmopolitan "new poets" have attempted, with varying degrees of success, to recreate in Japanese most of the Western poetic forms. However, public taste has continued to favor two enduring traditional forms, the *tanka* or *waka* of five lines and thirty-one syllables and the *haiku* of three lines and seventeen syllables.

CHARACTERISTICS
OF JAPANESE POETRY

Form These definitions immediately suggest that in traditional Japanese poetry, as in the English sonnet, length and form are very important—and indeed they are. The mainstays of English poetry are rhythm and rhyme even though some forms do not use them. The Japanese language has no stressed meter or much capacity for meaningful rhyme, though assonance and alliteration are important. Rather, the formal definition of poetry has to do with numbers of lines and syllables. Tanka and haiku are very short forms; their brevity excludes many forms—the epic, the narrative, the long lyric poem—that are important in Western verse. However, some compensation lies in the fact that in traditional Japanese literature poetry and prose are often combined. Works that employ both, such as the mythological epic and the unique "poetic diary," have been popular in the past; these are essentially composed of episodic narratives in which events climax in an insight, an exchange of notes, or a song expressed in verse. The prose often has a poetic flair, and the true poetry grows naturally out of it. Moreover, Zeami's No plays and Chikamatsu's puppet plays contain much that is really long poetry, and poetry of a very high order.

The definitions of tanka and haiku in terms of length may seem overly formal and arbitrary, but the poetry is not simple or perfunctory. Their brevity is in fact bound up with a whole concept of the poetic art that, in turn, offers profound insights into the Japanese experience.

Images The most important feature of all in Japanese poetry is the nature of its effect. Each poem in the traditional forms focuses on a single sight or human interaction and the momentary—though often subtle and complex—feeling it evokes. Japanese poetry is really an expression of emotional response rather than description or narration. It is concerned with the "feel" of things. The poet does not attempt to tell everything in order to capture and communicate the feel of a sight or experience. Rather, he or she will select a tiny clue from within the whole, a particular nuance or symbol that seems to encapsulate the totality in emotionally manageable terms. Just as a snapshot can sometimes catch the certain smile that somehow seems to sum up the whole personality of a loved one—even if that person may actually display the smile only occasionally—so, for the Japanese poet, the fall of a single cherry blossom can powerfully suggest not only the wistful mood called forth by the ending of spring's beauty, but the poignant transitoriness of all that is lovely.

As a modern commentator has put it:[1]

When a Japanese is about to compose a poem, he observes his object until a certain definite feeling comes and crystallizes in his mind. Then he interprets that emotion, using whatever part of the object is necessary to attain the purpose. This means that the material he uses in his poem may be entirely different from what he has observed. Suppose he is writing a poem about a storm scene. He sees the lightning that daggers flying clouds, the wind that uproots towering pine trees, and the roaring billows that batter against frowning cliffs. But the thing he uses in his poem may not be the lightning, or the wind, or the billows, but a single leaf which whirls among driving rain. In order to appreciate a Japanese poem, therefore, one must see, not how true it is to nature, but how true it is to the feel of nature.*

Thus a haiku by the master of the form, Bashō Matsuo:

> Though the winds of autumn blow,
> How very green
> The chestnut burrs.†

Subjects preferred for these feeling-laden images are restricted by convention. Nature has been most popular for several centuries, especially since the emergence of the haiku form in the early Tokugawa period. When describing nature, a poet customarily employs a *kigo* (season-word) to set the scene in spring, summer, fall, or winter. The strictest classical school goes even further; for example, only twenty-five flowers are acceptable as topics for poetry, and such a standby of Western verse as the rose is not included. This comes out of the *miyabi* tradition and the ancient domination of poetry by courtiers who considered only certain topics and moods elegant. Modern poets have gone beyond such restrictions; they write about trash heaps as well as azalea beds.

In the Heian heyday of *miyabi*, when—as we have seen in the case of *Genji*—the exchange of notes inscribed with tankas was a major vehicle of social relationship, especially between the sexes, poetry of love and introspection took pride of place over nature; the incomplete medieval shift from social and amorous topics to nature reflects both the increasing aesthetic influence of Zen and the increasing formal rigor of upper-class morals in feudal times. Yet all the way through, love, and especially the heartache of parting, are common themes, and themes of universal meaning.

*From "The Spirit of Japanese Poetry," Ken Nakazawa. Copyright © by The Atlantic Monthly Company, Boston, Mass. Reprinted by permission.
†All translations, unless otherwise noted, are by the author.

Moods Tradition favors certain moods that are still widely regarded as particularly "poetic." These center around the yearning, melancholy quality suggested by the Japanese words *sabi* and *yūgen*, or the German *Sehnsucht*. Over and over, subtle and elusive beauty, as transitory as it is rich, is sung of, as is love that ends in tearful separation, or is unrequited. Beloved of poets also are the sad calm joys of solitary contemplation.

True, Japanese verse has other forms. The light humorous verse called *haikai* was very popular in the Tokugawa period, as was and is *senryū* (humor or satire in haiku form) like this one:*

> Now the man has a child
> He knows the names
> Of all the local dogs.[2]

Or this more recent one:

> European food—
> Every blasted plate
> Is round.[3]

Folk songs and verses also have presented a naive or festive joy too earthy for the refined blood of court poets, as in this Tokugawa period song for the dances performed as the Ōbon festival, the joyous Buddhist holiday when spirits of the dead in one's family are believed to return and join the living:

> "Are you dancing in the Bon?"
> "Yes—because this year
> There's no babe in my belly
> And I feel light as air."[4]

JAPANESE POETRY FROM A HISTORICAL PERSPECTIVE

We shall now look at poetry characteristic of each major period of its development in Japan. We can only present here a few representative writers, poems, and collections; many very important examples of each must be omitted. Nonetheless, something of the flavor and variety of Japanese poetry, so vital a part of the entire culture, can be gained.

*Haiku poems from *The Penguin Book of Japanese Verse*, translated by Geoffrey Bownas and Anthony Thwaite (Penguin Poets, 1964). © Geoffrey Bownas and Anthony Thwaite, 1964. Reprinted by permission.

The Kojiki

The oldest extant Japanese book is the *Kojiki* (*Record of Ancient Things*), which was ordered by the Emperor Temmu and presented to the court in A.D. 712. According to its preface, it was compiled from various sources by Ō-no-Yasumaro (d. 723) and others. Among the sources seem to be myths, folktales, folksongs, and songs of the court, as well as now-lost chronicles. These were all pressed into the service of a mythological-historical narrative that legitimated the rule of the imperial line by showing its divine origin.

The story begins with the descent of the primal parents, Izanagi and Izanami, from the High Plain of Heaven. After they mate and she gives birth to the gods and islands of Japan, Izanami dies giving birth to the fire god and descends to the Underworld. Her spouse Izanagi follows her, but she is unable to return because she has eaten the food of the land of the dead. Upon his reemergence above, Izanagi purifies himself by washing in the ocean. From his washings are produced Amaterasu, the lovely solar and sovereign goddess enshrined at Ise; Tsukiyomi the moon god; and Susa-no-o, a rambunctious deity associated with both storms and fertility. Amaterasu ascends to heaven, where Susa-no-o outrages her by grossly polluting her fields and hall on the eve of the Harvest Festival. Offended, she hides in a cave, darkening the world, until all the *kami* gather in conference. A goddess performs a ribald dance, and the solar deity sticks her head out to see what the raucous laughter is about. Then a mirror is held up to her face; charmed by her own beauty, she emerges.

Susa-no-o is penalized and expelled from heaven. On earth, however, he turns into a more appealing character. He rescues a maiden from a dragon and marries her, setting up his home in Izumo. Later, however, he becomes master of the Underworld and plays an inimical role against the hero Ōkuninushi, a deity who several times dies and comes back to life, and who himself becomes patron of marriages, the realms of the dead, and the Izumo Grand Shrine.

The next major stage of the *Kojiki* tells of the descent of Amaterasu's grandson, Prince Ninigi, from heaven to engender the imperial line. His grandson, the Emperor Jimmu, establishes the empire; he and his descendants subdue the "natives" and consolidate their rule. The *Kojiki* then gives the history—often legendary—of sovereigns up to the Empress Suiko.

The poems scattered through the *Kojiki* are of varying numbers of lines and syllables, though some have been recast, doubtless by the compilers, in tanka form. They seem mostly to be *uta* (old songs), which were popular as entertainment in the court or countryside. The relation of most of these 113 songs to their settings in the narrative seems to be highly contrived; perhaps they were put in to provide an ancient explanation for a favorite song of feasting or war whose original purport had been long forgotten. Whatever the reason, we can be grateful the *Kojiki uta* were preserved; they provide a rare insight into a robust and archaic world.

These poems serve the perennial function of Japanese verse in a narrative context. They do not tell the story; they highlight the mood and capture the "feel" of each incident they crown. In the *Kojiki*, this mood and feel is brighter and simpler than in later courtly verse. They reflect an earlier and heartier era in which pleasures and sorrows were uncomplicated. In lusty songs of love and desire, the maiden is simply conquered without hint of subsequent pathos or parting. Foemen are vanquished without troublesome thoughts of the visit death will pay in the end to the victors as well. Banquet songs enhance a timeless present of festive joy, and mourning songs—as for the brave Prince Yamatotakeru—are sheer grief for a beloved hero and kinsman without thought of those taken by his own sacred sword.

Each song succinctly rounds off a single vibrant, very human, mood. Few if any of the poems can be called religious (though some may have been rituals or charms), despite the fact that many of the singers were supposedly *kami*. Rather, they are exuberantly earthy songs of loving, drinking, fighting, rejoicing in life, and bewailing death.

As an example, we can look at the first poem that appears in the book, which traditionally has been regarded as the oldest Japanese poem. That is not likely, if only because its extant version is in tanka form. However, the original was undoubtedly very old and may have been a ritual blessing for a new house. We are told that Susa-no-o, after slaying the dragon, came with his bride to the land of Izumo and built a palace for her there at a place called Suga. He said his heart was refreshed—*sugasugashii*, a word that suggests the bright, fresh, clean, pure feeling appropriate to Shinto shrines and moods. Clouds rose above the new home. Susa-no-o then sang:

> A splendid enclosure in Izumo
> Of the eightfold rising clouds—
> To dwell with my wife
> Do I build a splendid enclosure. . . .
> Oh, that splendid enclosure.

The second line, "of the eightfold rising clouds" (or simply "many rising clouds," for the old word for eight, *ya*, often means "many" or "manifold"), is a *makura-kotoba* (pillow word or conventional epithet) for Izumo. Many names had such epithets, often rather bizarre-sounding to modern ears, which were always used with them. They may have originally been charms for the protection of the person or place.

The Manyōshū

The late seventh and the eighth centuries were a vigorous period of poetic activity, which culminated in the great Nara-period collection of some 4500 poems called the *Manyōshū* (*Anthology of Myriad Leaves*). Although some 90 percent of the verses are tanka, this anthology exhibits considerable diversity of style and form. Some of its greatest works are *chōka* (long poems) of up to 149 lines, a form that virtually died out shortly after. The *Manyōshū* is justly celebrated for the universality of its taste; it contains folk songs and courtly verse, songs of wandering beggars and refined lovers, poems reflecting passionate concern for the sufferings of the poor, and poems rejoicing in the elegant pleasures of the rich. What binds them together is skillful technical artistry and a much-praised quality that can only be described as a lively combination of vigor, directness, and sincerity.

Hitomaro The best writer in the *Manyōshū* is Kakinomoto Hitomaro (fl. 680–700). Indeed, some critics think that Hitomaro's best verse has never been excelled. The Western critic Earl Miner has particularly praised his simple maturity: Hitomaro's ability, beyond his consummate technique, to see life whole and to give due place to public and private concerns without either losing balance or sparing passion.[5] He feels deeply, yet he sees the world beyond his feelings. As a government official he knows the world, yet bureaucratic duties have not shriveled his heart. He feels a deep and wise sympathy for an unknown man whose corpse he sees washed up on a beach—and for the man's family. He knows a profound grief when duty separates him from his wife, yet he is not deterred from that journey in the emperor's service.

The longest poem in the *Manyōshū* is Hitomaro's *chōka* of 149 lines, "On the Lying-in-State of Prince Takechi." He describes the battle against rebels of this well-beloved heir to the throne, who died before he could succeed to it, with a sustained dramatic power and the "feel" of the archaic epic, full of war-trumpets, whirring arrows, and a climactic eclipse that gives the prince the victory. His narrative, and the solemn elegy that follows for this hero who died at the height of his power, is worthy of its approximate Anglo-Saxon contemporary, *Beowulf*. The same poet could also mourn the death of his wife, whose life was bent to his "like bending sea-weed," and who has now left, "flown like an early bird."

Another important *Manyōshū* poet was Yamanoue Okura (660-733), who wrote powerfully of the pitiful condition of the poor. This topic was not uncommon in the Chinese poetry exercising considerable influence in Japan at the time, for in China poets have had a traditional role as tribunes of the people. But such social realism was seldom again considered appropriate to the poetic voice in Japan until the advent of modern "proletarian" poetry.

Heian Poetry

The greatest poetic monument of the Heian era, the golden age of the *miyabi* spirit, is the *Kokinshū* (*Anthology [of Poems] Old and New*), issued in 905. It is the first and greatest of a series of twenty-one imperial anthologies, the last of which appeared in 1439.[6] These "official" collections made up by government commissions, together with a certain number of unofficial collections, contain a treasure of many thousands of poems from the classic period. Nearly all are tanka; in the *Kokinshū*, all but nine of its 1,111 verses are in that five-line form.

Monogatari At about the same time as the *Kokinshū*, and closely related to it, came the poetic diaries and tales, those uniquely Japanese forms in which the uttering of an appropriate verse provides the literary climax to a scene, experience, expression of friendship, or amorous encounter. The brilliant preface to the *Kokinshū*, which outlines the theory of classic Japanese poetry with incomparable vividness, is by Ki no Tsurayuki (868-945), also author of the *Tosa Diary* (935), first and among the best of the poetic diaries, though the fiction is maintained that it is by a woman.

The *Tosa Diary* is a travel narrative interspersed with poems inspired by various events; like most such works, it is no doubt largely fictional, though to exactly what extent is disputed. Its dominant themes are not romantic love, but the difficulties of the sea voyage and the protagonist's sorrow for her dead daughter.

The first and best *utamonogatari* (poem-tale) is the *Ise Monogatari* (*Tales of Ise*), produced some time in the first half of the tenth century. It is a collection of romantic episodes during the course of travels by a government official largely in Ise province; they each culminate in one or more poems. The stories are based on the adventures of an already legendary figure, Ariwara Narihira (825-880); the unknown writer of the *Ise* was clearly inspired by Narihira's journals, and about one-third of the poems in the *Ise* are by him. Narihira—handsome, dashing, hot-blooded lover, reflective and gifted poet, elegant courtier and official—was an ideal, almost archetypal *miyabi* figure.

Narihira is, in fact, listed by Tsurayuki in his preface to the *Kokinshū* as one of the six great poets of the age, though the critic does comment, perhaps too hastily, that "his emotional techniques prove too much for his techniques of expression."[7] Nonetheless, many of his poems appear both in the *Ise Monogatari* and the *Kokinshū*. The former shares with *Genji*, which may be partly modeled on it, a superficially plotless, random and episodic character, in part a conscious reflection in both of the idea of a transient world and of the importance of the aesthetic moment. Yet, as do Genji's, the *Ise* protagonist's seemingly casual affairs and aimlessly hedonistic life have about them a strangely moving quality and sense of rich but intangible meaning; one feels that both the hero and the lady were deepened in sensitivity by each encounter. That dimension is, especially in *Ise*, conveyed by the poetry; its dignity and sensitivity to the nuances of each situation tell us that, at least in Heian romances, casualness and refined sensibility need not be mutually exclusive. Indeed, the very ideal of *miyabi* (courtly elegance) casts a moonlight glow over these brief meetings of long ago.

An example from the *Ise Monogatari* (the poems also appear in the *Kokinshū*) can serve to illustrate such an exchange. The protagonist—and perhaps Narihira himself—during his official travels in Ise appears to have actually managed to insinuate himself into the quarters at the Saigū of the princess-priestess and to spend a night with that lonely exile from the palace. The next morning the vestal, clearly flustered and excited, sent the traveler this message in verse:

> Whether my lord passed the night with me
> Or I went out,
> I cannot think.
> Was it a dream or reality?
> Was I asleep or awake?

The second line alludes to a belief prevalent in the Heian period, referred to in *Genji*, that one could go out of one's body in spectral form during one's dreams to visit lovers, connected to one's body only by a tenuous cord. The theme of confusing dream and reality is pronounced in Buddhism, though of course it is common to many literatures.

Her visitor responded in these terms:

> I also am one who wanders after illusions
> Throughout the black nights of a heart
> Which has no certainty or rest.
> As for whether it was dream or reality,
> You are the one who tonight must tell me.

"Darkness of heart" is a Buddhist expression for attachment to this world of illusory goods, especially human love. In this splendid poem Narihira knows this, knows the fruitlessness and despair of pursuing illusion, yet at the same time he sees that, at least for him, it is only through love that the darkness can be dispelled. Like all compulsive conquerers of the other sex, he hopes and believes that the next tryst—tonight's—will be different, will pull away the curtains veiling the reality he gropingly pursues in serial love. Alas, the answer from the Ise sibyl was not given him; the wandering lover was compelled that night to attend an unexpected banquet given in his honor by the provincial governor and had to put duty ahead of pleasure—or truth.

One woman is named in the preface of the *Kokinshū* as among the six great poets of the age. She is Ono no Komachi (fl. c. 850), noted for the intensity of her poetic passion. One can only wonder, as does Earl Miner, what sort of relationship might have obtained between Komachi and Narihira, both fiery-hearted poets preoccupied with affairs of love.[8] They were contemporaries, and in the small hothouse world of the Heian court one finds it hard to believe they did not know each other. Yet no record, poetic or otherwise, of that particular conjunction of kindred souls remains.

The following poem by Komachi was obviously written in the absence of someone like Narihira to share her bedchamber. Few poems in any language have more powerfully expressed in a few words the frustration of strong feminine passion.

> On a night like this
> When no moon shows your way to me,
> I awake, passionate,
> In my breast a rushing fire,
> While my heart burns down to ashes.

Poetry in the Late Middle Ages

The Taira and Minamoto arose, fought, wrought widespread devastation in their struggles for power, and stripped all political meaning from the old Heian court. Yet that court, though impoverished, continued on in Kyoto after the establishment of the Kamakura shogunate in 1185. Its courtiers preserved their lives of refinement and poetry; seemingly unconcerned with what was going on in more barbaric parts of the nation, they remained arbiters in affairs of taste if not in affairs of state. The most important imperial anthology after the *Kokinshū*, the *Shinkokinshū* (*New Anthology [of Poems] Old and New*), was published in 1205. Its verse continues the dominance of the tanka form and the basic values and interests of the earlier collection. The poems show, however, a trend toward description rather than pure subjectivity, toward allowing a sensitive use of imagery from nature to speak for itself as an expression of the poet's mood.

Saigyō Saigyō (1118-1190) was a courtier who became a Buddhist priest and devoted himself, in the classic mendicant tradition, to travel and contemplative solitude. His change of vocation in no way diminished his acute powers of observation; some of his poems show a rare sensitivity to the life and work of ordinary people. In the poem that follows, however, a different observation appears. He knows that, as a Buddhist priest, he ought to have no attachment to delusive natural beauty; yet the *miyabi* soul within him, schooled in such opposite values, is not entirely stilled. He does, then, confess to a certain capacity for *aware* (the term here translated as "melancholy loveliness"), an expression, so important in Japanese aesthetics, for that sort of profound awareness that combines a sense of the beauty of things with knowledge of their transitoriness.

> Though he ought to deny his feelings,
> Even such a one as I cannot but know
> The melancholy loveliness of things:
> A longbill arises from the marsh
> Of an autumn evening.

Teika and Princess Shikushi   Another important poet of the times was Fujiwara Teika (1162-1241), a master of several styles. The following verse, composed late in his life, is remarkable in that it is a poem by a man that expresses vividly the subjectivity of a woman. It gives a powerful picture of a woman whose sexual activity makes her both passionate and sad, who has probably been betrayed, and who senses youth departing—leaving her with what?

> Ceaselessly rising up, going down, waiting
> Like the reeds underfoot
> Or the colors of the moon—
> And all the while I am buffeted about
> By the autumn winds around my bed.

Note here the moon imagery; the moon is a common and complex symbol in Japanese literature, which suggests change, impermanence, femininity; when it is full, it paradoxically suggests completion and even the Buddhist Nirvana. Equally complex and important is the word *iro* (here rendered "colors"). The basic meaning of *iro* is color, but in literature it bears provocative overtones of mood, feeling, and sexual arousal.

Another verse, by a feminine poet of the *Shinkokinshū* known as Princess Shikushi (d. 1201), uses the same word. This gifted aristocratic lady once penned these lines:

> The flowers are fallen;
> There is no certain color.
> And as I look,
> Out of the empty sky
> Falls spring rain.

Here we see a characteristically subtle use of what appears to be only description of nature to express a deeply personal and inward state of mind. One feels the lines might have been written during the heavy rains that come to Japan around June, and which, combined with oppressive heat and humidity, wilt and blur the rare beauty of the Japanese spring with its exquisite cherry blossoms. But the use of *iro* (color) gives it another twist; the poet is also saying "I have no special thoughts or feelings, no special romantic desires, right now—I am passive, empty." Emptiness is also a two-way, loaded term: it suggests meaninglessness, to be sure, but it also suggests the Buddhist Void, the realm of nonattachment, the calm bliss of nirvana, and the image in the Lotus Sutra of the Buddha's dharma or marvelous grace and teaching falling on the world everywhere like rain.

HAIKU AND RELATED FORMS

Renga and Haikai

One cannot fully understand traditional Japanese verse without understanding its social meaning. Not only was poetry the conventional way of expressing sentiment in notes passed from one to another, but poems were also vehicles of social competition and compatibility alike. One's ability to write a good poem really could affect one's status in the Heian court. The court instituted poetry contests as early as 809; in its ultrarefined atmosphere they offered excitement comparable to that of the World Series for American baseball fans.

As we have indicated, poetry also provided the life of social gatherings. "Verse capping" games, in which one player gave the first three lines of a tanka poem and the others had to add immediately two appropriate closing lines, were immensely popular. This entertainment led to a form known as *renga* (linked verse), in which a long series of poems would be composed by a group together; each poem "picked up" and developed an allusion in the previous verse. *Renga* became recognized as an art in the fourteenth century, when Nijō Yoshimoto (1320–1388) compiled an imperial anthology of it in 1356. But the greatest *renga* event was in 1488, when the Zen priest and poet Sōgi (1421–1502) met with two other poets, Shōhaku and Shōchō, at the village shrine of Minase and composed a hundred-verse poem.

Sōgi and his companions raised *renga* to more than light diversion, for much of their imagistic play is rich and subtle. However, its main value was transitional; by emphasizing the independence, or possible independence, of the tanka's first three lines, *renga* led the way to the haiku. Another style, transitional in that it helped break up the traditional associations of tanka, was *haikai* (light humorous verse in tanka form). It was very popular in Muromachi and early Tokugawa times. Ihara Saikaku, later famous as the author of colorful and bawdy novels of the Edo "floating world," was a fervent devotee of *haikai* as a young man. He once wrote an incredible 23,500 such verses in a twenty-four hour one-man poetry-composing marathon.

Haiku

Haiku was originally called *hokku* (starting lines); as we have seen, haiku was originally just the first three lines of tanka, used in "capping" contests and in the composition of *renga*. The master Bashō Matsuo (1644–1694) developed the haiku into an independent form with its own distinctive possibilities. Haiku was thus a new Tokugawa-period style of verse; it responded not only to the new manner of "seeing" fostered by Zen aesthetics, but also to the new townsman audience that was less bound by courtly convention. On the Zen side, people were prepared for crisp, direct, unmediated, perhaps enigmatic, and certainly unexplained perceptions bearing the clarity of a Zen painting and the thought-stopping force of a Zen koan. On the townsman side, the new readership was less interested than was the old in courtly conventions and amours, more in what everyone could see and feel if it was shown him by a gesture of bare pointing. The haiku, then, is a very spare, "one-pointed" indication without the obtrusive subjectivity of something to see or feel. In its bare seventeen syllables and three lines, no space is left for interpretation. Yet a good haiku has a sense of *yūgen*, of profound meaning beyond words latent in something simple and natural to which the writer points. Nature is the predominant theme, though haiku are also drawn from the lives of people—ordinary people, not courtiers. The poems reflect daily work, daily beauties and sorrows, rather than the sentiments of lovers' notes.

Bashō In 1679 Bashō wrote his first major verse in the new style, and it is a strangely effective example:

> On a withered branch
> A crow settles—
> Autumn nightfall.

Notice that the poem really consists of two parts: the first, a clear specific image of a black crow coming to rest on a black dead branch. The final "setting" statement suddenly expands the sense of blackness and death almost to infinity. Yet the two statements are of two phenomena, both natural; they are not metaphors or similes of one another, but represent what Harold Henderson has called the "internal comparison" of haiku.[9] The dynamics of this internal "spring" releases the mysterious sense of vast but unspoken meaning born by great haiku, a sense conveyed simply through uninterpreted, seemingly small and precise but inconsequential, natural images.

In 1681 Bashō began the study of Zen Buddhism. He did not become a priest, but he was a Zen wanderer and contemplative, so infused with Zen that, it has been said, his poems capture the ineffable vision of things seen in the inexpressible experience of Zen *satori* (enlightenment or surprising awakening) and reflect his own moments of *satori*. In any case, in the last ten years of his life, after his engagement with Zen, Bashō wrote his best haiku.

In 1686 Bashō composed his most celebrated poem:

> An old pond—
> A frog jumps in—
> The sound of water.

Commentators have said that this poem captures, for those who understand, the whole essence of Buddhism. The portly Buddha, seated in meditation, had been—sometimes irreverently—referred to as a frog in Japanese letters and art before. The old pond can be both the world and nirvana, for they are ultimately one, ageless and inseparable. The Buddha—Tathagata or *Nyorai*—has now simply "gone thus," gone beyond conditioned reality altogether, yet alike from his ministry in the world and his great entry into nirvana, water-sounds like ripples from the dropping of something into a rimless pond still circle into the world in the form of the Blessed One's grace and doctrine.

Again, Buddhism is reflected in Bashō's deep awareness of the delicacy and transitoriness of finite existence, and of the thrill of encounter with the nameless reality beyond it. On one of his travels, he had to cross a frail rope bridge over a high gorge. The bridge swayed harrowingly, and between him and a rushing stream thousands of feet below was only empty air. Yet, winding over the cords of this precarious support were fine, twisting tendrils of ivy. Bashō does not say whether he was exhilarated or terrified as he swayed in midair high above incomparable scenery, only a single broken strand or false step away from death. But he did write:

> A swinging bridge—
> Ivy vines entwine
> One's life.

In 1689 Bashō began a six-months journey from Edo into the North Country. He wrote about this journey a partly fictional travel book called *Oku no Hosomichi* (*Narrow Roads in the Northern Hinterland*), which in the classic manner consists of notes and narrative interspersed with poems—now haiku—seizing the "feel" of each episode. Toward the beginning of the trip, Bashō, a cultivated man from the great city, was impressed by the sturdy old-fashioned ways of the countryside and perhaps also by the ultimate dependence of the city on the farmer. He wrote:

> The beginning of refinement (*fūryū*)—
> The rice-planting songs
> Of the hinterland.

He spent an afternoon at Takadate, a high castle where a great battle had been fought in samurai days, and where before then the Fujiwara had maintained a splendid stronghold. All he could see beneath the ruined hilltop citadel were empty green fields. He thought of the glories of a past now gone forever and wrote:

> Summer grasses—
> All that is left from the dreams
> Of splendid warriors.

Buson Taniguchi Buson (1715-1783) is generally considered to be the second greatest haiku poet. He is more descriptive and less profound than Bashō, more of a society poet than a Zen mystic. But he was capable of unforgettable work, whether in capturing a charming scene or in adding to conventional beauty a strange, somber, or provocative twist. Here are two examples on highly traditional themes we have already encountered: the fall of cherry blossoms and the spring rains:

> The blossoms are scattered—
> Now one can see
> A temple between the trees.

In the spring rains
A child's cloth ball on the roof
Is getting soaked.

MODERN POETRY

Poets in Japan since the Meiji Restoration have produced volumes of excellent writing and have gone in many directions, as one would expect from a nation with so rich a heritage in the art. Apart from some rather unsuccessful early attempts at the emulation of Western verse styles, the most important first fruit of Meiji poetry was a "modern" revival of tanka and haiku, in which the style was maintained but the voice subtly updated. The great Shiki Masaoka (1867-1902) was the prolific reviver of haiku; he also called influentially for a recovery of *Manyōshū* catholicity of vision in Japanese poetic letters. A major poet in modern tanka is Yosano Akiko (1878-1942), a woman in the classic tradition of passionate, erotic feminine versifiers, yet one whose frank expression of such feelings was in her day a call for the emancipation of woman from traditional subordinate roles.

After the First World War came a swarm of poetic movements, mostly based on the vogues sweeping the West at the same time: surrealism, imagism, symbolism, neorealism, proletarian verse. Most of the writers associated with these styles rejected traditional Japanese forms in favor of freer forms that paralleled the versatility of Western lyricism or narrative. Many of their works are as effective as any international poetry, and some may be better known in translation outside Japan than at home. Perhaps the best modern poet is Hagiwara Sakutarō (1886-1942), the first major poet to employ colloquialisms.

To represent modern poetry, then, here are selections from two of the most important writers. They both write on a perennial topic, the sad convolutions of which relations between the sexes are capable. One poem is by a female poet and the other by a male, and so two perspectives obtain.

Of the following two tanka by Yosano Akiko, the first picks up the theme of the title of her justly famous book of modern tanka, *Midaregami (Tangled Hair)*.[10]

Black hair,
Hair of a thousand strands,
Tangled hair.
And besides, you tangled my thoughts—
Left me tangled thoughts of you.

And here is the second tanka:

> This soft skin,
> This hot blood,
> You never seem to touch.
> Don't you get lonely,
> Just talking philosophy?

(Literally, the last line is "Just explaining the Tao.")
Here is a poem by Hagiwara Sakutarō, entitled "Woman!"*

> With lips painted lightly pink
> And powder smelling white and cool about
>   neck hair—
> Woman!
> With your breasts like rubber balls,
> Don't press too hard against my chest,
> Nor with your whitebait fingers
> Tickle my back so cunningly—
> Woman!
> Ah, with a sigh so scented,
> Don't gaze too closely into my eyes—
> Woman!
> Drop your little tricks—
> Woman!
> You are sad,
> Because you can never do without them.[11]

---

*From *The Poetry of Living Japan*, Takamichi Ninomiya and D.J. Enright. (New York: Grove Press; London: John Murray Ltd., 1957). Reprinted by permission of D.J. Enright.

Prose Literature

10

In traditional Japanese literature, as we have seen, no sharp line can be drawn between prose and poetic works for the simple reason that most major prose works, from the *Kojiki* to the plays of Chikamatsu, rise into poetry at each moment of heightened *mono no aware*. In some cases narration seems little more than a device for splicing together and explaining the settings of poems, even though the poems themselves, usually tightly constructed tanka or haiku, are one-pointed evocations of a single mood or scene. Moreover, much dramatic work, such as the great No plays and those of Chikamatsu, use poetic rhetoric like Elizabethan drama, though they do not employ the short forms that to most Japanese are real poetry.

MONOGATARI AND NIKKI

The earliest important prose that ranks as literature, apart from mythological-historical texts like the *Kojiki* and *Nihonshoki*, are the *monogatari* (tales) of the Heian period. Also from the period, and closely related, are *nikki* (diaries), and *zuihitsu* (miscellanies).

Monogatari are stories told for entertainment, properly to the accompaniment of the *koto*. The older examples are fanciful tales, such as the charming *Taketori Monogatari* (*Tale of the Bamboo Cutter*).[1] It is sometimes called the oldest of the *monogatari*, though the evidence is inconclusive. The present version is from the late ninth or early tenth century, and combines Buddhist, Chinese, and Japanese sources. It is a fairy tale of an old bamboo cutter who finds a tiny maiden in a stalk of bamboo. He raises the child; she turns into a ravishing beauty who causes her three suitors to attempt impossible tasks. After the emperor himself approaches her with amorous intentions, she returns to the palaces of the moon that are her true home.

Later *monogatari*, especially the *uta-monogatari* with verse (such as the *Ise Monogatari*) were set in the contemporary upper-class society in which they were heard or read. Indeed, much of the material in them is fact—or at least current gossip—rather than fiction.

The emergence of the novelistic *monogatari* is bound up with the *nikki* (diary form), and the two forms are best considered together. The *nikki* are less true diaries than a literary convention in which reminiscences and sometimes fiction are put in *nikki* form, together with poetry and elegant twists of phrase that explore events in terms of sensitivity to the beauty and pathos of things. They often most closely approach a genre that might be called autobiographical novel and show considerable introspective insight.

The earliest example, the *Tosa Nikki*, penned by the leading poet and critic Ki no Tsurayuki around 935, is in many ways also the best.[2] It pretends to be written by a woman; subsequently, nearly all important Heian prose literature was actually written by women. It is an account of the journey by ship of an official's wife home to Kyoto from a post on Shikoku, in the company of a number of others of her class. The extent to which it is fictionalized is much disputed, but there can be no doubt that emotionally the *Tosa Nikki* is a mature and true tale. This is no narrative of serial amours like much of the period's literature. Rather, the putative author is a matron who sorrows for the loss of her daughter during the stay on Shikoku. She is a stable, mature person who is not uncontrollably overwhelmed by grief. She is able to recount effectively the joys and frustrations of the sea journey: the parties, the stops along the way, the loss of time from bad weather, the friendships and tensions among passengers tightly confined together. Only occasionally does the sorrow, always just beneath the surface, break through, and then in those sharp little reminders that bring it all back: seeing shells along the seashore and thinking how the child would have loved to play with them, watching other parents hand their small ones down to waiting relatives when they finally disembark. The emotion is very adult and very convincing; one knows that is how grief for a lost child really is for a parent of both strength and sensitivity.

The *Kagerō Nikki* (translated as *The Gossamer Years*) records the years 954–974 in the life of the second wife of a prime minister. It too deals movingly with universal emotions, centering around the writer's unhappy marriage, though it is marred by her distasteful self-centeredness. Other important *nikki* include the *Izumi Shikibu Nikki*, a considerably fictionalized account of the loves of a court lady; and the *Sarashina Nikki* (translated as *As I Crossed a Bridge of Dreams*), a girl's account of her travels from her father's provincial post and her life as a retiring and sensitive soul in the exciting capital of which she had long dreamed.[3]

Murasaki Shikibu   The *monogatari* tradition began in fantasy like the *Taketori* or highly episodic entertainments like the *Ise Monogatari* or the *Utsubo Monogatari* (*Tale of the Hollow Tree*) written by Minamoto Shitagau in the late tenth century. This heritage combined with the realism and emotional maturity of the best *nikki* in the greatest work of the period, and indeed in Japanese literature, the *Genji Monogatari*, completed by Murasaki Shikibu (978?-1026?) about 1010.[4]

The writer of the *Genji* was married to Fujiwara Nobutaka, who died in 1001. From 1005 on, she served at the court of the Empress Akiko; her diary, the *Murasaki Shikibu Nikki*, provides valuable and delightful insights into the life of that court.[5] Many scholars believe that at least the bulk of the writing of the great novel was produced in the intervening years 1001-1005. Murasaki is not the real name of the author, which is unknown; it is a nom de plume probably taken from the heroine of her book.

Murasaki was clearly a highly intelligent observer who was trained from childhood in the intricate ways of the courtly Heian society she chronicled and in the nuances of its values; accepting those values and comprehending deeply the tone and quality they gave to human life, she painted an incomparable picture of what her society was like. We know relatively little of peasant and provincial life in the Heian period; however, largely through Murasaki's writing, there are few past societies whose intimate details of daily life and subtlest patterns of thought are as well communicated across the centuries as those of courtly Heian. And what a strange society, by twentieth century standards, it was—a world in which skill in poetry and calligraphy really affected advancement, whose entertainments included "verse capping" and incense smelling, and in which courtship was an art form and a major preoccupation. The tone of this world, above all its deep sense of *mono no aware*, of delicate awareness of the passing beauty conjoined with deep sadness of natural and human affairs, she captures through her own exquisite sense of *mono no aware*.

Genji is, however, more than just a novel of manners or a portrait of a society. Its central theme is the tracing of the career of the young prince, Genji, paragon of the man about court. Genji is widely admired, not as a knight or a statesman, but as a supreme exemplar of the court's canons of gentility and above all as practitioner of love. The core of the long work is Genji's relationship with a succession of women. Each companion is splendidly portrayed, as are the contours of each relationship; Genji, deeply sensitive to the personality of each paramour, adapts his own manner to hers. The prince appears as a wonderfully sensitive and almost infinitely complex man. He is able to play countless roles while remaining convincing and somehow true in each to his fundamental vision of life as a pluralism of many shadings, calling not for rigidity but flexibility guided by awareness. The last third of the novel, after Genji's death, becomes more somber; those whom he had known seem only shadows, and the light of the Shining Prince is gone from the world. Some attribute this change to a growing Buddhistic pessimism on the part of Murasaki; others believe the ending of the novel is by another hand.

Zuihitsu The *zuihitsu* (miscellany) genre is best represented by the *Makura no Sōshi* (*Pillow Book*) of Sei Shōnagon. She was a contemporary of Murasaki and also a court lady but one more given to witty epigrams than to deep-seeing penetration of life.[6] Her book is a collection of very short pieces on a variety of topics, ranging from her favorite things in each of the four seasons to why preachers ought to be handsome to what it feels like when a lover leaves at dawn. Her book is a classic of its sort and reflects a lively and irrepressible spirit undimmed by time. It gives a rich insight into her time that complements Murasaki's.

MEDIEVAL LITERATURE

The literary Kamakura and Muromachi periods are a long twilight following the splendid Heian high noon. Not only was poetry still dominated by the shadow court and the values shaped by the *Kokinshū*, but prose literature tended to be infused with nostalgia for the faded *miyabi* spirit and to be alive to the decline into violence and decay that so obsessed sensitive minds of the age. Even the brilliant new form that the Middle Ages produced, the Nō play, is haunted by ghosts of the past, which often, as in *Nonomiya*, come from the world of the prince of hearts, Genji. Even the *gunki* (chronicle of war), as typical of its age as the chronicle of love and sentiment was of the gentler Heian, covered its subject with a patina not of glory but of melancholy.

An example of the medieval spirit is the *Hōjōki* (*Lines from a Little Hut;* the title has also been translated as *Account of my Hut* or *The Ten Foot Square Hut*) of 1212 by the Buddhist priest, Kamo no Chōmei (1153-1216).[7] As the title suggests, the author retired to a lonely hermitage, where he wrote in elegiac tones of the evils of the world, sparing nothing in his accounts of war, famine, plague, and earthquake.

Even more representative and influential is the *Tsurezuregusa* (*Essays in Idleness*), the miscellany by Yoshida Kenkō (1283-

1350).[8] After around 1600, this little book was part of the education of every cultivated person; it not only expressed, but did much to create, the values of traditional *fūryū* culture and was the definitive theoretical statement on taste and feeling.

Yoshida's concept of taste was shaped by what it meant to be a man of cultivation and a Buddhist monk in the era when only the last sunset rays of the Heian brilliance were still visible and the nation was racked by war and its attendant destruction, poverty, and suffering. Unlike Kamo no Chōmei, Yoshida does not dwell explicitly on those grim matters, but their influence is visible in his high valuation of that which is old, laden with nostalgia, imperfect, incomplete, asymmetrical. He loves the *sabi* quality of old things passed on from another age and bemoans the shabbiness with which courtly courtesy is observed in his own age, even as he treasures shabby objects because they come from the better times of the past.

Another sort of evidence of the lingering Heian presence was the continuation, especially in court circles, of literature in the familiar genres. We have already mentioned tanka. The Kamakura age also produced such travel *nikki* and court ladies' memoirs as the *Izayoi Nikki*, the memoir of a journey made in 1277 by a nun named Abutsu; and the *Towazu-gatari* of the Lady Nijō (discovered in 1940), a final example of the long heritage of psychologically sensitive remembrances by women of high place.[9]

Gunki

The soul of the new age, however, was represented in a new genre, the *gunki*, which told of men and arms. The greatest is the *Heike Monogatari*, the tale of the twelfth-century wars between the Minamoto and the Taira (Heike) clans, in which the latter were finally vanquished.[10] At this time the proud chivalric tradition of the samurai warriors was in its first great flowering. In meeting the enemy, knights would call out their full names and pedigrees, hoping to attract opponents of equal stature who were worthy of their mettle.

Heike Monogatari The *Heike* is often considered to be the second greatest classic of Japanese prose literature after the *Genji*, and one can well appreciate this recognition. While it is uneven in literary power and does not provide the rounded psychological portraits of the best Heian literature or of good modern novels, it is nonetheless gripping reading. Its descriptions of the great battles and political issues of the era are lucid and dramatic. Swords and armor flash in the sun; courtiers whisper intrigue in palace corridors at midnight.

The book is deepened by another motif—a somber, elegiac tone that commemorates the ultimate futility of striving for power and glory on the field of honor, even though it does not deny the heroism and splendor of the endeavor. The more sensitive of the knights, appalled finally by the carnage that was the price of their fame, turned in the end to religion, taking Buddhist vows. The theme of the evanescence of the things of this world, influenced also by Amidist pietism and its paradise beyond, is strong.

All this is expressed in the famous opening lines of the *Heike:*

> The bell of the Gion Temple tolls into every man's heart to warn him that all is vanity and evanescence. The faded flowers of the sāla trees by the Buddha's deathbed bear witness to the truth that all who flourish are destined to decay. Yes, pride must have its fall, for it is as unsubstantial as a dream on a spring night. The brave and violent man—he too must die away in the end, like a whirl of dust in the wind.[11]

Gion is the Japanese rendering of the Jetavara temple and monastery at Srāvastī, India, which had a hall for sick priests; the temple bells tolled whenever a priest lay dying. The sāla is the teak tree; according to the *Nirvana Sutra*, one stood at each corner of the Buddha's deathbed.[12]

The *Heike Monogatari* tells us that the reason for the final fall of the Taira, and especially of Kiyomori, their leader until his death in 1181, was their failure to realize that all human life and glory is but vanity and evanescence. In their pride they thought themselves exceptions to the lot of mortals and showed only contempt for others. At the height of their ascendancy, Kiyomori's brother-in-law, Tokitada, boasted, "Unless a man is a Heike, he is not a human being!" Their fortunes then ebbed until defeat in the disastrous sea battle of Dannoura in 1185. At the end of the book we read: "This suffering was in retribution for the evil deeds of Kiyomori, the leader of their clan. He had held in his palm both heaven and earth, but to the throne above he paid no respect, and to the people below he paid no heed."[13] The last chapter ends with the tolling of the Jokkō-in temple bell in Japan, as the first had opened with the somber chimes in far-away India, reminding all of mortality.

TOKUGAWA LITERATURE

The Muromachi and Momoyama periods produced little prose of importance. In the Tokugawa era, however, Japanese writing burst into new vitality.

We see Tokugawa Japan as the last great era of traditional culture. The country seems sealed off, self-contained, and dominated by a regime bent on maintaining above all else the status quo. But the major literature of the period, by contrast, strongly shows a very recognizable sense of being "modern." The Tokugawa people portrayed by a great novelist like Saikaku or a playwright like Chikamatsu are similar to modern Europeans and Americans. They are ordinary shopkeepers and struggling writers concerned with making a living and finding what pleasures they can; they are not the romantic knights and lordly lovers of the literature of the past. Moreover, they are quite conscious that somehow those days are gone and times are different. Despite their anachronistic government, Tokugawa people, if these authors are any guide, see themselves as skeptical, greedy, amorous, and sensuous men and women of few principles but much capacity to enjoy life. Rightly or wrongly, they view these as the new attitudes of a new secularized and sophisticated world in which old dogmas, inhibitions, and romanticisms have faded away—an innate feeling that has been the crux of modern literature in the West as well. They talk cleverly of their greater precociousness in worldly matters. One of Saikaku's characters tells us that now women are likely to have their first love affairs at an age when only forty years before they would have been swinging on the gate and riding hobby horses.

Probably most people in all ages have been concerned with making a living, even if in the Heian era one did not talk about money in good society; *Genji* certainly dispels any notion that young lovers were really more precocious in Edo than in Heian. But the important matter is self-perception; if people think they are a new and different breed, that in itself is important for understanding their literature.

And the new self-perception was partly true. As we have seen, a new class with values different from those of Heian aristocrats and medieval samurai was at the fore in cultural impact: the chōnin (townspeople), who were mainly shopkeepers and artisans. They were money oriented. Because sumptuary laws restricted them in house and dress, they spent much of their incomes, if they were well off, on entertainment. They were interested in themselves and liked to read or see plays about people like themselves, though they also wanted to feel in touch with the historical and cultural tradition.

Thus historical dramas were popular, but the best and most characteristic Tokugawa literature is of the how-we-live-now type. Much of it centers around the *ukiyo*, the floating world of the pleasure quarters in the great cities, with their rigidly organized and hierarchic regiments of geishas and prostitutes, and the musicians, dancers, Kabuki actors, gay blades, footloose artists, and sheepish husbands on a fling who made it whirl. These fabulous worlds within cities—the Yoshiwara area in Edo, Gion in Kyoto,

Shimmachi in Osaka—were often called *fuyajō* (cities without night). Sometimes writers drew proper morals from the downfall of the unwary in that maelstrom, but, as is usual in such literature, the temptations are at least as interesting as the morality that prevails in the end.

In general, the sober Confucianism officially promulgated by the shogunal court seems to have had remarkably little effect on the commercialism of the great business houses or on the irrepressible hedonism of the entertainment districts—partly because the Tokugawa had reasons of their own for being somewhat two-faced about controlling them. They often needed loans or cooperation from the businessmen whose commerce they professed to rank low in social worth, and they knew that most people in a restrictively organized state, including the now superfluous samurai, needed ways to let off steam.

Tokugawa Japan had, of course, its darker side: its toiling peasants, its periodic famines, its exploitative sale of daughters to staff the mills of "pleasure." Yet the melancholic tone of medieval literature was gone. The mood was one not of bending to fate but of fighting back, not of dwelling on the miseries of the world but on celebrating the joys that were possible. Despite hard blows of fortune, people bounced back; like the poignantly heroic shopkeepers of Chikamatsu, they enjoyed life when they could, even to the extent of folly, and braved it with stoic fortitude or even protested with suicide when that seemed the only way. The prostitutes of Saikaku complained less of life's injustices than did the wife of a Fujiwara prime minister who wrote the *Kagerō Nikki;* rather, accepting their station, they made the most of it and tried to get ahead and to save something for old age.

Saikaku Ihara Saikaku (1642-1693) superbly represents the Tokugawa spirit, especially that of the Genroku (late seventeenth century) period that is considered its absolute epitome. He manifests all its "modern" iconoclasm, hedonism, and love of the human pageant. He frankly says he is tired of nature and cherry blossoms. In leading the reader through his books on a tour of old Kyoto or Osaka, he brings them not to palaces and temples, but to the haunts of amusement. His greatest works are *ukiyo zōshi* (writings on the floating world), erotic picaresques. *Kōshoku ichidai otoko* (1682; *The Life of an Amorous Man*) was his first work; it describes a life given over to the pursuit of women from the protagonist's first attempts at the age of seven to his embarcation at sixty for an island entirely inhabited by females.[14] *Kōshoku gonin onna* (*Five Women Who Loved Love*) of 1686 looks at the subject from the opposite point of view; it relates the extramarital affairs of women of the merchant class.[15] In his later works, especially *Nihon Eitaigura* (*The Eternal Storehouse of Japan*), Saikaku explored the shadier side of a society devoted to pleasure, or more precisely to those pleasures that are bought with money.[16] With both humor and bitterness, he delineates the battles of townsmen to make fortunes, the despair of those who fail and cannot pay their bills, and the gyrations those who are neither rich nor destitute undertake to keep afloat.

MODERN LITERATURE

At the time of the Meiji Restoration, Japanese prose literature, for all its past glories, was at a low ebb. No fiction of the first rank had been written for more than a century, though the markets were full of fifth-rate humor, bawdy, and adventure—entertaining perhaps, but unless from the pen of a Saikaku, not the stuff of immortal literature. The flowering of contact with new cultures and the rapid evolution of Japan changed the state of writing, however.

In any such encounter between cultures, several diverse reactions are likely to obtain. Some will embrace wholeheartedly and uncritically the values of the new culture, overwhelmed by its novelty and its apparent superiority. Others react against it, building ramparts in defence of tradition. Still others, probably later, after things have jelled a bit, will seek a middle way between these extremes.

All of these responses can be observed in Japanese writers of the Meiji period; in the twentieth century a certain style has emerged that might be thought of as the ultimate reaction to the tensions of cultural confrontation and modernization. It would be very misleading to imply that all or most important novels and stories fall into this style, for Japanese fiction has been quite diverse, ranging from fantasy to the most gritty realism, from aesthetic detachment to the overt political advocacy of the "proletarian novel." Nonetheless, a certain quality links together the most frequently discussed Japanese novelists and short story writers of the twentieth century— Sōseki, Kafū, Tanizaki, Akutagawa, Kawabata, Mishima. We have already alluded to this quality: a deep psychological introspection combined with a sense that the writer is and must be an outsider precisely in order to make those searingly passionate or ironic observations that are his calling.

The Writer as "Outsider"

The fundamental problem the outsider-writers observe is the conflict of tradition and modernity, of East and West. Perhaps, like Kafū, they view it in terms of nostalgia versus the ugliness of much that is new; perhaps, like Tanizaki, they symbolize it in the very different attractions of different women. Their styles themselves reflect old and new; the intuitive, evocative quality is Japanese, but it is tinged by the brush of Western romanticism. The novelistic form—sense of plot, character development, consistency—is more coherent than in the *monogatari* or *ukiyo* tale and shows the influence of the great nineteenth-century Western novels. Even so, many Western readers at first find some highly regarded modern Japanese novels to be excessively episodic and oblique. They must make a cultural transition and learn to read in a more intuitive manner than is necessary in most mainstream Western fiction; atmosphere and implication are likely to play a more central role in the oriental work.

Perhaps as a result of the extreme pressures of the age and the outsider's role, the bizarre and grotesque have been important in Japanese fiction, especially when linked to sexuality. Tanizaki, Akutagawa, and Mishima have outdone Edgar Allen Poe or H.P. Lovecraft in imagining bizarre situations or strange erotic tastes and above all in making them more than chilling literary entertainments, but also vehicles for important statements about the serpentine twistings of the human psyche beneath the orderly social surface. The outsider's business is to stir up this snakepit, even if it drives him—as it has rather frequently driven writers in modern Japan—to madness or suicide.

This characteristic, incidentally, also marks more popular forms of Japanese fiction. Mystery stories and science fiction both have large and enthusiastic followings in Japan today. Significantly, the line between these two great modern genres is less well defined in Japan than elsewhere. The same writers and magazines will usually publish both. For in both the emphasis is likely not to be so much on hard science or police work as on fantastic situations that put weird psychological pressures on the principals. Whether the explanation is ultimately normal or paranormal, in getting there the reader will have vicariously gone through that partial collapse of ordinary reality that seems to be the real thrill in Japanese thrillers.[17]

All of these themes have a background in the Japanese tradition. But they are treated differently today. The sensitive psychological introspection of the modern Japanese novel certainly has sources in Murasaki and Ki no Tsurayuki, but these writers were hardly alienated from their societies in the manner that seems incumbent upon the serious modern writer. Erotic material is used much more unself-consciously for its emotional power and symbolic value by Japanese writers than by most Western writers; this derives from the long heritage of literary sexual love in Heian and Tokugawa letters and combines both the Heian's nuanced sensitivity and the

Tokugawa's bawdy realism. The writer's role as outsider has sources in the travel narrative (even if the writer was an insider at court, he or she was a detached observer on the road) and especially in the writings of priestly wanderers, hermits, and commentators of the Middle Ages and after, like Saigyō, Yoshida, or Bashō. Bizarre material has a goodly antecedence in the ghost and supernatural vengeance stories that have long been popular entertainment and that supplied themes to the No plays of Zeami. Yet in the twentieth century all this has been treated differently too.

Kinkakuji

We have already summarized the main schools and names of modern Japanese writing in Chapter 3. Rather than repeat or expand that list here, it might be more profitable to examine one important novel, looking in it for the dominant themes we have indicated. That novel will be Mishima Yukio's *Kinkakuji* (*The Temple of the Golden Pavilion*) of 1959.[18]

Kinkakuji is not necessarily the greatest Japanese novel, but it is very well done and, moreover, presents starkly and strikingly the tense, dark world of modern Japanese fiction. We mentioned in Chapter 3 the complex character and life of Mishima Yukio (pseudonym for Hiraoka Kimitake, 1925–1970), who was torn between the old samurai values and modern Westernized Japan, and between his inward convoluted obsessions and weaknesses and his increasing passion to create himself through body-building and deliberately fanatical commitments. These tensions were finally sprung in his dramatic suicide in 1970 in the presence of his private army, just after he had completed his four-volume *Sea of Fertility*.

At the time of *The Temple of the Golden Pavilion*, however, his mind was less set; indeed, much of the strength of the novel lies in the harsh, penetrating light it sheds impartially on Japan old and new. The story revolves around one of the most precious shrines of traditional culture, the Golden Temple built near Kyoto by the redoubtable Ashikaga Yoshimitsu. Although it resounds with accounts of the Zen life of the priesthood that controls the temple, this is no soft romantic view of a hallowed shrine and a venerable spiritual tradition. The tiny Zen community is ruled by a plump, worldly abbot, and the story's protagonist is a disturbed young novice with no real vocation for the priestly life. He is obsessed by the beauty of the temple, with its sides and phoenix-crown of gold and its shimmering golden reflection in the pond. The novel is based on a true event; in 1950 such an unbalanced young novice actually set fire to the Temple of the Golden Pavilion out of jealousy for its loveliness and perfection. (The edifice was rebuilt in 1955.)

Mishima brilliantly recreates the monk-arsonist, making him a prototype of the obsessed, introspective, suicidal "outsider" he was himself, and which he had portrayed in the earlier semi-autobiographical *Confessions of a Mask*. Mizoguchi, the temple-burner, is not particularly bright and he is no writer; perhaps therefore he has to express the rage that bubbles within him in deeds. He is ugly and a stutterer; these characteristics act as a heavy wall between his inner self and the world of others. He is preoccupied with the Temple of the Golden Pavilion, especially after he becomes a novice there upon the death of his father, a country Zen priest. He imagines it sometimes as a great golden bird about to take off across the lake, sometimes as a vast temple embracing the world. But it always seems a thing of absolute, unconditioned beauty and perfection; it fascinates him to the point of obsession because it is so opposite to his own inarticulate ugliness, and it lies like a yellow weight on his adolescent struggles to free himself from the walls of gracelessness and stammering around him.

Several events inaugurate that release—he kicks a drunken, pregnant harlot in the snow near the temple and he visits a brothel—and end his stuttering temporarily. But those breakthroughs are not enough. His great idea is suggested by the American fire-bombings of Japan in 1944 and 1945; Mizoguchi begins having the daring fantasy that an incendiary bomb might land near the golden temple and reduce it to ashes. (Actually, the ancient capital was spared bombing.) The fantasies are excited further by his meditation on the famous enigmatic Zen saying, "If you see the Buddha, kill him." Finally one dark rainy night the time has come: he sets fire to straw within the aged wood structure. He had initially planned to stay in the building and perish with his tremendous love-enemy, but he cannot open the door of the room where he had intended to await death. Suddenly he turns and runs as fast as he can into the nearby hills, where he quietly watches the spectacular conflagration. Indeed, a great change comes over the novice. For the first time, we are told in the last line of the novel, he wants to live.

The Temple of the Golden Pavilion shows the acute and paradoxical juxtapositon of extremes of violence and tranquillity that is perennially Japanese, which in particular has accompanied the Golden Temple since the days of Yoshimitsu, who himself found ample opportunity for both pursuits. The wind and flame of catastrophic war whirl just beyond the shrine by its lake; the shrine, nonetheless, remains the abode of utter peace, indeed of peace so profound as to be stifling. The Zen ideal sits ill with both the oppressive institutionalized form in which it is presented to Mizoguchi and with his own inner torment, which its consolations seem unable to touch.

Finally, we note a passionate Dostoevskian inward searching and struggle, involving complex engagement with the meaning of such eternal spiritual themes as love, freedom, and rebirth. Yet, as Nancy Wilson Ross has acutely observed, a sharp difference with the Russian writer obtains here: as one reads the story, one is drawn with absorption and even awe by the strange drama that unfolds, yet one is not led to identify emotionally with anyone or to sort it out in moralistic terms.[19] One both pities and is repelled by Mizoguchi in about equal measure, so that one is unable either to defend or to blame him. One simply watches the story unfold with a dreadful fascination, unable to turn one's eyes away.

Further, while the Buddhist concept of karmic moral cause and effect hangs in the air over the fateful unravelling of Mizoguchi's tale, the reader is not led to see the tragic fire as anyone's immediate fault. Guilt has nowhere to go. Only in the most superficial sense is Mizoguchi himself morally to blame, for he is clearly a very young person at the mercy of dark inner forces he only dimly comprehends. His well-meaning father cannot be blamed, nor can the abbot, for all his faults. The Golden Temple itself in a real sense *is* the villain, yet its only sin is that of being superlatively beautiful.

These features, which mark the book as different from much Western literature, in no way lessen the novel's force or diminish the fact that Mishima is ultimately concerned with the profoundest human and moral issues. Rather, it exemplifies the capacity, which most important modern Japanese novelists have had to a striking degree, to break through doctrine, euphemism, and abstraction to confront the human condition in all its extremes and perplexing ambiguities. This vision is not moralistic in the sense that it must look for the good and the bad in every situation, nor is it simply the mellow wisdom of such bromides as "To understand all is to forgive all."

Instead, it is the vision of the outsider pursuing an observant and introspective inquiry into the dynamics of human life, an inquiry that is moral because it seeks the sort of knowledge that can come only from empathy and compassion. It is the inquiry of men and women whose roots have been deeply shaken by the transformation of a society and by defeat, and who were never guided by the dualistic Judeo-Christian ethic. To Westerners they may seem often to begin their inquiry closer to point zero than we would have thought possible. If to many, including many Japanese, the society of the island nation seems so tightly structured as hardly to leave any breathing space, certain of its novelists have discovered just beneath the surface an abyss of fire and night.

Cinema:
A Distinguished Art

11

Although contemporary Japanese painting, sculpture, and stage drama are not quite equal to their best creative periods, a new art form, internationally recognized as second to none, has arisen to take their place and in a real sense to claim their heritage: cinema, the new art of the technological age. Some of the most gifted artists of the twentieth century have sought out the freedom and subtlety of which this medium is capable and have made of it work that, unburdened by the past, profoundly reflects the modern experience. Yet they are also heirs to Japan's artistic past, and in important respects the unique genius of Japanese cinema is built on special qualities of the nation's traditional drama and painting.

CHARACTERISTICS
OF JAPANESE CINEMA

Like Japanese painting and wood-block prints, Japanese cinematography tends to use a stark flat perspective, with detail precision but without wide-angle expanse or immense depth—unless it is the "vertical depth" opening into infinite nothingness of Sesshū's landscapes or the attention to one symbolic distant object of Hokusai's Fuji prints. But this lack of depth perspective hardly means that Japanese films, at their best, are shallow. They avoid the easy cinematic glories of vast settings and a "cast of thousands" in favor of studying the subtle tensions of small intimate groups—families, pairs of lovers, comrades in war—with the precision of subtle but exact symbols. Even within these tiny universes, the emotional tone may be presented in a more "flat," less jagged and "hot" manner than in Western cinema, manifesting a subtly different Japanese sense of emotional communication. An abandoned heroine, for example, may not be shown close-up, weeping, and with her face contorted; rather, the cameras may pull back to portray her small and far away, standing alone under a single tree blowing in the wind.

Basic Themes   Japan has had its share of "samurai westerns" and "monster from outer space" potboilers, but its serious films, including its best historical and science-fiction pictures, have been fundamentally social commentaries, concerned with the interaction of social rules and historical events with individual lives. Often the lives of obscure but representative people have been the subjects of films. This cinema explores the web of intricate social controls that the Japanese inevitably assume is the really important determinant in human life—a lesson brought home in cinema time and again.

Whether tragedy or comedy, the basic theme generally is "how we live now" (or lived then) and what the social system does to the individual: what duties it imposes, what opportunities it allows. More often than not, the final message is that the life of the individual, in the end, is a sacrifice to the ongoing life of society—though (to refer back to the two Kurosawa films discussed in Chapter 3) the sacrifice may be given joyously and even seen as an opportunity to live a truly meaningful life as in *No Regrets for Our Youth*, or it may be grudgingly interpreted as a defeat of individual honor and purpose as in the more pessimistic *The Bad Sleep Well*.

We may recall that this is also the fundamental theme of the major traditional drama, No and Kabuki. They usually emphasize the absolute priority of the social order, as represented by codes of honor and duty, for which one would sacrifice not only life and all its goods, but even the life beyond life. Tsunemasa, in the No play of that name, fought because he was of samurai class even though his greater love was music and even at the cost of Buddhist perdition. Kabuki heroes threw all else aside to wreck vengeance and satisfy honor. In the modern world reflected in the film, the social controls may be more nuanced and indirect, but they are nonetheless there in full force. In the hands of a master, the movie camera is an ideal instrument—with its ability to isolate significant gestures and subtle symbols—for unveiling the operation of social controls.

If "how we live now" in a society that dominates the individual's way of life is the persistent theme of Japanese cinema, then society and lifestyle have changed immensely in the decades cinema has been there to record it. In fact, we should not underestimate the power of the modern film itself to serve as a medium of that domination and as a molder of society and lifestyles. Japanese cinema has been extremely sensitive to the special mood and concerns of each passing, and often awesomely contrasting, decade of modern Japan: the xenophobic thirties, the wartime frenzy of the forties, the postwar idealism of the late forties and early fifties, the subsequent affluence and disillusionment.

FILMS AND DIRECTORS

Japanese cinema has been preeminently a director's art. Its magnificent achievements have centered on the distinct styles and perspectives of a small number of extraordinary masters of cinematic art, of whom the best known are Mizoguchi Kenji (1898-1956), Ozu Yasujirō (1903-1963), and Kurosawa Akira (1910-). They all produced films in the late prewar period, when social criticism was muted and traditional structures of culture and family life were ostensibly taken for granted, though an occasional implied question slipped in; during the wartime period, when the hand of the censor was heavy and films, though sometimes technically excellent, could only parrot the official values of militarism and total sacrifice for the cause; and the postwar era, when new freedoms and new ambiguities brought first a backlash against the madness of war in a spate of idealistic and antiwar films, and then a focus on the ironic problems of a society that was not as liberated as it thought.

Ozu Yasujirō Of these directors, the most traditionalist was Ozu Yasujirō. The highly Japanese quality of his aesthetics has made him less well known abroad than others, though his reputation is steadily growing. He made much use of asymmetry, empty space, restricted view, and fixed cameo-like scenes. His favorite subject was the Japanese family, both in its "ideal" form and in dissolution. His prewar and wartime films, such as *I Was Born, But . . .* and *There Was a Father*, are essentially dramatic documentaries of the Japanese family, studies of its small problems and triumphs. The conventional structure of benign but patriarchal father and subservient wife who lives to please others was assumed; as time went on, the argument that in the final analysis this arrangement works best was made more and more overtly.

Yet Ozu's traditionalism had little to do with the more strident Japanism of the military nationalists. Preferring to make his own kind of films, all through the war he evaded efforts of the government to recruit him to make propagandistic pieces. During this period he proposed a film about a soldier's last meal with his family before he left for the front; it was turned down by the censor because the family ate only tea over brown rice rather than the festive red rice a patriotic family ought to have set out on such an occasion. Ozu refused to rewrite it; he felt that the spare, ascetic meal he envisioned fitted the aesthetics and the message he wanted for that film.

In the postwar period, Ozu's work could only be a chronicle of the decline of the traditional family he had long observed. He worked in his usual restrained style and with his customary subtle sensitivity. *Tokyo Story*, for example, pictured a very ordinary family caught between tradition and modernity. In this 1953 film, an elderly couple travel to Tokyo to visit their grown-up offspring. The picture focuses on the contrast between the aged mother, who represents all that is best in old Japan, and her loud, domineering "modern" daughter, a beautician. When the old woman dies, it becomes clear that the daughter, for all her flashy exterior, has lost the capacity for deep feeling and can only respond with cliches that reveal the emptiness inside. Her widowed sister-in-law, with whom the mother had much closer rapport, represents the possibility of keeping up with the old values in the uncongenial postwar city. She uncomplainingly works hard to support herself and remains loyal to her dead husband, killed in the war. When death comes, her quiet presence says more than the daughter's hollow talk.

Kurosawa Akira Ozu's films offer an invaluable mirror of old Japan and Japan in transition for anyone who would understand the society in depth. However, the movies of Kurosawa Akira have attracted more international attention, both because of their more universal themes and their less austere cinematography.

Kurosawa's films have been remarkably diverse in mood and topic, ranging from samurais to the contemporary business world epics, and he has produced the recognized classics of many genres. In all of them, however, runs a serious inquiry that marks his work as serious drama. As one critic has put it, each film is asking the basic question, What should we do with our lives?

Kurosawa does not give wholly consistent answers to this all-important question, and it is undoubtedly a mark of his honesty that he does not. Sometimes his answer is to give oneself idealistically to the service of others or to a great cause; sometimes to find an inner integrity in the midst of the world's ambiguities; sometimes to combine service with a good death that inspires others.

We have considered examples of the first two answers in *No Regrets for Our Youth* and *The Bad Sleep Well*. The first is also the message of his wartime films, which understandably extol sacrificial labor, though sometimes with subtle lingering questions, and of his great *Seven Samurai* (1954), which ends by shifting our feelings from the warriors to the peasants and their collective struggles to survive and live. In *Ikiru* (*To Live*) he advocates a good death.

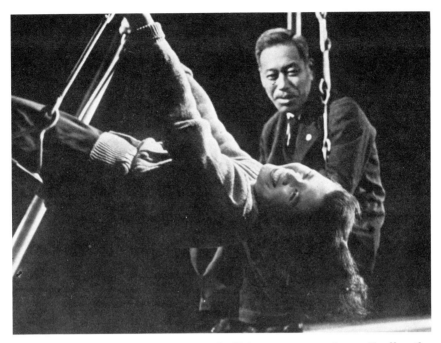

This still from Kurosawa Akira's Ikiru *portrays dramatically the strange but vital relationship between a government official dying of cancer and a lively young woman who inspires him to spend his last year living for others. (Courtesy The Museum of Modern Art. Film Stills Archive.)*

This film also vividly depicts the cultural confusion and the decline of manners and morals in the younger generation that came to maturity during the Americanization of culture and the "democracy" of the Occupation years. But in *Ikiru* (1952) Kurosawa refuses to place all the blame on outside forces. Rather, he sees corresponding though different evils inherent in the traditional Japanese hierarchical society and bureaucratic government and insists that, whatever the social context, each person must decide individually whether to live a meaningful or an empty life.

The protagonist of *Ikiru* is a petty bureaucrat who learns that he will die within a year of stomach cancer. At first he seeks solace in the gaudy pleasures of Westernized night clubs and in an affair with a girl who is wild about Western stockings and the like; she quits her government job to work in a factory making Western-style toys. Significantly, she is by no means the wholly negative figure she might have been in an Ozu movie. Instead, she tells the dying official how much she enjoys working in the toy factory because she thinks of all the pleasure its products will give children. This impresses the protagonist, and he changes his outlook. He devotes all his energies to helping a group of mothers who had been petitioning to have drained a polluted swamp that endangered their children; in usual bureaucratic manner they had been shunted from one office to another while the danger remained. Ignoring proper procedure and respect for seniority, he fights until the task is accomplished; so impressed are his colleagues that they vow in the future to put the needs of citizens first. At the hero's funeral signs appear that the reform will not last long, and that soon the officials will fall back into their self-serving and time-serving ways.

Here, the answer to the question of how to live is that one must serve others, and that even death can be a good if by its onset one is led to this realization. Death, in fact, is the omnipresent human reality that can force us to live well and for others, especially for the next generation. Death reminds us that living only for self cannot last long in any case, and that in a finite life decisions cannot be put off forever. A good death—one sanctified by the decisions for selfless service its coming has evoked—is then the true gauge of worth in this film by the profoundly moral director, Kurosawa Akira.

Mizoguchi Kenji   In some ways the most interesting of all the great Japanese directors is Mizoguchi Kenji. His major concern has been women and their ambivalent role in Japanese society; the tensions and changes in their position become touchstones for grappling with the perennial issue of tradition versus modernity in Japan. Mizoguchi's films tend to be period pieces, set in the Meiji or Tokugawa or another bygone era. The anger and compassion they express over the suffering of women, and the sensitivity they ascribe to the redemptive power of women's love, is timeless. Mizoguchi studies women in a society whose major institutions—government, religion, family structure, economic life—are all essentially repressive of women, teaching them only to accept the lot given them in life and forcing them into lives of dependence upon men. Although nothing can diminish the basically degrading structure of this pattern, women can and do find dignity within the social structure by seeing through the hypocrisy around them. The love they show for their men is so pure that it transcends the unequal dependence forced by the system within which it must be expressed.

Partly because it opens up the world of Kabuki and Kabuki actors, one of the most fascinating of Mizoguchi's pictures is *The Story of the Last Chrysanthemum* (1939). Set in the Meiji period, this is the tale of the indulged young scion of a great Kabuki acting family who is making his way into the theater mostly on his family's credentials. His dedication to his craft becomes more serious after

This scene from The Story of the Last Chrysanthemum, *directed by Mizoguchi Kenji, shows the protagonist with his beloved, a serving maid in the famous Kabuki family's house. The expressions and poses seem understated and frozen as though from a tableau, yet they are powerfully expressive. (Courtesy The Museum of Modern Art. Film Stills Archive.)*

he falls in love with a maid in his house. However, when his mother learns of this inappropriate relationship, she promptly fires the maid.

The young actor, Kikunosuke, leaves home, finds his love, and, forsaking the advantages he might have had, becomes a second-rate traveling actor in the country. He and the former maid live together the demanding life of the struggling trouper; he slowly masters his art the hard but thorough way. She sustains him with her love, encouragement, and extra income earned by sewing, asking nothing for herself. When he finally triumphs in Osaka as a star and is received back by his family, they still refuse to allow him to marry her. As Kikunosuke makes a triumphal tour of the city, his paramour lies dying; he stops only briefly to see her and promises to allow her to die as his wife. He is riding victoriously down the canal in a boat past cheering throngs as she slips away later that night.

The meaning of this film is obvious. Mizoguchi honors the oft-sung capacity of traditional Japanese women for almost limitless self-sacrifice, yet he does not blur the fact that the heroines are also victims. Even in this prewar film, he makes apparent the black side of the Japanese family, celebrated as the bulwark of society: its near-total domination of each member that forces them to either conform or face exile; its callousness toward those, especially of lower class, outside its charmed circle. And *Last Chrysanthemum* gives us a glorious picture of Kabuki in its Meiji heyday, when performances were mounted with magnificence and its great stars lived as raucously and opulently, and were as wildly idolized, as rock stars are today.

Other Directors and Films   Certain other distinguished directors and films could be cited, such as Naruse Mikio's *The Whole Family Works*, about poverty and hope in the rural Japan of the thirties; Ichikawa Kon's *The Harp of Burma*, a Buddhistic picture of a mystical Japanese officer in wartime Burma; Teshigahara Hiroshi's unusual allegory *Woman in the Dunes;* and Inamura Shohei's *History of Postwar Japan as Told by a Bar Hostess*, a flavorsome account of the hardscrabble Occupation years and a celebration of the eternal Japanese ability to survive by adaptation to new realities.

Through these films run certain deep structures and tensions that virtually can serve to sum up Japanese culture as a whole, from the primordial myths of Amaterasu through the *miyabi* refinement and realism of Genji, the elegant warriors of Kamakura and Muromachi, the mysteries of No and the spectacle of Kabuki, down to the shocks and breakthroughs of the twentieth century. Always the theme of the presence of the past, with its lost glories and sacrifices, haunts the present like the shade of Tsunemasa. Always these dreams and the duties they impose must tangle with the present and its practicalities. Always a tight social order, perhaps vibrantly graceful in its symbols and ideals, but suffocating in effect, does subtle war with a questing, remarkably free spirituality: *giri* versus *ninjō.* And unceasingly, Japanese exponents of the spirit turn to women, repressed yet somehow the still center of things like Amaterasu in the cave, who in suffering reflect, interpret, and redeem these paradoxes.

Notes

CHAPTER 1

1. Murasaki Shikibu, *The Tale of Genji*, 2 vols., trans. by Edward G. Seiden-sticker (New York: Alfred A. Knopf, 1976), vol. I, pp. 189-90. For further discussion of the Ise princess-priestess, see Robert S. Ellwood, Jr., "The Saigū: Princess and Priestess," *History of Religions* 7, no. 1 (August 1967): 35-60.
2. For useful discussions of *ikebana*, the *fūryū* concept, and Higashiyama culture, see Thomas Hoover, *Zen Culture* (New York: Random House, 1977); and Issotei Nishikawa, *Floral Art of Japan* (Tokyo: Japan Travel Bureau, 1964).
3. See Jack Seward, *Hara-Kiri: Japanese Ritual Suicide* (Rutland, Vt. and Tokyo: Charles E. Tuttle Co., 1968).
4. *The Love Suicides at Amijima* is translated and discussed in Donald Keene, *Four Major Plays of Chikamatsu* (New York: Columbia University Press, 1961), p. 208. See also Donald Keene, *Bunraku: The Art of the Japanese Puppet Theatre* (Tokyo: Kodansha International Ltd., 1973).

CHAPTER 2

1. Donald Keene, *Four Major Plays of Chikamatsu* (New York: Columbia University Press, 1961), p. 33.
2. See Carmen Blacker, *The Catalpa Bow: A Study of Shamanistic Practices in Japan* (London: George Allen & Unwin, 1975).
3. See Ichirō Hori, *Folk Religion in Japan* (Chicago: University of Chicago Press, 1968), especially pp. 49-81; and Robert J. Smith, *Ancestor Worship in Contemporary Japan* (Stanford, Calif.: Stanford University Press, 1974).
4. Chie Nakane, *Japanese Society* (Berkeley and Los Angeles: University of California Press, 1970), p. 7.
5. Nakane, *Japanese Society*, p. 42.

CHAPTER 3

1. Translation by the author.

CHAPTER 4

1. Sokyō Ono, *Shinto: The Kami Way* (Rutland, Vt.: Charles E. Tuttle Co., 1967) is one of the few reliable introductions to Shinto for the Western reader.

2. Kenzo Tange and Noboru Kawazoe, *Ise: Prototype of Japanese Architecture* (Cambridge, Mass.: MIT Press, 1965) is a spectacularly illustrated introduction to the Grand Shrine.

3. See Robert S. Ellwood, Jr., "Harvest and Renewal at the Grand Shrine of Ise," *Numen* 15, no. 3 (November 1968): 165-90.

4. Richard H. Robinson, *The Buddhist Religion* (Belmont, Calif.: Dickenson Publishing Co., 1970) is a good, vividly written introductory textbook.

5. See Harper Havelock Coates and Ryugaku Ishizuka, *Hōnen the Buddhist Saint* (Kyoto: Choin-in, 1925).

6. See Alfred Bloom, *Shinran's Gospel of Pure Grace* (Tucson: University of Arizona Press, 1965).

7. See Masaharu Anesaki, *Nichiren the Buddhist Prophet* (Cambridge, Mass.: Harvard University Press, 1916).

8. One good study of modern Nichirenism is James W. White, *The Sōkagakkai and Mass Society* (Stanford, Calif.: Stanford University Press, 1970).

9. Of the many books in English on Zen, Thomas Hoover, *Zen Culture* (New York: Random House, 1977) can be especially recommended for its readability and its emphasis on the general cultural impact of Zen.

10. Interview statement in *Wind Bell* 8, no. 1-2 (Fall 1969): 29.

11. An interesting introduction to the New Religions is Harry Thomsen, *The New Religions of Japan* (Tokyo and Rutland, Vt.: Charles E. Tuttle Co., 1963).

CHAPTER 5

1. See *Kūkai: Major Works*, trans. by Yoshito S. Hakeda (New York: Columbia University Press, 1972).

2. A good source on Dōgen and other Zen intellectuals is Heinrich Dumoulin, *A History of Zen Buddhism* (New York: Pantheon, 1963).

3. From the commentary by Yeh Ts'ai on the *Chin Ssu Lu*, compiled 1175 by Chu Hsi and Lu Tsu-chien, in Wing-tsit Chan, ed. and trans., *Reflections on Things at Hand: The Neo-Confucian Anthology Compiled by Chu Hsi and Lu Tsu-chien* (New York: Columbia University Press, 1967), p. 83; cited in Laurence G. Thompson, "Confucianism as a Way of Ultimate Transformation," in *East/West Cultures: Religious Motivations for Behavior: A Colloquium* (Santa Barbara, Calif.: Educational Futures International, 1977), pp. 1-38, to which article I am much indebted for insights into the meaning of Neo-Confucianism.

4. See M. Maruyama, *Studies in the Intellectual History of Tokugawa Japan* (Tokyo: University of Tokyo Press, 1974).

5. See Robert N. Bellah, *Tokugawa Religion* (Glencoe, Ill.: The Free Press, 1957).

6. See G. Piovesana, *Recent Japanese Philosophical Thought 1862-1962: A Survey* (Tokyo: Sophia University Press, 1968); Kitarō Nishida, *Intelligibility and the Philosophy of Nothingness* (Tokyo: Maruzen, 1958); Hajime Nakamura, *Ways of Thinking of Eastern Peoples: India, China, Tibet, Japan* (Honolulu: University Press of Hawaii, 1974).

CHAPTER 6

1. Peter C. Swann, *An Introduction to the Arts of Japan* (New York: Frederick A. Praeger, 1958), p. 166.

CHAPTER 8

1. See *The Nō Plays of Japan*, trans. by Arthur Waley (New York: Grove Press, 1957), p. 82.

2. Robert Garfias, *Gagaku: The Music and Dances of the Japanese Imperial Household* (New York: Theatre Arts Books, 1959).

3. William P. Malm, *Japanese Music and Musical Instruments* (Rutland, Vt.: Charles E. Tuttle Co., 1959) is by far the most thorough, scholarly, and reliable book in English on the subject.

4. A splendid historical and dramatic introduction to No is Donald Keene, *Nō: The Classical Theatre of Japan* (Tokyo: Kodansha, 1966).

5. Donald Keene, ed., *Twenty Plays of the Nō Theatre* (New York: Columbia University Press, 1970). *Nonomiya*, pp. 180-92, is translated by H. Paul Varley.

6. A good introduction is Earle Ernst, *The Kabuki Theatre* (London: Secker and Warburg, 1956).

CHAPTER 9

1. Ken Nakazawa, "The Spirit of Japanese Poetry," *Atlantic Monthly* (Feb. 1929), p. 212.

2. *The Penguin Book of Japanese Verse*, trans. by Geoffrey Bownas and Anthony Thwaite (Baltimore, Md.: Penguin Books, 1964), p. 131.

3. *The Penguin Book of Japanese Verse*, p. 177.

4. *The Penguin Book of Japanese Verse*, p. 150.

5. Earl Miner, *An Introduction to Japanese Court Poetry* (Stanford, Calif.: Stanford University Press, 1968), p. 51.

6. For a description of the twenty-one imperial anthologies see Robert H. Brower and Earl Miner, *Japanese Court Poetry* (Stanford, Calif.: Stanford University Press, 1961), pp. 482-86. This book is the standard English discussion of the tradition.

7. *The Tales of Ise*, trans. by H. Jay Harris (Rutland, Vt.: Charles E. Tuttle Co., 1972), pp. 16-17.

8. Miner, *An Introduction to Japanese Court Poetry*, p. 84.

9. Harold G. Henderson, *An Introduction to Haiku* (Garden City, N.Y.: Doubleday & Co., 1958), p. 19. This is the best introductory book on haiku for the general reader or beginning student.

10. A good version, with both English and the original Japanese, is Sanford Goldstein and Seishi Shinoda, *Tangled Hair: Selected Tanka from* Midaregami *by Akiko Yosano* (Lafayette, Ind.: Purdue University Studies, 1971).

11. Takamichi Ninomiya and D.J. Enright, *The Poetry of Living Japan* (New York: Grove Press, 1957), pp. 49-50.

CHAPTER 10

1. *The Taketori Monogatari* is translated by Frederick Victor Dickens as *The Old Bamboo-Hewer's Story or the Tale of Taketori* (Tokyo: San Kaku Sha, 1934).

2. The *Tosa Nikki* is translated by Earl Miner, in *Japanese Poetic Diaries* (Berkeley: University of California Press, 1969).

3. The *Kagerō Nikki* is translated as *The Gossamer Years* by Edward Seidensticker (Tokyo: Charles E. Tuttle Co., 1964); the *Izumi Shikibu Nikki* as *Shikibu Izumi Diary: A Romance of the Heian Court*, trans. by Edwin A. Cranston (Cambridge, Mass.: Harvard University Press, 1969); the *Sarashina Nikki* as *As I Crossed a Bridge of Dreams*, trans. by Ivan Morris (New York: Dial Press, 1971).

4. The *Genji Monogatari* is translated as *The Tale of Genji* by Arthur Waley (New York: Modern Library, 1960) and by Edward Seidensticker, (New York: A.A. Knopf, 1976).

5. Lady Murasaki, *Murasaki Shikibu Nikki*, trans. by Annie Shepley Omori and Kochi Doi (New York: AMS Press, 1970. Originally published in 1920).

6. Sei Shōnagon, *The Pillow Book of Sei Shōnagon*, ed. and trans. by Ivan Morris (New York: Columbia University Press, 1967).

7. *The Ten-Foot Square Hut and Tales of the Heike*, trans. by A.L. Sadler (Tokyo: Charles E. Tuttle Co., 1972).

8. *Essays in Idleness: The Tsurezuregusa of Kenkō*, trans. by Donald Keene (New York: Columbia University Press, 1967).

9. *Izayoi Nikki*, in Edwin O. Reischauer and Joseph K. Yamagiwa, *Translations from Early Japanese Literature* (Cambridge, Mass.: Harvard University Press, 1951, 1970); *The Confessions of Lady Nijō*, trans. by Karen Brazell (Garden City, N.Y.: Anchor Books, 1973).

10. *The Tale of the Heike*, trans. by Hiroshi Kitagawa and Bruce T. Tsuchida (Tokyo: University of Tokyo Press, 1974).

11. Ibid., p. 5.

12. Ibid., p. 6, notes.

13. Ibid., p. 781.

14. *The Life of an Amorous Man*, trans. by Kengi Hamada (Rutland, Vt.: Charles E. Tuttle Co., 1964).

15. *Five Women Who Loved Love*, trans. by William Theodore de Bary (Tokyo: Charles E. Tuttle Co., 1956).

16. *The Japanese Family Storehouse or the Millionaires' Gospel Modernized*, trans. by G.W. Sargent (Cambridge: Cambridge University Press, 1959).

17. For some gripping examples of Japanese mysteries, see Ellery Queen's *Japanese Golden Dozen: The Detective Story World in Japan* (Rutland, Vt. and Tokyo: Charles E. Tuttle Co., 1978).

18. Mishima Yukio, *The Temple of the Golden Pavilion*, trans. by Ivan Morris (New York: A.A. Knopf, 1958). Introduction by Nancy Wilson Ross.

19. Ibid., see Introduction.

Glossary

This glossary provides brief identifications of certain important Japanese terms used in this book. Less important words used only once may not be included, since they are defined in the text at the place of their sole use. Only Japanese terms are defined, not those from Sanskrit or Chinese. Proper names of persons, places, books, sects, historical periods, and so forth are not given; they can be easily identified by looking them up in the index and ascertaining the major reference.

Bakufu "Tent government"; the government of a shogun.
Bonsai Miniature trees made by careful pruning.
Bunraku The classic puppet theater, named for a district in Osaka where it developed.
Chanoyu "Hot water for tea," the classic "tea ceremony."
Chōka Long poems of the *Manyōshū* period.
Daimoku Nichiren Buddhist chant to the powers of the Lotus Sutra.
Daimyō Feudal lord.
Fūryū Refined elegance achieved through simplicity and seeming imperfection.
Giri Sense of duty and obligation toward a benefactor.
Gunki A tale of war.
Haiku Seventeen-syllable poem capturing a single scene.
Haniwa Clay figurines from ancient tombs.
Ikebana The classic art of flower arrangement.
Jidaimono Historical play.
Jōdo "Pure Land"; the paradise of Amidist Buddhism.
Jōruri Dramatic ballad sung during the course of the classic puppet theater; the puppet theater itself.
Kabuki The classic theater of the Tokugawa period, noted for its stylized but skillful acting.
Kagura Shinto sacred dance, the ultimate source of much Japanese theater.
Kami Shinto deity.
Kannon A popular bodhisattva noted for compassion, often loosely spoken of as a Buddhist "goddess of mercy."
Kigo Word indicating season in poetry.
Koan (Kōan) A short riddle-like saying used as a focus for meditation in Zen training.
Koto Traditional lute-like musical instrument.
Matsuri Shinto festival.
Miko A shaman, or a maiden who performs sacred dance at Shinto shrines.

Miyabi "Courtly beauty"; the ideal of refined elegance of the Heian court and its arts.

Monogatari A tale; the classical long fictional narrative.

Nembutsu The devotional chant to Amida of Pure Land Buddhism.

Nikki Diary; a classical literary form, presented as a diary but often fictionalized.

No (Nō) Classic theater originating in the Ashikaya period, noted for its mystic quality.

On The kindness and favor of a benefactor or parent to client, child, or someone in the child's role.

Renga Linked verse; a classic poetic form.

Ri Principle or essence, a Neo-Confucian concept.

Sabi The quality of appearing aged, worn, or antique, and thereby evoking feelings of nostalgia, pity, and wistful yearning for what is gone.

Saigū Palace of the vestal princess at Ise.

Samisen Stringed banjo-like musical instrument.

Senryū Light, humorous verse in classic form.

Shinden Architectural style of the Heian period.

Shingeki or Shingeki Shibai Modern Western-type drama.

Shinto (Shintō) The indigenous polytheistic religion of Japan.

Shogun (Shōgun) Military dictators who ruled Japan in the name of the emperor during most of the period 1192-1867.

Shoin Traditional architectural style employing paper screens and *tokonoma*.

Sōhei Soldier-monks.

Suiboku sumie Painting with ink and wash.

Tanka Traditional 31-syllable poem.

Tokonoma Alcove in home for such traditional ornaments as *ikebana* and hanging scroll.

Uji Clan; ancient social unit.

Ujigami Patronal Shinto *kami* or deity of a clan or extended family.

Ukiyo "Floating world"; term applied especially to the Tokugawa period world of fashion and entertainment.

Ukiyo-e "Floating world pictures"; genre of art depicting Tokugawa-era actors, courtesans, and scenes of daily life; usually wood-block prints.

Wabi Loneliness, poverty; an aesthetic quality evoking a sense of the ordinariness and pitifulness of the object.

Waka Classic Japanese poem; same as *tanka* in most usage.

Yūgen Aesthetic quality initially used in discussion of No; the almost indefinable sense of profundity, mystery, and sublimity evoked by great art.

Zuihitsu A miscellany of epigrams and very short essays; literary form originating in the Heian period.

Bibliography

Of the hundreds of valuable books on Japan in the English language, space allows us to list here only fifty-five. I have endeavored to select five books suitable for further reading by students in each field, to go with each of the eleven chapters of this volume. In some areas of Japanese studies, five is a ridiculously small number to cite in even the most rudimentary bibliography; in others, it takes a bit of digging to find even five worth recommending. Nonetheless, the choices have had to be made. In many instances books just as good as those cited have had to be left out, and other authors might have made different selections. These are, however, books that those interested in Japan will not waste time reading, and many of them contain excellent bibliographies for further research in particular aspects of Japanese civilization.

INTRODUCING JAPAN AND THE JAPANESE HERITAGE

Bacon, Alice Mabel. *Japanese Girls and Women.* New York: Gordon Press, 1975. First published 1891. *An interesting introduction to the feminine side of traditional life.*

Lebra, Takie S. and William P. Lebra. *Japanese Culture and Behavior: Selected Readings.* Honolulu: University Press of Hawaii, 1974. *Discussions by authoritative scholars.*

Morris, Ivan. *The Nobility of Failure: Tragic Heroes in the History of Japan.* New York: Holt, Rinehart, and Winston, 1975. *A brilliant study that gives a deep insight into Japanese culture and character.*

Murakami, H. and E. Seidensticker. *Guide to Japanese Culture.* Tokyo: Japan Travel Bureau, 1976. *An introduction by two excellent authorities.*

Reischauer, Edwin O. *The Japanese.* Cambridge, Mass: Belknap Press, 1977. *A readable, highly regarded introduction to Japanese life and culture.*

THE VALUES OF JAPANESE CULTURE

Beardsley, Richard K., John W. Hall, and Robert E. Ward. *Village Japan.* Chicago: University of Chicago Press, 1959. *An anthropological study that gives valuable insight into the structures and values of rural Japanese life.*

DeVos, G. *Socialization for Achievement: Essays on the Cultural Psychology of the Japanese.* Berkeley: University of California Press, 1973. *The interworking of the Japanese mind and Japanese society.*

Miller, Roy Andrew. *The Japanese Language.* Chicago: University of Chicago Press, 1967. *An admirable linguistic study that in the course of introducing the language gives rich insights into how the Japanese think and how the society works.*

Nakane, Chie. *Japanese Society.* Berkeley: University of California Press, 1970. *A landmark sociological interpretation of modern Japan.*

Yanagida, Kunio. *Japanese Folktales: A Revised Selection.* Trans. by Fanny Hagin Mayer. Tokyo: Tokyo News Service, 1966. *An initial step into the world of Japanese folk culture and folklore by one of Japan's greatest folklorists.*

PERIODS IN JAPANESE HISTORY

Reischauer, Edwin O. *Japan: The Story of a Nation,* rev. ed. New York: Alfred A. Knopf, 1974. *A reliable history, emphasizing the modern period.*

Sansom, George. *Japan: A Short Cultural History.* New York: Appleton-Century-Crofts, 1931. *A classic introduction to Japanese cultural history.*

Shively, Donald H. *Tradition and Modernization in Japanese Culture.* Princeton, N.J.: Princeton University Press, 1972. *A respected study of the basic tensions of recent Japanese life.*

Statler, Oliver. *Japanese Inn: A Reconstruction of the Past.* New York: Random House, 1961. *A brilliant fictionalized but authoritative visit to Tokugawa Japan; should be read by everyone interested in the country and the period.*

Varley, H. Paul. *Japanese Culture: A Short History.* New York: Praeger, 1973. *A readable and reliable survey.*

RELIGION: A NATION SECULAR AND SACRED

Blacker, Carmen. *The Catalpa Bow: A Study of Shamanistic Practices in Japan.* London: George Allen & Unwin, 1975. *A carefully researched and beautifully written summary of shamanism, the background of so much else in Japanese religion.*

Earhart, H. Byron. *Japanese Religion: Unity and Diversity.* Encino, Calif.: Dickenson Publishing Co., 1974. *A fine introductory text, oriented toward history.*

Hoover, Thomas. *Zen Culture.* New York: Random House, 1977. *A good introduction to the aspect of Japanese spiritual life that has most interested non-Japanese.*

Kitagawa, Joseph M. *Religion in Japanese History.* New York: Columbia University Press, 1968. *An authoritative historical survey, emphasizing the modern period.*

Ono, Sokyo. *Shinto: The Kami Way.* Rutland, Vt.: Charles E. Tuttle Co., 1967. *A basic introduction, from the point of view of a leading Japanese Shinto scholar.*

PHILOSOPHY: THINKING ABOUT ULTIMATES

Bellah, Robert N. *Tokugawa Religion.* Glencoe, Ill.: The Free Press, 1957. *A classic study of popular philosophies in the Edo period.*

Kim, Hee-Jin. *Dōgen Kigen, Mystical Realist.* Tucson: University of Arizona Press, 1975. *An introduction to Japan's most provocative Buddhist philosopher.*

Maruyama, M. *Studies in the Intellectual History of Tokugawa Japan.* Tokyo: University of Tokyo Press, 1974.

Moore, Charles, ed. *The Japanese Mind: Essentials of Japanese Philosophy and Culture.* Honolulu: East-West Center Press, 1967. *Valuable insights from a collection of writers both Eastern and Western.*

Piovesana, G. *Recent Japanese Philosophical Thought 1862–1962: A Survey.* Tokyo: Sophia University Press, 1968. *The standard introduction to modern Japanese philosophy.*

SCULPTURE AND PAINTING

Anesaki, Masaharu. *Art, Life, and Nature in Japan.* Boston: Marshall Jones Co., 1933. *A successful philosophical interpretation.*

Grilli, Elise. *Japanese Picture Scrolls.* New York: Crown, 1958. *Well-illustrated presentation of the* emakimono.

Michener, James A. *The Floating World: The Story of Japanese Prints.* New York: Random House, 1954. *A thorough introduction to the art and artists of the* ukiyo.

Munsterberg, Hugo. *The Arts of Japan: An Illustrated History.* Rutland, Vt.: Charles E. Tuttle Co., 1958. *An attractive historical survey.*

Swann, Peter C. *An Introduction to the Arts of Japan.* New York: Praeger, 1958. *A reliable scholarly introduction.*

ARCHITECTURE, GARDENS, AND OTHER ARTS: MINIATURE PARADISES

Drexler, Arthur. *The Architecture of Japan.* New York: Museum of Modern Art, 1955. *A lavishly illustrated introduction.*

Engel, Heinrich. *The Japanese House.* Rutland, Vt.: Charles E. Tuttle Co., 1964. *A survey, with emphasis on the impact of traditional Japanese styles on contemporary architecture.*

Fukukita, Yasunosuke. *Tea Cult of Japan.* Tokyo: Japan Travel Bureau, 1957. *A balanced overview of the tea ceremony and its traditions.*

Itō, Teiji. *The Japanese Garden.* New Haven: Yale University Press, 1972. *A good study of the forms and philosophy of the garden.*

Teshigahara, Wafū. *Japanese Flower Arrangement.* Tokyo: Kodansha, 1966. *A beautifully illustrated guide to the art.*

DANCE, MUSIC, AND DRAMA: THE PAST IN THE PRESENT

Ashihara, Hidesato. *The Japanese Dance*. Tokyo: Japan Travel Bureau, 1964. *An overall introduction to a complex field.*

Keene, Donald. *Bunraku: The Art of the Japanese Puppet Theatre*. Tokyo: Kodansha, 1973. *An excellent introduction.*

Keene, Donald. *Nō: The Classical Theatre of Japan*. Tokyo: Kodansha, 1966. *A brilliant study of the history, theory, and practice of No.*

Malm, William P. *Japanese Music and Musical Instruments*. Rutland, Vt.: Charles E. Tuttle Co., 1959. *The standard book on this subject.*

Toita, Yasuji. *Kabuki*. Trans. by Don Kenny. New York and Tokyo: Walker/Weatherhill, 1970. *A competent survey of Kabuki, its arts and lore.*

POETRY: A NATION OF POETS

Bownas, Geoffrey, and Anthony Thwaite. *The Penguin Book of Japanese Verse*. Baltimore: Penguin Books, 1964. *A standard introductory anthology.*

Brower Robert H., and Earl Miner. *Japanese Court Poetry*. Stanford, Calif.: Stanford University Press, 1961. *An excellent scholarly survey.*

Henderson, Harold H. *An Introduction to Haiku*. Garden City, N.Y.: Doubleday & Co., 1958. *The best general introduction to the form.*

Kijima, Hajime. *The Poetry of Postwar Japan*. Iowa City: University of Iowa Press, 1975. *Annotated translations of modern Japanese verse.*

Ueda, Makoto. *Modern Japanese Haiku: An Anthology*. Toronto and Buffalo: University of Toronto Press, 1976. *An attractive and representative collection.*

PROSE LITERATURE

Hibbett, Howard. *The Floating World in Japanese Fiction*. New York: Oxford University Press, 1959. *A good introductory anthology of the Tokugawa period "floating world" literature.*

Keene, Donald. *Anthology of Japanese Literature*. New York: Grove Press, 1955. *An excellent introductory anthology of classical literature.*

Keene, Donald. *Modern Japanese Literature*. New York: Grove Press, 1956. *A good introduction to modern writers, especially writers of stories.*

Miner, Earl Roy. *Japanese Poetic Diaries*. Berkeley: University of California Press, 1969. *Sensitive translation with an excellent introduction. Together with translations cited in the references to chapter 10 and Ivan Morris's splendid* The World of the Shining Prince: Court Life in Ancient Japan. *New York: Alfred A. Knopf, 1964, a fairly complete picture of Heian aristocratic culture can be gathered.*

Miyoshi, Masao. *Accomplices of Silence: The Modern Japanese Novel.* Berkeley: University of California Press. *A good critical overview of the literature, emphasizing tensions between the native literary tradition and the modern Western forms in contemporary Japanese fiction.*

CINEMA: A DISTINGUISHED ART

Anderson, Joseph L., and Donald Richie. *The Japanese Film: Art and Industry.* New York: Grove Press, 1959. *A valuable introduction and survey to the date of publication.*

Mellen, Joan. *The Waves and Genji's Door: Japan through its Cinema.* New York: Pantheon Books, 1976. *A valuable study, emphasizing the social meaning of films.*

Richie, Donald. *Japanese Cinema: Film Style and National Character.* Garden City, N.Y.: Doubleday & Co., 1971. *An interpretation by the leading Western critic of Japanese cinema.*

Richie, Donald. *The Films of Akira Kurosawa.* Berkeley: University of California Press, 1965.

Richie, Donald. *Ozu: His Life and Films.* Berkeley: University of California Press, 1974.

Index

80; Shōdō, 76; in the theater, 131.
See also Pure Land; Shingon; Tendai;
Zen Buddhism
Bugaku (court dances), 133-136, 138;
screens of, 110
buke (samurai, warriors), 35, 37
Bunraku (puppet theater), 13-15, 143;
music of, 137. See also *ningyō jōruri;*
Puppet theater
bunrakujin (outcasts), 24
Bushidō, Code of, 12, 90
Buson, Taniguchi (1715-1783; poet),
163
byōbu (screens), 97
Byōdōin temple, 103, 120

Calligraphy, 110
Capping game, 149, 160, 161, 169
Castles, 43, 44, 163; art in, 108
chadō (the way of tea), 117
chanoyu (tea ceremony), 9, 123
Charisma, importance of, 22, 65, 83
chigi (high, crossing beams), 120
Chikamatsu.Monzaemon (1653-1725;
dramatist), 13-16, 17, 23, 44, 46, 75,
143, 150, 173
China: cultural influence of, 99-100,
101, 102, 106-107, 108, 109, 121-
122, 133, 136, 138; defeat of, in
1890s, 49; occupation of, 54; trade
with, 41; war with, 54-55
China Incident (1937), 54
Chionin temple, described, 76-77
Chōjū Giga (Frolicking Animals; paint-
ing by Kakuyū), 105
chōka (long poems), 155
chōnin (townman), 46, 173
Chōshū, feudal state of, 47, 48
Christianity, 43-44, 51-52, 84
Chu Hsi (1130-1200; philosopher), 89
Chūgū temple, 100
Cinema, 58-59, 181-188
Classes, social: four, 45-46; outcasts, 24
Climate, 3-4
Cold War, 57
Confessions of a Mask (novel by
Mishima), 59, 178
Confucianism, 87-88; influence of, 25,
32, 44, 88-90, 174

Confucius, 87-88
Constitution: of 1889, 49; postwar, 57;
Ritsuryō, 32, 88; Seventeen Article,
31-32
Creel, Harlee, 87
Culture: conflict as a dynamic of, 6,
17-19; elegance of, 35, see also Heian
court and *miyabi;* folk, 19-23; influences on, 43, 99-100, see also
China, cultural influences of; high,
17-19; importation of, 4-5, 31, 50;
popular, 17, 92; prehistoric, 3; sources
of, 31; [794-1185], 35; [1568-1600],
42-43; [1392-1569], 9; [1600-
1868], 45-46; [1868-1912], 50;
[1926-1945], 55-56; [1945-], 57-60

Daibutsu, see Great Buddha of Nara
Daimoku (Buddhist chant), 79
daimyō (feudal lord), 25, 45
Dainichi, 74. See also Vairocana
Dance, 132-134; in No, 130, 141
Dance(s): court, 133-136; folk, 139;
Gigaku, 102, 138; lion, 138; masks
for, 102, 138; sacred, 131, 132, 144
Dannoura (Dan-no-Ura), battle of, 37,
172
Daruma (Bodhidharma; Zen master), 82
Decision making, 25-26
Deguchi Onisaburō (religious leader), 65
Deities, 66-67. See also Gods; *kami*
Democracy, 52
dengaku (field music) dances, 139
Dengyō Daishi (762-822; Tendai
leader), 74
Dharma, the (Buddha's teaching), 69
dharmakaya ("clear light of the void"),
106
Diamond, the (Shingon mandala), 73
Diaries, 36, 150, 170; first poetic, 156.
See also *nikki*
Diary of a Mad Old Man (Tanizaki), 56
Discrimination (class), 24
dō (a *tao* or way), 117, 118, 124
Dōgen (1200-1253; philosopher), 82,
86-87

Osaka castle, siege of, 44
Outsider-writers, 56, 175-177, 178-179
oyabun (parent-like figure), 25
Ōyōmeigakuha school (of philosophy), 90
Ozaki Kōyō (1867-1903; novelist), 50
Ozawa, Seiji (conductor), 138
Ozu Yasujirō (1903-1963; film director), 183-184

Painting, 105-111; Heian period, 105; Japanese (*yamato-e*), 104-105, 110; modern, 50, 115; Momoyama period, 97-98; oldest extant examples of, 100, 104-105, 110; silk screen, 43; in temples, 102, 103; Tokugawa period, 109-111; Zen, 81
Pearl Harbor, 55
Peasants, 12, 46, 92, 174
Perry, Commodore Matthew, 47
Perfect Liberty (religion), 83
Philosophy, 61-62, 85-93
Pilgrimage, 19, 20, 65, 84
Pimiko (ruler), 30
Plays: Kabuki, 145-146; poetry in, 150. See also Cinema; Drama
Poetry, 17, 34, 36-37, 50, 149-165; characteristics of, 150-152; collections of, 153, 155, 156, 158; colloquialisms in, 164; forms of, see *chōka, haikai*, Haiku, *renga*, tanka, *uta, utamonogatari*; in narrative context, 154; moods in, 150, 152; oldest, 154; on paintings, 110-111; social meaning of, 160
Poets, role of, 156
Polytheism, 66-67
Popular culture defined, 17
Portraiture, 106
Portuguese, influence of. See *namban*
Postwar period, 56-60, 184
Pottery, 29, 110-111
Printmaking, 109, 111-112
Prose, 167-179; earliest, 167; with poetry, 150
Primal parents, 1, 153
"Prince Takechi, On the Lying-in-State of" (poem by Hitomaro), 156

Puppet theater, 13-15, 46. **See also** Bunraku; *ningyō jōruri*
Pure Land Buddhism, 23, 25, 39-40, 74, 75-77, 102, 103
Purity, 20; expressed in art, 107

Raigō-zu (paintings of Amida), 104
Rangaku (Dutch Studies) school, 91-92
Realism: in art, 106; in literature, 50; in poetry, 156
Reality, 11; concept of, 85; essence of (*dharmakaya*), 106
Recent period (1945-), 56-60
Religion, 39-40, 61-84; in art, see Art; compared with philosophy, 85; influence of shamanism on, 22; relativism and pluralism of, 63. See also Buddhism; Pure Land; Shinto
renga (linked verse), 160-161
ri. See *li*
rikka (school of flower arrangement), 125
Rikyū, Sen no (1521-1591; master of the tea ceremony), 43, 123
ringisho (memos), 26
Rinzai Zen, 82
Ritsuryō (Laws and Regulations), 32
Rock garden of Ryōanji, 80, 122
roji (dewy path/stepping stones), 123
Rokkakudō temple, 10
Rokujō, Lady (in *Genji . . .*), 8, 142
rōnin (masterless samurai), 136
rōshi (Zen masters), 81
Ross, Nancy Wilson, 179
Russian, Japanese war with, 49
Ryōanji monastery/temple, 80, 122
Ryōbu Shintō (religion), 73
Ryūkyū Islands, 3, 137; annexation of, 49

sabi (yearning melancholoy), 42, 152, 171
Saichō. See Dengyō Daishi
Saigyō (1118-1190; priest-poet), 159, 177; scrolls on life of, 110
Sakata Tojirō (1647-1709; performer), 13
Sakhalin Island, 3; annexation of, 49
Sakya clan, 68

Sakyamuni (560-483 B.C.; Buddha), 68
sambhogakaya (heavenly), 106
Samgha (Buddhist order), 69
samisen (banjo-like instrument), 15, 16, 137
Samurai (warriers), 12, 35, 39, 42, 45-46, 82, 90, 136, 171, 174; Bushidō code of, 12, 90; dominant class, 12; ideals, 39; war between, 37
sangaku. See sarugaku
Sangatsudō (or Hokkedō) temple, 72
Sanjūsangendō temple (Hall of the Thirty Three Bays), described, 72
Sanmon (temple gate at Chionin), 76
Sarashina Nikki (Sarashina Diary), 168
sarugaku ("monkey music"; entertainment), 138-139
sato kagura (village sacred dances), 133
satori (sudden awakening), 81, 82, 162
Satsuma (feudal state of), 47, 48
Science fiction, 176
Screens, 97, 108, 110
Scrolls. See *emki; kakemono*
Sculpture, 98, 106; Buddhist, 103, 106; Heian, 105; portrait, 101; in temples, 70-72, 100-101, 103; themes of, 99-100
Sea of Fertility, The (novel by Mishima), 60
Sei Shōnagon (c. 968–c. 1025), 36, 170
Seichō no Ie (House of Life; religion), 83
seii taishōgun (generalisimo), 88
Sekigahara, battle of (1600), 44
Self-Defense Force, the, 57, 60
senryū (humor or satire in verse), 152
seppuku (*hara-kiri*, suicide), 12
sesshō (regent for an emperor), 34
Sesshū (1420-1506; priest-painter), 107-108
Seven Samurai (film by Kurosawa), 184
Seventeen Article Constitution, 31-32
Shaka; Shakamuni (Buddha), 68
Shakamuni Triad (Buddhist sculpture), 100
shakuhachi (Japanese flute), 136
Shaman, 30, 137; defined, 22
Shamanism, 22, 65, 133

Sharaku, Tōshūsai (fl. 1794-1795; artist), 109, 112
shiki (outdoor sanctuaries), 19
Shiki Masaoka (1867-1902; poet), 164
Shikushi, Princess (d. 1201, poet), 159-160
Shimmachi, in Osaka, 174
Shimonoseki, bombardment of, 48
shin (will), 90
shinden style of architecture, 120-121
Shingaku (Heart- or Mind-Learning), 92
shingeki shibai ("modern" drama), 15, 146-147
Shingon Buddhism, 35, 72-74, 86, 102
Shinkokinshū (New Anthology [of Poems] Old and New), 158-160
Shinran (1173-1263; priest), 39-40, 61, 65, 77
Shinto, 20-23, 35, 61, 64, 65, 66-67, 74, 88, 121, 131; separation of, from Buddhism, 49
shite (main No performer), 141
shō (reed pipes), 136
Shōchō (c. 1488; poet), 161
Shōdō (holy paths) Buddhism, 76
shōen (tax-free estate), 35
Shogun (shōgun), defined, 6, 38
Shogunal system, 38; weakness of, 47
Shoguns: Ashikaga, 6, 9; last of, 42
Shōhaku (c. 1488; poet), 161
Shōhondō temple, described, 79-80
shoin (writing room) style of architecture, 121
shōji (sliding doors and screens), 121
Shōkokuji Zen monastery, 107
Shōmu, Emperor (r. 724-749), 33, 68, 102
Shopkeepers, 12, 173, 174
Shōsōin, 102
Shōtoku Taishi (573-621; prince regent), 31-32, 88
Shōwa periods, (1926-1945, 1945-), 53-60
Shrine(s): dancers at, 132-133; family, 23-24; at Izumo, 153; Kasuga, 33, 139; Matsu-no-o, 103; Nonomiya, 8; Shinto, 21, 23-24, 65-67, 73, 120, 121; Tamanushi, 100. See also Grand Shrine of Ise
Shūbun (d. 1450; priest-painter), 107